JOHN CALVIN AND THE
NATURAL WORLD

Davis A. Young

University Press of America,® Inc.
Lanham · Boulder · New York · Toronto · Plymouth, UK

Copyright © 2007 by
University Press of America,® Inc.
4501 Forbes Boulevard
Suite 200
Lanham, Maryland 20706
UPA Acquisitions Department (301) 459-3366

Estover Road
Plymouth PL6 7PY
United Kingdom

Library of Congress Control Number: 2006941022
ISBN-13: 978-0-7618-3712-1 (clothbound : alk. paper)
ISBN-10: 0-7618-3712-4 (clothbound : alk. paper)
ISBN-13: 978-0-7618-3713-8 (paperback : alk. paper)
ISBN-10: 0-7618-3713-2 (paperback : alk. paper)

To Dan, Tim, and Tracy

Three treasured gifts from God

TABLE OF CONTENTS

PREFACE

From beginning to end the Bible tells a story of unique events of profound religious significance that transpired in the locations now known as Israel, Syria, Jordan, Iraq, Iran, Egypt, Turkey, Greece, and Italy. Far from being a textbook of abstract religious philosophy or a manual of ethics, the Bible conveys its message by firmly situating the redemptive acts of God in specific, real-world geographical sites. The story begins with Genesis telling us in its very first words that God created the material cosmos and all the creatures, including humans, that inhabit the cosmos. God then placed two human beings into a park-like garden well stocked with trees, fruits, a variety of animals, and identifiable rivers. After Adam and Eve disobeyed God by eating fruit from the prohibited tree of the knowledge of good and evil, they were driven out of the garden into a world of thorns and thistles. We read that their descendants grew crops and raised animals. Because wickedness quickly prevailed, God sent a great deluge to decimate birds, livestock, wild animals, creeping creatures, and humans. In time, God called Abram out of Ur, a city in Mesopotamia, and covenanted with him to make his offspring as numerous as the stars of heaven. On and on the Old Testament continues to tell its unfolding story of God's dealings with human beings in the context of our physical and biological surroundings.

When we arrive at the New Testament, we find Jesus routinely teaching his disciples by means of parables replete with allusions to the natural world: sheep, fig trees, soils, wheat and weeds, mustard plants, rock and sand as building sites, and vineyards. In the book of Acts we encounter storms, snakes, and earthquakes. The Apocalypse closes out Scripture with a host of references to thunder, lightning, earthquakes, stars, the sea, grapes, and flesh-eating birds. The biblical story from beginning to the end records the judging, guiding, and saving acts of God in the lives of people and nations who lived in a material world that is full of organic beings. Because of its character as a story set squarely in this material world, the biblical text contains a stunning wealth of references to natural features and phenomena that form the physical environment in which we live: the stars, the Sun, the Moon, land, sea, rocks, gemstones, earthquakes, mountains, trees, fruit, crops, seeds, grass, birds, fish, lions, bears, dogs, snakes, ants, and so on. Because the Bible contains so many allusions to the natural world, it is appropriate to ask how Christians living in different times have understood the Bible's references to the natural world in the context of the knowledge and ideas of their own times.

Commentators from the earliest centuries of the Christian church such as Clement of Alexandria, Basil of Caesarea, and Augustine of Hippo to those of the present day have discussed the biblical mention of various natural phenomena in light of the scientific understanding of their own day. In that regard, John Calvin (1509-1564), the great theologian of the Protestant Reformation in the sixteenth century, was no exception. Like everyone else who has walked the face of the Earth, Calvin was very much a product of his own time, inescapably molded in his thinking by the contemporary understanding of the way in which the world is constructed and in which it behaves.

The voluminous writings of John Calvin have exercised a pervasive influence on many aspects of modern western culture. As a result, his thought has been subjected to intense scrutiny and critical analysis by a never-ending stream of both admirers and detractors. Although the bulk of critical attention has been devoted to Calvin's theology, ecclesiology, and ethics, much has also been written about the political, philosophical, and sociological aspects of Calvin's thought-world. In contrast, very little has been written about Calvin's understanding of the natural world and its investigation or about the impact of his theological thought on how Christians should regard nature and natural science. There exists no comprehensive, English-language assessment of Calvin's attitudes toward science. To fill this void, I have written this book to point out how Calvin explained biblical references to natural phenomena and to shed some light on his own ideas about the natural world and scientific explanations of that world. The book has been written primarily for historians of science, Calvin specialists, and the many Christian pastors and lay people who have been strongly influenced by the thought of the great theologian of the Protestant Reformation and also have some interest in nature and science.

My work complements an anthology of papers on Calvin and the sciences edited by Richard C. Gamble, most of which deal with Calvin's opinion of the Copernican hypothesis, as well as more technical treatments of the allied topic of Calvin's doctrine of creation by Richard Stauffer (*Dieu, la Création et la Providence dans la Prédication de Calvin*) and Susan Schreiner (*The Theater of his Glory: Nature and the Natural Order in the Thought of John Calvin*). Inasmuch as none of these works deals with Calvin's comments about animals, earthquakes and other geological phenomena, the age of the Earth, or meteorological phenomena such as rainbows, wind, and clouds, my book contributes to our understanding of a generally overlooked aspect of Calvin's thought-world.

This study is timely in light of some seemingly never-ending controversies that disturb much of the English-speaking ecclesiastical world, particularly in the United States, Australia, and New Zealand. These controversies entail questions in relation to the bearing of Scripture on the practice of natural science. Does the infallibility of the Bible extend to scientific matters? Should the Bible serve as a judge among competing scientific theories? Does Genesis confine the church to a particular understanding of the age of the Earth? Is it permissible for Christians to accept any kind of theory of organic evolution? Is intelligent design theory consistent with the biblical message? In what way did the fall affect the physical universe and our ability to understand it? Contemporary discussion about these and related questions has commonly been conducted with little reference to the views of Calvin, no doubt because many of these questions were not asked in Calvin's day. Nevertheless, even though the issues and questions of today are addressed in the context of a scientifically-oriented culture and a body of scientific knowledge that is radically different from that in which Calvin was situated, the church may still profit from Calvin's approach to the question of the proper application of Scripture to the interpretation of the created order. Unfortunately, Christians, particularly those of the Reformed tradition who claim deep allegiance to the theology and ecclesiology of John Calvin, are generally unaware of Calvin's ideas about the natural world and science. But just as Christians eagerly consult Calvin on a host of other biblical issues, they ought also seek to learn from his application of Scripture to the scientific issues of his own day. Perhaps contemporary Christendom could avoid some of the flawed approaches to the issues noted above if participants in the discussions would appropriate some aspects of the thinking of Calvin. There is need, therefore, for an in-depth study of Calvin and science that is also accessible to lay Christians, many of whom have intensely held, but poorly informed, ideas about the place of science in relation to belief in the Christian doctrines of creation and providence and in relation to appropriate interpretation of Scripture. I am hopeful that this book, especially the final two chapters, will satisfy that need.

This study was a natural outgrowth of several personal and professional interests. As someone who was raised in a passionately Calvinistic home who developed an early love for geology at the age of 12, I developed an intense desire to understand the relationships among Scripture, Christian theology, and geology. My work on those issues quickly led to a study of the history of geology. Most of my professional writing has concerned those fields. Investigation of how various Calvinistic theologians faced the scientific issues of their day, most of it done in the context of a teaching position in geology at Calvin College, inevitably led me to wonder how the "prince of theologians" dealt with the science of his own time. Curiosity led me to a thorough reading of the entire corpus of Calvin's commentaries, the *Institutes of the Christian Religion*, selected sermons on Job, the booklet entitled *A Warning against Judiciary Astrology*, *The Secret Providence of God*, and Calvin's early commentary on Seneca's *De Clementia*. It is almost entirely from these works that I have drawn my findings and on which I have based my conclusions. Because I have consulted only a few of Calvin's latest letters and have ignored most of his briefer writings, I would very much appreciate hearing from readers who are familiar with any of Calvin's writings that I have neglected if they are aware of items of scientific relevance in those writings. I would also encourage others who have a strong interest in Calvin studies to build on what I have done here so that our understanding of the reformer's views on nature can be expanded and refined.

I am deeply grateful to Dr. Karin Maag, director of the H. H. Meeter Center for Calvin Studies at Calvin College for her support for and interest in the project. Through her efforts, the Meeter Center provided not only office space but also funds that enabled me to devote a substantial portion of the Fall, 2001, semester at Calvin College on the project. Thanks are also due to Susan Schmurr and Paul Fields for their assistance in regard to the use of the Meeter Center collection.

Thanks are also due to Dr. James D. Bratt, director of the Calvin Center for Christian Scholarship (CCCS) for guiding my proposal to study Calvin's views on the natural world through the review process of the CCCS Governing Board. A substantial reduction in teaching load during the entire 2002-2003 academic year was made possible by the very generous financial support provided by the CCCS.

This work has come to final fruition during my first two years of retirement following 36 years of teaching geology, the last 26 at Calvin College. Inspiration for thinking and writing comes easily in the spectacular beauty of the Arizona desert and mountains. The glorious lack of committee meetings from my daily routine likewise serves as a stimulus to the craft of writing! The manuscript has benefited from the patient and kind labors of a number of individuals. My wife read the entire manuscript and offered numerous invaluable stylistic suggestions. The text has also been greatly improved and some of the errors have been thinned out thanks to the careful reading of specific chapters by Christopher Kaiser, Paul Seely, Ralph Stearley, and John Zwart. Ronald Numbers graciously uncovered information about Benedict Textor in the archives in Geneva for me. Many thanks for your help. William B. Eerdmans Publishing Company and Westminster John Knox Press are gratefully acknowledged for granting permission to use quotations from writings of John Calvin, and Concordia Publishing House is acknowledged for granting permission to use quotations from the works of Martin Luther. Excerpts from Luther's Works Vol. 1 © 1960 Concordia Publishing House. Used with permission. All rights reserved.

Tucson, Arizona
October, 2006

CHAPTER 1

CALVIN ON SCIENCE, THE ARTS, AND LEARNING

John Calvin approached life whole-heartedly. Full of the Holy Spirit like the Apostle Paul, he was driven to proclaim Christ and him crucified. So dedicated to the cause of the gospel and the reformation of the church was Calvin that he was consumed by preaching the Word of God to his congregations in Strasbourg and at St. Peter's Cathedral in Geneva, by almost daily lecturing to theology students at the fledgling university in Geneva, by writing an unending stream of biblical commentaries, and by refuting heresy. He was so pressed for time that he frequently delivered his lectures on the Scriptures with virtually no preparation, and yet he did so with remarkable competence because his mind and heart were so thoroughly permeated by the text of Holy Scripture.[1]

Given Calvin's near total absorption in the exposition of Scripture and commitment to the cause of the Protestant Reformation, one might be excused for imagining him as a person who regarded the pursuit of knowledge as frivolous, if not outright useless, for the life of the Christian unless that knowledge was immediately related to biblical, theological, or ecclesiastical concerns. Might Calvin have agreed with the assertion of St. Ambrose (c. 339-397), the Bishop of Milan, that discussing the nature and position of the Earth does not help us in our hope of the life to come? Some expressions in Calvin's writings could be interpreted to mean that he was favorably disposed toward the sympathies expressed in Ambrose's comment. Consider, for example, the following selections from Calvin's commentaries on Hosea, John, and I Corinthians:

Let us suppose men endued, not only with great clearness of mind, but also with the knowledge of all the sciences; let them be philosophers, let them be physicians, let them be lawyers, let nothing be wanting to them, except that they have no true knowledge of eternal life, would it not be better for them to be mere cattle than to be thus wise, to exercise their minds for a short time on fading things, and to know that all their highly valued treasure shall perish with their life? Surely to be thus wise is far more wretched than if men were wholly void of understanding.[2]

Natural reason never will direct men to Christ. The fact that they are furnished with wisdom for ruling their lives, and are formed for the humanities and sciences, disappears without effect.[3]

Knowledge of all the sciences is so much smoke apart from the heavenly science of Christ.[4]

No teaching can be approved which is not 'baptized' in the love of God.[5]

But was Calvin really as unappreciative of scientific knowledge in particular and higher learning in general as these assertions seem to suggest?

A careful study of Calvin's writings, however, strongly indicates that he was, in reality, extremely appreciative of scientific work. A theologian at University of Chicago Divinity School and Union Theological Seminary, Brian Gerrish, for example, insisted that it simply is not true that Calvin appeared to have no taste for the sciences. "On the contrary," Gerrish argued, "he writes almost enviously of the astronomer, to whom the intricate workings of providence were more openly displayed than to other men."[6] Why then the seemingly negative statements like those listed above? When the context of these evaluations is reckoned with, it becomes clear that Calvin was always concerned to point out the inability of science to lead people to the true knowledge of God or to the way of salvation. In his judgment, science was of little aid in opening up *spiritual* knowledge. He was very concerned to urge those who were satisfied with explanations of phenomena that were couched strictly and purely in terms of secondary causes not to remain entrenched at the scientific level of thinking but to rise beyond that level by acknowledging and praising the author and sustainer of all the phenomena of nature. In that respect, Calvin differed little from some of his predecessors such as medieval philosopher Manegold of Lautenbach (c. 1030-c. 1112) who, according to Christopher Kaiser, a professor of historical and systematic theology at Western Theological Seminary, complained that the natural philosophers had become so preoccupied with the physical nature of things that they had difficulty any longer conceiving of anything beyond the natural order.[7] In this connection, there comes to mind Jesus' that there is no profit in gaining the whole world if we forfeit our soul in the end. As soon as we recognize the spiritual concern that motivated Calvin to make these apparently anti-scientific statements, we can begin to appreciate that he approved of science and that he frequently said so. He was immensely positive in regard to all liberal learning and very open to its discoveries.

Calvin used the Latin words *scientiae* and *artes* (sciences and arts) dozens of times, particularly throughout his commentaries. In the sixteenth century, the term "science" did not carry the technical meaning that it does today. For example, when Calvin used the term "science" he did not necessarily have "natural science" in mind. He did not immediately think of "biology," "astronomy," "geology," "chemistry," "physics," and so on to the exclusion of other areas of knowledge. For one thing, apart from "astronomy" and "physics," the terms for those disciplines within the natural sciences did not yet exist. Calvin did not specifically think of different kinds of sciences such as the "social sciences" in distinction from the "natural sciences." Neither did he distinguish between "applied" science and "pure" or "theoretical" science. Rather, he used the terms *scientia*, *scientiae*, *ars*, and *artes* broadly for all sorts of genuine knowledge obtained by a variety of methods. Moreover, he used the terms "science" and "art" interchangeably. For example, Calvin occasionally referred to astronomy as an art and music as a science. Elsewhere he designated music as an art and astronomy as a science.[8] Even crafts and forms of technology such as glass manufacture were commonly designated as arts or sciences. Often Calvin simply referred to "liberal learning" or just "learning." It is clear, however, that he regarded the disciplined investigation of the natural world as one set of activities to be included among the various sciences and arts or considered under the rubric of liberal learning.

No matter what terminology Calvin used, it is evident that he had a deep appreciation for the study of the natural world and respect for those who studied it even though he personally had no time to indulge in such study. His deep study of and thorough devotion to Scripture as the pointer to the sole way of salvation through Jesus Christ contributed to his conviction that the Bible should not be considered as the sole source of all knowledge and truth, infallible though it might be. He plainly understood that a wide range of knowledge may be obtained from sources and by methods that lie outside of the Bible. For Calvin, however, the God of the Bible remained the ultimate source and giver of all true knowledge and of the ability to seek and discover knowledge, including knowledge of the natural world.

Learning and the Liberal Arts

Calvin's interest in the natural world was only one manifestation of his general love of learning, knowledge, and the liberal arts. That love of learning has been pointed out repeatedly. Kenneth Howell, in his book on the relationship between the cosmology of Copernicus and the interpretation of the Bible, remarked that Calvin's understanding of the search for knowledge as a worthy pursuit revealed itself from his earliest days as author of a commentary on the book of Seneca (c. 4 B. C.-A. D. 65) *De Clementia* until the end of his life.[9] Calvin's passion for learning came to the surface in a more mature work, *De*

Scandalis, a lengthy tract completed in late 1550 in which he provided some encouragement for those adherents of the Reformed faith who were enduring various stumbling blocks. In that tract, he also addressed individuals who were put off by the Reformed faith on account of the various scandals that were rightly or wrongly associated with it. To those who were troubled by some of these scandals, Calvin suggested that they should "learn to become fools in this world in order to become capable of the heavenly wisdom." He quickly pointed out, however, that to become a fool, he did not mean that we should become stupid, "nor do we direct those who are learned in the liberal sciences to jettison their knowledge, and those who are gifted with quickness of mind to become dull, as if a man cannot be a Christian unless he is more like a beast than a man. The profession of Christianity requires us to be immature, not in our thinking, but in malice."[10]

Expressions extolling learning and the arts pervade the *Institutes* and the commentaries, and it is to them that we now turn. Calvin's generally positive attitude toward learning in general and science in particular is especially striking in view of his strong opinions regarding the fall of Adam, original sin, and the depravity of the fallen human race. One might expect that a depraved human race would be incapable of developing science or that its science might be irreparably corrupted and misguided. Or one might expect that only redeemed humanity might be able to produce genuine science. But that is not at all what we find in Calvin. Without hesitation, he squarely faced the fact that some of the highest intellectual attainments have been accomplished by individuals and cultures that have not experienced the light of the gospel. He saw that the children of darkness have often exceeded the children of light in science and the arts. Despite this situation, Calvin's verdict is one of unhesitating approval of science and the arts. He believed that God is free to use even wicked reprobates in the disclosure of truth.

One of Calvin's strongest affirmations of the validity and praiseworthiness of much of the learning of the heathen occurs in Book II of the *Institutes*. In the first chapter of Book II he had discussed the fact that "by the fall and revolt of Adam the whole human race was delivered to the curse, and degenerated from its original condition." Then, in the second chapter, he argued that "man has now been deprived of freedom of choice and bound over to miserable servitude." This does not sound promising! And yet in the second chapter we also encounter the following powerful affirmation:

> Whenever we come upon these matters [i.e., the arts] in secular writers, let that admirable light of truth shining in them teach us that the mind of man, though fallen and perverted from its wholeness, is nevertheless clothed and ornamented with God's excellent gifts. If we regard the Spirit of God as the sole fountain of truth, we shall neither reject the truth itself, nor despise it wherever it shall appear, unless we wish to dishonor the Spirit of God. For by holding the gifts of the Spirit in slight esteem, we contemn and reproach the Spirit himself. What then? Shall we deny that the truth shone upon the ancient jurists who established civic order and discipline with such great equity? Shall we say

that the philosophers were blind in their fine observation and artful description of nature? Shall we say that those men were devoid of understanding who conceived the art of disputation and taught us to speak reasonably? Shall we say that they are insane who developed medicine, devoting their labor to our benefit? What shall we say of all the mathematical sciences? Shall we consider them the ravings of madmen? No, we cannot read the writings of the ancients on these subjects without great admiration. We marvel at them because we are compelled to recognize how preeminent they are. But shall we count anything praiseworthy or noble without recognizing at the same time that it comes from God? Let us be ashamed of such ingratitude, into which not even the pagan poets fell, for they confessed that the gods had invented philosophy, laws, and all useful arts. Those men who Scripture calls "natural men" were, indeed, sharp and penetrating in their investigation of inferior things. Let us, accordingly learn by their example how many gifts the Lord left to human nature even after it was despoiled of its true good.[11]

Should we discredit and scorn the careful observations and descriptions of nature, developments in medicine, and advances in mathematics simply because unbelievers might have made them? Calvin emphatically said no.

Similar commendations of the science of the heathens occur throughout the commentaries. The Old Testament makes clear that two of the greatest leaders of Israel received their preparation and education in pagan courts. Calvin made much of the fact that Moses was thoroughly educated in the schools of Egypt and that Daniel and his three friends were trained in the learning and literature of the Chaldeans. Of the reference made by Stephen during his defense before the Sanhedrin to the fact that "Moses was educated in all the wisdom of the Egyptians," Calvin wrote that Moses "was instructed in the noble arts,"[12] and where discussing the dimensions of Noah's ark, he observed that "Moses was educated in all the science of the Egyptians and was not ignorant of geometry."[13] Regarding the educational experience of Daniel and his three friends, Calvin suggested that they "might have learned these arts; that is, astrology, and other liberal sciences, just as Moses is said to have been instructed in all the sciences of Egypt." "It is said both of Moses and of our Prophet," he continued, "that they were imbued with a knowledge of the stars and of the other liberal sciences."[14] Calvin claimed that Daniel and his three companions "were divinely adorned with this gift, well versed in the Chaldean literature and true and natural science."[15] He observed that "Daniel made rapid progress in all sciences, and flourished much in intellectual quickness" because of the liberality of God. Not once in his reflections on the educational experiences of Moses and Daniel in these pagan environments did Calvin criticize the Egyptians or the Chaldeans for educating their young men. He did not cast aspersions on the content of their "heathen" training by making negative comments about the liberal arts in general or by intimating that Moses and Daniel had to unlearn most of what they had learned. On the contrary, Calvin viewed the liberal training with which Daniel and his friends had been adorned as a "gift" and their progress in learning as the product of the "mere liberality of God."[16]

Calvin's remarkable acceptance of the learning of the Chaldeans and Egyptians, peoples that practiced a brand of superstitious astrology that he so uncompromisingly condemned elsewhere, was completely in keeping with the attitude that he expressed in the passage from the *Institutes* just quoted toward knowledge emanating from pagan sources. So were his comments on Paul's reference to the adage in Titus 1:12 that "Cretans are always liars, evil brutes, lazy gluttons." Here he took advantage of Paul's mention of a heathen writer to castigate those people as "superstitious" who refused to "make any use of secular authors." Calvin insisted that, if "any ungodly man has said anything true," Christians should not reject what they said because "all truth is of God." One may dedicate to the glory of God "everything that can be rightly used in that way."[17] For Calvin, valid knowledge that was developed by unbelievers could be dedicated to God's glory. He was not about to reject a fragment of knowledge on the grounds that a wicked person might have stated it or even discovered it. The validity of knowledge, including even knowledge of nature, was independent of its discoverer or of its proponent because that knowledge originated in God.

It is one thing to give lip service to liberal learning in writings and in sermons. It is another thing to promote knowledge through action, and Calvin was a man of action. Throughout his tenure in Geneva, he was eager to establish educational institutions because he was convinced that the cause of the Reformation would more likely flourish with an educated populace. Not only did he want to encourage the development of educated clergy to provide sound instruction, but he also believed that the people must be educated so that they might effectively receive and appropriate that instruction. Calvin's educational efforts culminated in the establishment of the Academy of Geneva in June, 1559. The Academy consisted of the *schola privata* for students to about the age of sixteen and the *schola publica* for older students. The latter provided essentially university education and marked the beginnings of the University of Geneva. Although the curriculum was strong in humanistic studies such as French, Hebrew, Greek, Latin, classical literature and history, and theology, Calvin was insistent that instruction also be devoted to the natural sciences. That was the responsibility of the professor of arts. According to W. Stanford Reid (1913-1996), a historian at the University of Guelph, "Calvin believed that physical science should be taught simply because nature was God's vesture in which He continually reveals Himself to all men everywhere. Stressing the idea of Creation he held that man should investigate and study nature in order to understand its Maker."[18] For Calvin, affirmation of liberal learning was not simply a matter of talk but a matter of the utmost urgency. He, therefore, took steps to educate people and not just talk about educating them.

Sciences and Arts as a Gift of God Worthy of Praise

That Calvin could so freely accept knowledge from unbelievers flowed from his conviction that knowledge is a gift of God. As Reid put it, Calvin "accepted all scientific investigation as God-given for the use and profit of man."[19] We will look at these two aspects of science in turn: first, its character as a gift from God and, secondly, its utility. The notion that science and the ability to gain scientific knowledge are gifts of God, given even to the heathen, features prominently throughout the commentaries. The account in Genesis 4 of the development of culture by the descendants of Cain elicited an extensive discussion from Calvin regarding the arts and sciences. After discussing the wickedness of Cain's descendant Lamech, he turned to the descriptions of the cultural achievements of Jabal, Jubal, and Tubalcain, Lamech's accomplished offspring. Acknowledging that some good had been blended with the evils in the family of Cain, Calvin wrote that "the invention of arts, and of other things which serve to the common use and convenience of life, is a gift of God by no means to be despised and a faculty worthy of commendation." Even though the line of Cain had fallen from integrity, they still exceeded the race of Adam in rare endowments, which Calvin considered a wonderful thing. As Cain and his descendants were endued with gifts "of no despicable kind," even so in Calvin's own day, the "excellent gifts of the Spirit" had been diffused throughout the entire human race.

"The liberal arts and sciences," Calvin asserted, "have descended to us from the heathen" to such an extent that we must "acknowledge that we have received astronomy, and the other parts of philosophy, medicine, and the order of civil government from them." God had liberally enriched the heathen with "excellent favours" to the end that they would have less excuse for their impiety before God. Christians, Calvin thought, should admire the riches of God's favor that had been bestowed on the heathen.[20]

If there is a passage in Scripture that might readily lend itself to an interpretation that is condemnatory of science or even higher learning generally, it is the first chapter of I Corinthians, a text that roundly repudiates the wisdom of the world. Calvin, however, did not view the passage that way. Instead he took great pains to point out that the apostle Paul was not issuing a blanket condemnation of all human knowledge and learning. He insisted that it was unreasonable to think that Paul would "condemn out of hand those arts, which, without any doubt, are splendid gifts of God, gifts which we could call instruments for helping men carry out worthwhile activities." What sorts of arts did Calvin have in mind? There is nothing irreligious about those arts, "for they contain sound learning, and depend on principles of truth." Such arts are "useful and suitable for the general affairs of human society" so that one cannot doubt that "they have come from the Holy Spirit." Paul is "not to be taken as disparaging to the arts, as if they were working against religion."[21] Nor was Calvin here confining the acceptable arts to practical skills, for he claimed that knowledge "is well known to be the chief gift of God in this world." After all, what is more noble than a man's reason, the faculty in which he excels the animals?[22] When arriving at I Corinthians 3:19 where Paul says that "the wisdom of this world is foolishness in God's sight," Calvin almost seemed to have turned Paul's assertion on its head by claiming that "natural insight is a gift of God. The arts men naturally pursue, and all the disciplines by which wisdom is acquired are also gifts of God."[23]

The final verses of Isaiah 28 also provided an opening for Calvin to reflect on science and knowledge. These verses refer specifically to farming as a skill whose practitioners have been instructed by God. The farmer's knowledge and ability have come, said the prophet, from the Almighty himself. Calvin remarked that "not only agriculture, but likewise all the arts which contribute to the advantage of mankind, are the gift of God, and that all that belongs to skilful invention has been imparted by him to the minds of men." As a result, men have no excuse for being proud "or to arrogate to themselves the praise of invention." Then Calvin proceeded from the practical arts and skills to other sciences of a more abstract and theoretical nature.

> If we ought to form such an opinion about agriculture and mechanical arts, what shall we think of the learned and exalted sciences, such as medicine, jurisprudence, astronomy, geometry, logic, and such like? Shall we not much more consider them to have proceeded from God? Shall we not in them also behold and acknowledge his goodness, that his praise and glory may be celebrated both in the smallest and in the greatest affairs?[24]

Some of Calvin's most instructive and delightful passages pertaining to the study of nature were uttered in his sermons on Job. By way of example, in his first sermon on Job 28, Calvin preached on Job's discourse about mines and mining. Calvin instructed his congregation that knowledge of nature is a gift of God that he has lavished on believers and unbelievers alike.

> When he says that man's wit is by nature able to conceive the things that are here beneath, and which concerned the present life, the word "nature" does not bar it from being God's gift, but serves to do us to understand that the thing is given to the unbelievers also and to those whom God has not forgotten again by his Holy Ghost. . . . Although we have not the Holy Ghost, to be regenerated . . . . yet may we well have understanding. For it is a common thing both to the believers and unbelievers, to judge of the things that are here beneath, yea and oftentimes the wicked, and the despisers of God, to be the sharper witted, and more skillful in their doings.

> Although there be a great number of secrets in nature . . . yet has God given men ability to attain unto them. . . . The thing then that I mean, is that there is some capacity in men to comprehend natural things, notwithstanding that they be dark at the first entrance. And although men be hard and gross of understanding, yet do they attain to the cast of this earthly life, because God gives them the aids and means wherewith to pass through the world.[25]

At times, Calvin went beyond referring to science and knowledge as gifts of God by suggesting that knowledge is a kind of revelation from God. Such knowledge included not simply that which is drawn from the Bible. Any valid knowledge is revelatory. Calvin wrote that "Christ condemns only such probing as goes beyond the limits set by God's revelation." By this assertion he was not restricting revelation to the Bible or condemning extra-biblical learning, for he went on to say that "such matters as philosophers or farmers have come to understand by their art, by learning, by judgment, or by experience, God is not described as having kept to himself, since he has in a sense put all that into their hands."[26] He has, in effect, revealed it to men.

Because the arts and sciences are the gifts of a God who lavishes good things upon the human race for our enjoyment, the sciences are eminently worthy of our praise and admiration. "How richly deserving of honour are the liberal sciences, which polish man so as to give him the dignity of true humanity!" Calvin enthused.[27] He frequently singled out astronomy as praiseworthy. He realized, of course, that the study of the heavens had commonly been prostituted and debased to mere fortune-telling. In reference to Daniel's response to Nebuchadnezzar's desire to have his dream about the great statue with the feet of clay interpreted, Calvin recognized the dual character of the study of the heavenly bodies in his day by writing that he excluded from praiseworthiness those superstitions that vitiated true and genuine science. As to its principles, however, he said that he could not condemn astronomy and whatever belonged to a consideration of the order of nature.[28] Elsewhere, he cast his view in much more positive terms by asserting that astronomy "is indeed worthy of praise, were men to preserve moderation," or that because astronomy considered the wonderful workmanship of God involved in the placement of the stars, in their variety, and in their moving, force, and secret offices, it is, therefore, a profitable and praiseworthy exercise.[29]

If science is a praiseworthy activity, and if we have been placed in this world as in a spacious theater to behold the works of God, as Calvin was so fond of pointing out, then we can understand why he claimed that "there is no work of God so small that we ought to pass by it lightly, but all ought to be carefully and diligently observed."[30]

The Utility of Sciences and Arts

As Reid noted, Calvin also recognized that God had given the gift of science for our use and profit. The arts and sciences are praiseworthy not simply because they are gifts of God but also because they are useful and valuable to human life. The liberal sciences yield "a great number of rare products."[31] According to Calvin, Isaiah commended "the mechanical arts, agriculture, manual occupations of every description, architecture, and such like," all of them endeavors we cannot dispense with. "Artisans of every kind, who contribute what is useful to men, are the servants of God," and have the preservation of mankind in view.[32] As we saw in his discussion of Paul's rebuff to human wisdom in I Corinthians, Calvin rejected the thought that the apostle condemned the arts that serve as instruments to assist men in the accomplishment of important purposes.

Arts that are useful and suited to the common transactions of human life have undoubtedly come from the Holy Spirit and the advantage derived from them ought to be ascribed exclusively to God.[33]

Calvin singled out astronomy, the legitimate form of astrology, as a science that is "not only pleasant, but also very useful to be known." Not least of its benefits is that it "unfolds the admirable wisdom of God."[34] Just like the study of nature or the practical arts, music, too, has its value. When Isaiah pronounced woe and judgment on the rebellious people of God who stayed up late at night until they were inflamed with wine, and played harps, lyres, tambourines, and flutes at their banquets, Calvin wrote that Isaiah was not blaming or condemning music *per se*, "for it is a science which ought not to be despised."[35] Even though the harp and similar instruments minister to our pleasure rather than to our necessity, music is not altogether superfluous and does not deserve to be condemned. Moreover, music can be adapted to the offices of religion and made profitable to men. But, Calvin warned, music needs to be freed from "vicious attractions" and from foolish delight by which it seduces men from better employments and occupies them in vanity.[36]

The consequence of the fact that science, the arts, scientific ability, and artistic ability are good gifts of God that make life more pleasant and productive is that honor and respect are due to those who possess these gifts and employ them in the pursuit of science and the arts. The ingenious men who expended labor in the pursuit of astronomy ought to be honored, Calvin said. He urged those who had the time and ability not to neglect such exercises but to seek the "more exalted" knowledge that astronomers possess.[37] One passage illustrates in particularly stunning fashion Calvin's high regard for experts in various fields of knowledge. In discussing the shipwreck of the apostle Paul and his companions on the way to Rome as described in Acts 27, Calvin commended the Roman centurion for listening to the captain of the ship rather than paying attention to Paul's "divinely inspired" advice about how to survive the tempest! In effect, he commended the centurion for heeding the advice of a man rather than "the word of God!" He wrote that "the centurion is not blamed because he listened to the captain and owner rather than Paul. In fact what should he have done? For although he deferred very much to Paul's advice on other matters, yet he knew that he had no skill in navigation. Therefore, like a prudent and modest man, he allows himself to be guided by those who were trained and experienced."[38]

Criticism of Those Who Espouse Ignorance

Unlike many contemporary Christians, Calvin was not the sort of person who always tried to cast his message in positive terms. He did not hesitate to point out and condemn erroneous belief or deficient behavior. Not being content with the positive stress that the pursuit of science is a good thing, he also reasoned more negatively that the downgrading, neglect, or willful ignorance of science and learning were reprehensible. Calvin leveled harsh terms like "fanatic" at folk who outright opposed learning, favored ignorance, or were content with limited knowledge. In regard to Paul's claim in I Corinthians 8 that "knowledge puffs up," he castigated "certain extremists, who furiously protest against all the liberal arts and science" because they are of the mistaken opinion that the only purpose of the arts and sciences was to "encourage men's pride" rather than to have any "valuable contribution to make to our everyday life." He berated the arrogance of those who are willfully ignorant.[39] Paul's request to Timothy that he bring him his scrolls and parchments moved Calvin to write that this request refuted "the madness of the fanatics who despise books and condemn all reading and boast only of their ενθυσιασμους, their private inspirations by God. But we should note that this passage commends continual reading to all godly men as a thing from which they can profit."[40] Calvin bemoaned what he perceived as a very anti-intellectual attitude in his own day. While musing on the education of Daniel by the Chaldeans, he complained that

> learning and the liberal arts were not then so despised as they are in this age, and in those immediately preceding it. So strongly has barbarism prevailed in the world, that it is almost disgraceful for nobles to be reckoned among the men of education and of letters! The chief boast of the nobility was to be destitute of scholarship—nay, they gloried in the assertion, that there were no scholars, in the language of the day.[41]

In what is arguably the best known passage pertaining to the sciences in all of Calvin's writings, he chided individuals who rejected the study of the stars. "This study is not to be reprobated," he asserted, "nor this science to be condemned, because some frantic persons are wont boldly to reject whatever is unknown to them."[42] He roundly criticized the anabaptists "for boasting of being spiritual persons" on the grounds "that they are grossly ignorant of all science." He further criticized them because they presumed to be following the example of David and thereby said that all learning and liberal sciences should be despised.[43] Calvin also rebuked those who condemned philosophy because they thought that the apostle Paul had issued a blanket indictment when he warned against being taken captive "through hollow and deceptive philosophy." "Many have mistakenly imagined that Paul here condemns philosophy," Calvin averred. He seriously doubted that Paul was referring to philosophical thinking in general but rather to "everything that men contrive of themselves when wishing to be wise in their own understanding." Philosophy in this context is "only a corruption of spiritual doctrine if it is mixed up with Christ."[44]

Although recognizing that there were numerous instances in which the Lord employed poorly educated men and women, Calvin thought that there was no excuse for turning that precedent into a norm and thereby exalting ignorance as a virtue. When the Lord chose several plain working folk who lacked a great deal of education to serve among his apostles, he did not choose them because he preferred "ignorance to learning, just as some crazy fellows applaud themselves for their ignorance, and reckon they are closer to the Apostles for being further from their books." The point of Jesus' choosing fishermen like Peter and Andrew was not to commend ignorance but to "bring down the lofty looks of those who thought heaven was closed to the uneducated classes." Calvin reminded his readers that the Lord later added the very highly educated Paul to the apostolate.[45]

Calvin rebuked those who might not explicitly condemn learning but yet showed indications of mental laziness, considered much learning to be too taxing, or were so content with their own limited knowledge that they could not be further instructed. He knew that there are people "who chatter away that on difficult problems they rightly suspend their judgment because they must wait for a sure definition of it," but what really irritated him was that some people went farther and used that plea as an excuse "that it is wisdom to avoid deliberately any inquisition into the truth." He complained that it was "wicked slothfulness" that, although people might "take so much trouble about fleshly and earthly things," they neglected their eternal salvation and contrived "empty excuses for their gross and supine ignorance."[46] Although criticizing those who found it too difficult to do any hard thinking about spiritual matters, Calvin was also put off by general unwillingness to exercise the mind. In another context, he complained about people who were "overtaken at once by the irksomeness of learning" and considered them as much "too capricious or pleasure-loving."[47]

Calvin was particularly scathing toward those who were content with limited knowledge but acted as if they knew everything. "There is no worse plague than when men are so drunk with their belief in their little learning," the reformer fumed, "that they boldly reject everything contrary to their opinion."[48] He lamented that

> many are immediately satisfied with but moderate information, and as soon as they understand a portion of any subject, they reject every addition, and many too often settle down at the first elements, and their obstinacy prevents that complete knowledge which is necessary.[49]

Calvin's general attitude toward intellectual apathy may be summed up by his observation that "sometimes ill disposed, shameless ignorance creates more difficulty and trouble than great cleverness and learning."[50]

We plainly see that Calvin did not suffer from the malady, not unknown in our own day, that afflicts people who take perverse delight in mocking or scorning the counsel of experts or who consider themselves to be just as qualified to make pronouncements in some field of knowledge as the experts in that field even though their knowledge of that field may be negligible.

The Discoveries of the Philosophers

Calvin's admiration for science was not restricted to broad generalities. He was not like individuals in our own day who pay great lip service to science and wish to be considered as scientifically minded people while taking the opportunity to announce their rejection of fundamental theoretical explanations that have been painstakingly developed by the scientific community. In the sixteenth century, of course, there were no "scientists" as there are today. Natural knowledge was gleaned by scholars who demonstrated very wide-ranging interests. Calvin and others generally referred to these scholars as the "philosophers." Not only did he regularly pay homage to liberal learning as having great value in the enrichment of human life, but he also frequently acknowledged the validity of specific contributions that had been made to an understanding of the natural world by the "philosophers." Despite his suspicion of some of their metaphysical, epistemological, and religious claims, Calvin rendered due honor to the philosophers when they dealt with the structure and functioning of the natural world. He believed they had more penetration into astronomical matters than did other people.[51] He acknowledged that there were people who were "exceedingly acute in discerning the natural cause of things."[52] He commended the astronomers for investigating with great labor whatever the sagacity of the human mind could comprehend.[53] "The philosophers," Calvin preached in his second sermon on Job 28, "have well conceived the reason of the things that are seen in this world."[54] And in his fifth sermon on Job 36, he said that it was God who "gave wit to the heathen philosophers" to treat the secrets of nature so skillfully.[55]

What specifically was it that the philosophers had discovered by virtue of their acumen? "Astronomers prove, by conclusive reasons," Calvin claimed, "that the star of Saturn, which, on account of its great distance, appears the least of all, is greater than the moon."[56] He said that the philosophers understood "how the stars are arranged in such beautiful order" and that "notwithstanding their immense number there is no confusion."[57] Philosophers brought some probable reasons as to the extent of the heavens.[58] They also conjectured about the dimensions of the Earth.

In his commentary on Exodus 7:8-13, a passage that refers to the changing of the rods by the magicians of Egypt, Calvin asserted that the "philosophers are not ignorant of the great variety of transmutation which occur in nature."[59] Among those phenomena that the philosophers had been able to account for by transmutation, he included atmospheric phenomena such as rain, snow, clouds, hail, wind, thunder, lightning, and comets. The philosophers knew a great deal about rain, wind, and other atmospheric manifestations. In an extended discussion of Jeremiah 10:12-13, a passage that extols the power and wisdom of God in creating and governing the heavens and earth, we read that "philosophers find out the cause why the winds arise from the earth."[60] He then proceeded to discuss their explanation. Elsewhere he wrote that "philosophers discover the origin of rain in the elements."[61] The philosophers also discoursed properly about the origin of snow. As he said in his fourth sermon on Job 38:

> Have we not cause to magnify the inestimable power of God when he covers the whole earth with snow? Whence takes he so great a quantity of waters? Truly men will say it is engendered in the middle rooms of the air which is cold, and that when a great quantity of vapours is drawn up there, at length the

same comes together and freezes, and thereof engenders the snow: and if the same stuff is more harder bound, then hail is engendered, because the thing has become more fast and substantial. Men may well say so, and it is true.[62]

Calvin maintained that philosophers had obtained genuine knowledge about the behavior of animals. Deuteronomy 28 recites a very lengthy litany of curses that would befall the Israelites if they failed to live in obedience to Yahweh. One curse threatens that harvests would be slight because locusts would devour the crops. The reference to locusts prompted Calvin to write that the philosophers had discovered the reason why more little creatures are generated in one year than another.[63]

We Must Rise above Science to God

Now that we have established that Calvin was very favorable toward scientific activity and thinking, let's consider some of the apparently negative assessments that were introduced at the beginning of the chapter. A synopsis of Calvin's attitude toward science would be incomplete without some attempt to place it within a larger context and to take note of some caveats he issued with regard to science. It is appropriate, therefore, to point out that, despite his interest in and respect for investigation of the natural world, Calvin, as a Christian theologian, consistently stressed that science was not the pinnacle of knowledge beyond which one need not or cannot advance. He insisted that a practitioner of science who remained content solely with science and did not rise to the knowledge of God was ultimately engaging in a barren and useless enterprise. Although science is a praiseworthy activity that may be practiced to the glory of God by the Christian believer and that may lead to many worthwhile benefits when practiced by the unbeliever, science is incapable of leading anyone to eternal life or of instructing anyone in spiritual matters. For the person who gains the whole world, or gains eminence in science, but loses his own soul, science avails nothing in the end. It is in light of these observations that many of the following comments from Calvin must be understood.

In addressing Paul's quotations from Psalm 14 and 53 to the effect that no one seeks after God, Calvin opined that "the man in whom there is no knowledge of God, whatever other learning he may otherwise possess, is empty, and even the very sciences and the arts, which are good in themselves, are emptied of significance when they lack this basis."[64] Like Paul, Calvin warned that natural knowledge was of no value when it came to acquiring spiritual wisdom. Without Christ the sciences in every department are vain, and "the man who is well grounded in every aspect of learning, but is yet ignorant of God, has nothing."[65] In the Genesis passage where he extolled the wonderful gifts of God that had been lavishly bestowed upon the heathen, Calvin maintained that "Christians should value even more highly the grace of regeneration than all the gifts of intellect and aesthetics."[66] He warned that those who practice science and art need to give due regard to moderation. Astronomy is praiseworthy "were men to preserve moderation." The problem was, however, that "the curiosity of men is insatiable, so they wandered here and there, and overleaped all limits, and thus perverted the whole order of nature." As a result, the Chaldeans "were not genuine, but, on the contrary, spurious astrologers."[67] Where dealing with the episode in which the apostles drew lots to discern the replacement for Judas, Calvin again castigated the Chaldeans, saying that the casting of lots is no more depraved by corrupt usage than genuine astrology is by the vain and counterfeit devices of the Chaldeans. He charged that they had gone about cloaking and coloring their "wicked curiosity" under the guise of astrology, and, in so doing, brought into disrepute a science that is "both useful and praiseworthy."[68] Science is a handmaid, not a mistress, and so the sciences are empty and worthless until they have become entirely subject to the word and Spirit of God. If those engaged in science and the arts set themselves in opposition to Christ, then they must be looked upon as dangerous pests.[69]

The Philosophers Do Not Go Far Enough

Despite the significant contributions to scientific knowledge by the philosophers, contributions that he willingly granted and even admired, Calvin taught that "the chief thing in philosophy is to have regard to God, who brings the winds out of his treasures."[70] He thought it was fine that philosophers mentioned the causes of things in the natural world, but he urged that "we ought to come to the fountain itself, and the original cause, even this, that things are so arranged in the world, that though there are intermediate and subordinate causes, yet the primary cause ever appears eminently, even the wisdom and power of God." It may be possible to account for the different winds in terms of exhalations, he conceded, but we must also ask who created the exhalations.[71] So concerned was Calvin that people rise to the knowledge of God that he went so far as to suggest that to be scientifically knowledgeable but lacking the knowledge of heavenly things was almost a worse condition than being ignorant.[72]

Of Peter's passage about the scoffers of the last days who would repudiate God's creation and action in history, Calvin wrote that

> the world does not stand properly by any other power than that of the Word of God, that secondary causes derive their power from Him, and that they have different effects as they are directed. Thus the world was established on the waters, but they had no power of themselves, but were rather subject to the Word of God as an inferior element. . . . We can now see how wrong people are who stop at the bare elements as though perpetuity was to be found in them, and not rather that their nature is amenable to the will of God.[73]

One reason that Calvin constantly stressed the importance of going beyond science and rising up to God is that, in so many cases, the philosophers had failed to do just that. He realized that those who are most acute in the discerning of natural causes are many times the "most blind in reference to the divine judgments."[74] Calvin constantly castigated the philosophers, especially Aristotle, because they did not rise up in praise to God for the wonderful things they had learned. He refused to "excuse the profane subtlety of Aristotle, who, when he disputes so acutely concerning second causes, in his *Book on Meteors*, buries God himself in profound silence."[75] Elsewhere he lamented that "philosophers think not that they have reasoned skilfully enough about inferior causes, unless they separate God very far from his works." Calvin regarded it as a "diabolical science" that would focus our attention on the works of nature and then turn them away from God. He spoke of the great folly of "those philosophers, who, out of mediate and proximate causes, weave themselves vails, lest they should be compelled to acknowledge the hand of God, which manifestly displays itself in his works." Here, too, Calvin singled out Aristotle for special criticism:

> Aristotle, in his book on *Meteors*, reasons very shrewdly about these things, in so far as relates to proximate causes, only that he omits the chief point. The investigation of these would, indeed, be both a profitable and pleasant exercise, were we led by it, as we ought, to the Author of Nature himself. But nothing is more preposterous than, when we meet with mediate causes, however many, to be stopped and retarded by them, as by so many obstacles, from approaching God; for this is the same as if a man were to remain at the very rudiments of things during his whole life, without going further. In short, this is to learn in such a manner that you can never know any thing. That shrewdness alone, therefore, is worthy of praise, which elevates us by these means even to heaven, in order that not a confused noise only may strike our ears, but that the voice of the Lord may penetrate our hearts, and teach us to pray and serve God.[76]

Calvin was also piqued that even the general populace was inclined not to see God's activity in nature. In a fascinating passage about the wheels of the cherubim described in Ezekiel 10, he wrote that "not even the slightest motion happens without that secret instinct" whereby all creatures hear God's voice. And yet, he complained, "when the air is serene and calm, we do not think that God's voice reigns there, but we imagine some natural cause: so also when the sky is clouded, when it rains, when storms rise, when other changes happen, in some way or other we exclude God from these actions."[77]

The reformer also scolded those who did seek to rise beyond second causes, but then pursued improper avenues. On this score he particularly condemned what he regarded as the foolish and vain speculations of "judicial astrology." The Chaldeans were discontented with genuine science, and, as a result, they corrupted the legitimate study of the stars.[78] The Egyptians, too, were not content with the simple order of nature and, like the Chaldeans, had wandered into many foolish speculations.[79]

Calvin further warned against being puffed up with profane sciences. More generally, in his discussion of Paul's warning to Timothy to turn away from godless chatter and knowledge falsely so called, Calvin wrote that Paul had pronounced any science that exalts itself over the simple and humble doctrine of godliness is not knowledge at all. This should be carefully noted so that we may learn to ridicule boldly and pour scorn on that feigned knowledge which fills the world with admiration and amazement, but in which there is no solid edification. The only thing which on Paul's authority truly deserves to be called knowledge is that which instructs us in the confidence and fear of God, that is, in godliness.[80]

Calvin's view of scientific activity that should give due honor to God is well summarized in the Argument to the *Commentary on the Book of Genesis*:

> Men are commonly subject to these two extremes; namely, that some, forgetful of God, apply the whole force of their mind to the consideration of nature; and others, overlooking the works of God, aspire with a foolish and insane curiosity to inquire into his Essence. Both labor in vain. To be so occupied in the investigation of the secrets of nature, as never to turn the eyes to its Author, is a most perverted study; and to enjoy everything in nature without acknowledging the Author of the benefit, is the basest ingratitude.[81]

Science of Itself Cannot Lead to God

For all his desire that the philosophers and the general public should go beyond a mere knowledge of the natural world to acquire the knowledge of God, Calvin was very cognizant that human learning and science in themselves are incapable of leading us to God or helping us to understand spiritual matters. Men may think that they can discern the mysteries of heaven by their own intelligence, but humanity cannot rise up to God through its own wisdom or effort. In his first sermon on Job 28, Calvin preached that intelligent people are prone to think that "because they be sharp witted and subtle in these lower things: they are able also to judge of all God's secrets, of the whole doctrine of the law, of the prophets, and of the gospel. But God makes them double blind, when they be so presumptuous. For faith is a spiritual light."[82] In analyzing Paul's visit to Athens and his distress at seeing the city full of idols, Calvin observed that

> the Holy Spirit convicting the whole world of ignorance and stupidity, says that all the teachers of liberal science were spell-bound by an unusual madness; and from that we gather what use human shrewdness is in the things of God. And there is no doubt that God allowed the Athenians to fall into extreme folly, so that they might be a warning to all generations that all the acuteness of the human mind, aided by learning and teaching, is nothing but foolishness, when it comes to the Kingdom of God . . . and that human wisdom is nothing else but a factory of all the errors.[83]

Along the same lines, Calvin's remarks on light entering the darkness as recorded in the beginning of John's gospel led him to observe that "natural reason will never direct men to Christ. The fact that they are furnished with wisdom for ruling their lives and are formed for the humanities and sciences disappears without effect."[84] There is a difference in the mode of acquisition between the truth of God and that of the human sciences. "Knowledge," said Calvin, "is joined to faith, because we have a sure and undoubted conviction of God's truth, not in the same way as human sciences are apprehended, but when the Spirit seals it in our hearts."[85] Despite the fact that the sciences are good gifts from God and are to be extolled, the sciences are sufficiently limited that they cannot penetrate into God's heavenly kingdom.[86] Science is only a handmaid and not a mistress. Following Paul, Calvin warned again and again that natural knowledge availed nothing when it came to attaining spiritual wisdom.[87]

As a striking example of the contrast between science and divine revelation, Calvin wrote that

> these two things are opposite to each other and do not mutually agree, general and perpetual science, and special revelation. Since God claims this power of opening by means of a dream, what he has engraven on the minds of men, hence art and science cannot obtain it, but a revelation from the spirit must be waited for.[88]

In summary, Calvin wished that all people would be led into fellowship with God through saving faith in his Son Jesus Christ. That saving faith would be imparted by the application of the divine revelation of Holy Scripture to the heart of the believer by the Holy Spirit. Those who had been given the gift of scientific ability by God would then, with joy and delight, explore, describe, and come to understand the workings of God's magnificent creation, and in their activity they would give him glory, praise, and honor for the wonder of his handiwork and for the privilege of investigating it.

NOTES

1. For some recent studies of the life and thought of John Calvin see William Bouwsma, *John Calvin: A Sixteenth-Century Portrait* (New York: Oxford University Press, 1988) and Bernard Cottret, *Calvin: A Biography* (Grand Rapids, Mich.: William B. Eerdmans, 2000).

2. Commentary on Hosea 14:9. All quotations from Calvin's Old Testament commentaries have been drawn from the Calvin Translation Society of Edinburgh edition published between 1845 and 1855 in Great Britain. The entire edition was reprinted during the 1990s by Baker Book House of Grand Rapids, Mich. Virtually all quotations from the New Testament commentaries were drawn from the edition of David W. Torrance and Thomas F. Torrance and published by Oliver and Boyd and by William B. Eerdmans during the 1960s. Quotations throughout the text from Calvin's New Testament Commentaries are reproduced by permission of the William B. Eerdmans Publishing Company. All subsequent notes pertaining to quotations from the commentaries follow the format used at the beginning of this note.

3. Commentary on John 1:5.

4. Commentary on I Corinthians 1:20.

5. Commentary on I Corinthians 8:1-3.

6. Brian A. Gerrish, "The Reformation and the Rise of Modern Science: Luther, Calvin, and Copernicus," in *The Old Protestantism and the New*, ed. Brian A. Gerrish (Chicago: University of Chicago Press, 1982), 163-78.

7. Christopher B. Kaiser, *Creational Theology and the History of Physical Science: The Creationist Tradition from Basil to Bohr* (Leiden: Brill, 1997), 52.

8. The terms "astronomy" and "astrology" were used interchangeably during the first half of the sixteenth century, but Calvin consistently employed the Latin word *astrologia* or the French word *astrologie* whenever he was talking about either what we would consider the legitimate science of astronomy or what we now consider the illegitimate use of the stars for horoscopes. The context invariably makes clear what meaning Calvin had in mind when he used the words *astrologia* or *astrologie*. Calvin, following in the line of medieval scholars, regarded legitimate scientific astrology as encompassing the notion that heavenly bodies (not just the Sun and Moon) exert a profound influence on the Earth. Medical practice of Calvin's time, for example, relied on the positions of stellar constellations in the sky. This topic will be explored more thoroughly in Chapters 2 and 6. Because the term "astrology" has a negative connotation for contemporary Christians and because most educated people today make a distinction between astronomy and astrology, I will normally use the terms "astronomy" and "astronomer" in reference to what Calvin considered legitimate "astrology," and I will restrict the terms "astrology" and "astrologer" in reference to what Calvin considered as an illegitimate brand of astrology, namely, "judicial astrology."

9. K. J. Howell, *God's Two Books: Copernican Cosmology and Biblical Interpretation in Early Modern Science* (Notre Dame, Ind.: University of Notre Dame Press, 2002).

10. John Calvin, *Concerning Scandals*, trans. J. W. Fraser, (Grand Rapids, Mich.: William B. Eerdmans, 1978).

11. Unless otherwise noted, quotations from Calvin's *Institutes* are reproduced from *Calvin: Institutes of the Christian Religion* (Library of Christian Classics Series) edited by John T. McNeill. Used by permission of Westminster John Knox Press. This is the English translation of the 1559 Latin text by Ford Lewis Battles. The quotation here cited comes from *Institutes* 2.2.15, referring to Book 2, Chapter 2, Section 15.

12. Commentary on Acts 7:22.
13. Commentary on Genesis 6:14.
14. Commentary on Daniel 1:4.
15. Commentary on Daniel 1:17.
16. Commentary on Daniel 2:30.
17. Commentary on Titus 1:12.
18. W. S. Reid, "Calvin and the Founding of the Geneva Academy," *Westminster Theological Journal* 18, (1955): 1-33.
19. W. S. Reid, "Natural Science in Sixteenth-Century Calvinistic Thought," *Transactions of the Royal Society of Canada* 1 ser. 4, (1963): 305-19.
20. Commentary on Genesis 4:20-22.
21. Commentary on I Corinthians 1:17.
22. Commentary on I Corinthians 1:20.
23. Commentary on I Corinthians 3:19.
24. Commentary on Isaiah 28:29.
25. The quotation is from the First Sermon on Job 28. See John Calvin, *Sermons on Job* (Edinburgh: Banner of Truth Trust, 1993). This is a facsimile of the 1574 edition (London: George Bishop), a translation into English from French by Arthur Golding. All further citations of the sermons on Job will simply be identified as a specific sermon on a specific chapter of Job as above. Because the English translation from which the sermon quotations have been taken is centuries old, the author has modified the translations where appropriate.
26. Commentary on Acts 1:7.
27. Commentary on I Corinthians 1:20.
28. Commentary on Daniel 2:27-28.
29. Commentary on Jeremiah 50:35-36 and Acts 7:22.
30. Commentary on Isaiah 57:1.
31. Commentary on I Corinthians 1:20.
32. Commentary on Isaiah 3:4.
33. Commentary on I Corinthians 1:17.
34. Commentary on Genesis 1:16.
35. Commentary on Isaiah 5:12
36. Commentary on Genesis 4:20.
37. Commentary on Genesis 1:16.
38. Commentary on Acts 27:11.
39. Commentary on I Corinthians 8:1.
40. Commentary on II Timothy 4:13.
41. Commentary on Daniel 1:4.
42. Commentary on Genesis 1:16.
43. Commentary on Psalm 71:15.
44. Commentary on Colossians 2:8.
45. Commentary on Luke 5:10.
46. Commentary on Matthew 16:2-3.
47. Commentary on Acts 19:9.
48. Commentary on John 7:28.
49. Commentary on Daniel 8:15.
50. Commentary on II Timothy 4:14.
51. Commentary on Psalm 19:2.
52. Commentary on Genesis 20:2.
53. Commentary on Genesis 1:16.

54. Second Sermon on Job 28.
55. Fifth Sermon on Job 36.
56. Commentary on Genesis 1:16.
57. Commentary on Psalm 19:2
58. Commentary on Jeremiah 31:37.
59. Commentary on Exodus 7:8-13.
60. Commentary on Jeremiah 10:12-13.
61. Commentary on Psalm 147:7-8.
62. Fourth Sermon on Job 38.
63. Commentary on Deuteronomy 28:38.
64. Commentary on Romans 3:11.
65. Commentary on I Corinthians 1:20.
66. Commentary on Genesis 4:20.
67. Commentary on Jeremiah 50:35-36.
68. Commentary on Acts 1:26.
69. Commentary on I Corinthians 3:19. Calvin would, I believe, have thrilled to the scientific labors of men and women today who have committed their lives to Christ and who seek to bring glory to God in their effort to explain some of the wonders and mysteries of God's creative handiwork. He would, I believe, have greatly appreciated the work that is done in the various science departments of Christian colleges and universities to train young Christian students in how to interpret the created order in the context of Christian faith. And, I believe, Calvin would have rejoiced to see the flourishing of Christian scientific organizations like Christians in Science and the American Scientific Affiliation (ASA) whose members are practicing scientists in a wide variety of fields but whose primary allegiance is to Jesus Christ. ASA publishes a quarterly journal entitled *Perspectives on Science and Christian Faith*. Information about the Affiliation may be found on its website at www.asa3.org.
70. Commentary on Jeremiah 10:12-13.
71. Commentary on Jeremiah 51:16-17.
72. Commentary on Hosea 14:9.
73. Commentary on II Peter 3:5.
74. Commentary on Genesis 20:2.
75. Commentary on Genesis 19:24.
76. Commentary on Psalm 29:5-8.
77. Commentary on Ezekiel 10:13.
78. Commentary on Daniel 1:17.
79. Commentary on Acts 7:22.
80. Commentary on I Timothy 6:20.
81. Commentary on Genesis, Argument.
82. First Sermon on Job 28.
83. Commentary on Acts17:16.
84. Commentary on John 1:5.
85. Commentary on John 6:69.
86. Commentary on I Corinthians 3:19.
87. Commentary on Romans 3:11.
88. Commentary on Daniel 2:4.

CHAPTER 2

CALVIN ON THE HEAVENS

We have seen that John Calvin deeply appreciated the sciences for their ability to shed greater light on the works of God as well as for their utility to humankind. He regarded the sciences as one of the choicest gifts of the creator, and he judged that they provide occasion for offering praise to God. But what was the content of Calvin's scientific knowledge about the natural world? To what extent did his views comport with or differ from those of his contemporaries? We will seek to answer such questions in the next few chapters. In this chapter we will begin by examining Calvin's conception of the overall structure and behavior of the universe and of the place of the Earth within the universe. In the next chapter we will examine his ideas about the nature of matter and atmospheric phenomena. In Chapter 4 Calvin's "geological" ideas will come into view. What did he think about earthquakes, mountains, rocks, and fossils? In Chapter 5 we will explore Calvin's ideas about animals and plants, and our overview of his scientific ideas concludes with a survey of his knowledge of human biology, disease, and medicine in Chapter 6. Along the way we will try to uncover the major influences on Calvin's scientific thinking.

Let's begin with cosmology. John Calvin probably wrote more about the heavens than about any other aspect of the physical creation. There are several reasons for this emphasis. In the first place, Calvin's conceptions about nature were profoundly shaped by Scripture. He was, after all, a *biblical* theologian. The Bible is steeped in talk about the heavens from its very first page. The biblical writers all lived in a part of the world that is remarkable for its arid climate and its crystal clear skies. Shepherds who kept watch over their flocks by night on the Palestinian hillsides could not help but be awestruck by the dazzling heavenly host of the stars. It is small wonder that the psalm-writing shepherd

David would write that the heavens declare the glory of God, and it is small wonder that God directed Àbram's attention to the night sky and promised Abram that his descendants would be as numerous as the stars. The night-time heavens of the ancient Near East were undoubtedly much more brilliant than are the skies of modern industrialized Europe and North America, strongly affected as they are by high humidity and haze, frequent clouds and storms, air pollution caused by particulate matter, and light pollution in the vicinity of sprawling cities. If contemporary North American Christians desire a semblance of the night-sky experience of Abram or David without traveling to the Near East, they should camp out in the open spaces of the American Southwest, far removed from large population centers. The millions of denizens of American cities who are familiar only with the washed out skies of the northeastern United States would be stunned at how awesome, black, and deep the night sky actually is, how brilliant the stars are in places like Monument Valley on the Utah-Arizona border, and how many stars are visible. The night sky of sixteenth-century France and Switzerland was, no doubt, clearer than that of modern Paris or Geneva, but even so, the humidity of the European climate would have rendered the sky that Calvin saw dimmer than the sky visible to the biblical writers. As a faithful expositor of the biblical text, however, he was much influenced by the conception and impression of the heavens with which the biblical writers operated. Few things convey a sense of awe and an awareness of our smallness, fragility, and seeming insignificance as effectively as a panoramic view of the desert sky on a clear night, the kind of view well known to the biblical writers.

In the second place, Calvin wrote about the heavens because he was well aware of their utility. He understood that sailors used stellar positions as aids in navigation. In common with his contemporaries, he also recognized the effect that the Sun (and, he thought, the Moon and the constellations) had on the seasons and on agriculture. Genesis 1, of course, confirmed that God had given the Sun and the Moon to humanity to rule the seasons and, with that, the times for planting and harvesting.

Thirdly, the study of the stars and planets was more advanced than was the study of plants, animals, substances, rocks, fossils, and mountains in Calvin's day. Terms like "biology," "botany," "zoology," "chemistry," and "geology" were not yet in use. "Astrology" and "astronomy," however, were. Astronomy in the sixteenth century was heir to a long tradition that began millennia before Christ in Sumer and Egypt where the positions of stars throughout the year had been catalogued. The tradition passed on to Greece where a host of major advances occurred. The Greeks refined measurements of stellar positions, discovered the precession of the equinoxes, measured distances to the Sun and the Moon, measured the sizes of the Sun and the Earth, and learned to predict eclipses.

Cosmology Before Calvin's Time

Greek cosmology was profoundly shaped by Plato and Aristotle. Plato (428-347 B. C.) advanced his cosmological ideas in the dialogue *Timaeus*.[1] He postulated that a divine creator, operating with the idea of an orderly cosmos, imposed order on pre-existing undifferentiated raw matter in a state of inharmonious motion. The world, for Plato, was also a living thing that possessed soul and intelligence. In his conception, the universe was spherical and had a circular motion. He considered the Earth to be a stationary globe located at the center of the universe. The Sun, the Moon, the five known planets (Mercury, Venus, Mars, Jupiter, and Saturn), and all the stars were thought to revolve daily around the central Earth. Plato's cosmology was systematically developed and refined by Eudoxos (c. 408-355 B. C.) and by Plato's most brilliant student, Aristotle (384-322 B. C.).[2] Aristotle envisioned the Sun, the planets, and the stars being carried around the Earth on a series of nested "homocentric" spheres. The sphere of the Sun was considered to be more distant from the Earth than the sphere of the Moon. The spheres of the planets were believed to be more distant than the sphere of the Sun. The sphere of the fixed stars was thought to be highest of all. In Aristotle's thought, this outer sphere of fixed stars revolved the most rapidly of any of the spheres, imparting circular motion successively to inner spheres by something akin to frictional drag. Aristotle also envisioned the spheres as having an animated nature with objects farther from the Earth and nearer to the high heavens possessing a higher degree of spirituality. He also introduced the idea of an unmoved mover who set the entire cosmic mechanism into motion. Because, as we now know, Mars and the other planets revolve about the Sun at different rates of speed from that of planet Earth, the planets display the phenomenon of apparent retrograde motion. From the vantage point of the Earth, a planet sometimes appears to move westward relative to its background if observed at a specific hour on a succession of nights, whereas it appears at other times to reverse direction and move eastward relative to its background when observed at the same hour on a succession of nights. This phenomenon of planetary retrograde motion posed one of the major challenges to the conceptual apparatus of Greek cosmology, but thinkers like Eudoxos and Aristotle and, later, the astronomer Claudius Ptolemaeus of Alexandria (Ptolemy) (A. D. c. 100-c. 170) conceived a variety of ways to explain the relative motions of the various spheres. Aristotle accounted for the retrograde motions of planets by proposing a set of several linkages between the various nested spheres that controlled the relative motions. Ptolemy introduced the notion of planetary epicycles in which the planets were said to move on small circles around a center that itself followed a circular path about the central Earth. In addition, he introduced eccentrics, suggesting that the centers of some of the rotating spheres did not coincide with the center of the universe but circled around it.

Aristotle also maintained that there is a fundamental distinction between the region beneath the sphere of the Moon, known as the sublunary realm, and the realm beyond the Moon. In Aristotle's view, the sublunary realm is the part of the cosmos that is characterized by change and impermanence. Objects within that realm are composed of one of four fundamental elements: fire, air, water, and earth. Sublunary motion is generally linear, and objects tend to move up or down.

In contrast, the realm above the sphere of the Moon was very different in Aristotle's scheme. This part of the cosmos partakes of imperishability, unending perfection, static permanence, and eternity. The substance of the heavens differs from that of the four elements. That region, said Aristotle, is composed of a fifth ethereal substance that he called the αιτηερ (aether) or the quintessence, literally the fifth essence. According to Aristotle, the motion in the region beyond the Moon is circular. Circles are, after all, the perfect geometrical shape. Furthermore, the "celestial element" is eternal, because there is no beginning or end to a circle. Thus circular motion must be continuous. The entire system of spheres was enclosed by another revolving sphere, the *primum mobile*, that imparted motion to these inner spheres. Aristotle's prime mover, or unmoved first mover, set the *primum mobile* in motion.

The primary dissenter to the generally accepted view of the structure of the universe in Greece was Aristarchos of Samos (310-230 B. C.). He postulated that the Sun occupies the central position and that the Earth and all other heavenly bodies orbit the Sun. The heliocentric universe of Aristarchos would have been considerably larger than the geocentric universe accepted by virtually everyone else. Lacking sufficient confirmatory evidence, however, the hypothesis of Aristarchos soon fell by the wayside. Consequently, the geocentric picture of cosmic structure developed by Plato and refined by Eudoxos, Aristotle, Hipparchos (second century B. C.), who observed the precession of the equinoxes and developed the system of latitude and longitude for terrestrial geography, and Ptolemy was the dominant view that was adopted by Jewish and early Christian thinkers. The theologians of the early Christian church envisioned the geocentric cosmos developed in Greek thought as generally compatible with biblical texts. They sought to refine the world picture, however, by making it even more consistent with Christian teaching. Basil, Bishop of Caesarea (330-379), for example, rejected the idea that the stars were divine intelligences. Early Christians rejected Aristotle's dualism separating heaven and earth, and other unbiblical elements, such as the claim that the circular motion of the heavens had no beginning, were jettisoned. After all, that assertion smacked of an eternal universe and a denial of creation. In general, early Christian thinkers attempted to retain the biblical emphasis on the unity of heaven and earth.[3]

During the Middle Ages, Aristotle's scheme of homocentric spheres was modified by Islamic scholars such as astronomer Alpetragius (Nur al-Din Ibn Ishaq al-Bitruji) (d. 1204). Four of the greatest medieval thinkers like Roger Bacon (1214-1292) and the great theologians Albertus Magnus (c. 1200-1280), Bonaventure (1221-1274), and Thomas Aquinas (1225-1274) sought to make the scheme more consistent with the Christian doctrine of providence. In Aristotle's cosmology, the *primum mobile* was the only part of the universe with which God had any immediate contact, but placement of the prime mover (God, in Christian terms) beyond the *primum mobile* placed God's activity too remote from the Earth for the liking of Christian scholars. As a result, theologians restricted God's use of the spheres to purely physical effects to allow for God's immediate action on humanity in the spiritual realm. As Kaiser observed:

> the configuration of the heavens was responsible for the creation of worms and insects from putrefaction, for instance, and the sun could influence the birth and death of higher animals—all, of course, under God's ultimate control. There were two channels open, however, for the more immediate influence of God in human life under normal conditions (de potentia ordinata): God could enlighten the soul or affect the will directly, and he could, and regularly did, infuse grace through the seven sacraments, particularly through the Eucharist.[4]

The notion became more entrenched that God providentially directs actions and events on the Earth through the intermediary influence of the heavenly bodies.[5] Christian thinkers also tacked on additional spheres beyond the spheres of the Sun, the Moon, five planets, and starry firmament. These included the waters above the firmament, typically conceived as being crystalline, the outermost created sphere that was the abode of angels called the empyrean, and lastly the heaven of the Holy Trinity.[6]

By Calvin's day astronomy was on the verge of a profound conceptual revolution that was initiated by Nicole Oresme (c. 1320-1382) and Nicolas da Cusa (1401-1464). Nicole Oresme, royal chaplain to King Charles V of France, was a critic of astrology, asserted that so-called magical events could be explained in terms of natural causes, and, although he accepted the geocentric cosmology, taught that terrestrial motion could not be disproved. He proposed that, to a person standing on an object in the heavens, it would appear that the Earth was revolving around that object. Nicholas da Cusa, cardinal of the church of St. Peter ad Vincula in Rome, argued that the Earth is a star, that it is not at the center of the universe, and that it is not at rest. Moreover, he claimed that appearances in the sky could be accounted for by *relative* motion.

A later proposal by Polish astronomer Nicholas Copernicus (1473-1543), who had been unaware of Nicholas da Cusa's radical suggestions, became public in the year of his death through the publication of *De Revolutionibus Orbium Coelestium* (On the Revolution of the Heavenly Spheres), a book that precipitated intense discussion that lasted for decades.[7] The radical idea of Copernicus was that the Sun is located at the center of the cosmos, that the Earth and the five planets all revolve around the Sun, and that the Earth rotates on its axis. Terrestrial rotation, he claimed, gives not only the appearance of the Sun and planets revolving around the Earth but also the appearance that the stars do likewise. Although the Roman Catholic Church was willing to accept his claims about cosmic structure as a hypothesis or a calculating device, physical proof for the heliocentric conception of the universe was needed before full acceptance as a true description of reality could be granted. Copernicus, however, was unable to supply the requisite physical demonstration. Supporting evidence for Copernican heliocentrism was not even sufficient to induce an immediate acceptance among astronomers. As a result, most people continued to accept that the Earth is the center of the cosmos. Although John Calvin preached sermons and wrote commentaries for 21 years after the death of Copernicus, the heliocentric hypothesis had still by no means become firmly established among astronomers during that time, although Copernicus did have strong supporters like Georg Joachim Rheticus (1514-1576), a professor at the University of Wittenberg. Consequently, there was no compelling reason for Calvin to adopt the Copernican hypothesis. Later in the chapter we will examine the evidence pertaining to Calvin's attitude toward the heliocentric proposal of Copernicus.

Widespread acceptance of the Copernican universe came only after discoveries made by Galileo Galilei (1564-1642), who held positions in mathematics at the Universities of Pisa and Padua; formulation of the laws of planetary motion by Johannes Kepler (1571-1630), who taught mathematics in Graz, Prague, and Linz; and the physical explanation of planetary motion in terms of inertia and gravitation by Isaac Newton (1642-1727), professor of mathematics at Cambridge. Given that Galileo was born in the year that Calvin died, Calvin did not live to see the completion of the revolution in astronomy and cosmology.

True and False Astrology

Calvin, therefore, was profoundly impressed by the heavens and by those who studied and progressed in understanding them. If he displayed a deep regard for the sciences throughout his literary corpus, nowhere was this more evident than in his lavish praise for the science of "astrology." To Calvin, astrology was not a bad thing, in principle. Astrology, however, was subject to distortion. As Christine Probes pointed out, there was a great resurgence of interest in astrology during the Renaissance and "thirty thousand sorcerers, alchemists, diviners and astrologers lived on the credulity of sixteenth century Paris."[8] To combat the abuses of astrology, Calvin published a little booklet, *Advertissement contre Astrologie* (variously known in English as *Admonition against Astrology* or *A Warning against Judiciary Astrology*), devoted to the subject of astrology in 1549.[9] The title intimates that he opposed astrology, but the entire book is a pointed polemic against the abuses of astrology. In this little work Calvin repeatedly drew a distinction between legitimate or true astrology (what is closer to what we call today the science of "astronomy," although Calvin drew the line a bit differently from what we would do today) and "judicial" astrology (what we would today call simply "astrology").[10]

Calvin was not the first to draw the distinction between astronomy and astrology (Isidore of Seville, for example, had done so in the seventh century), but his analysis of the two kinds of astrology and his criticism of "judicial astrology" was one of the most thorough and scathing. In this pamphlet Calvin complained insistently about those who "borrow, or rather steal, the title of a good and legitimate science to lend credence to their own fantasies, which are wholly contrary to the truth of the science which they pretend is theirs." He also castigated them for calling themselves by the worthy name of "mathematician," an honored profession, to serve as a cloak for their machinations.[11]

Calvin frequently praised astronomy, the "true astrology." He wrote that God "does not condemn that astronomy which surveys the courses of the planets, in which we ought to acknowledge the wonderful majesty of God."[12] Despite their pagan theology and despite even their abuses of astrology, he commended the Egyptians and the Chaldeans as "true astrologers" who

> understood the art, which in itself is praiseworthy; for to observe the stars, what else is it, but to contemplate that wonderful workmanship, in which the power, as well as the wisdom and goodness of God, shines forth? And, indeed, astrology may justly be called the alphabet of theology; for no one can with a right mind come to the contemplation of the celestial framework, without being enraptured with admiration at the display of God's wisdom, as well as of his power and goodness. The Chaldeans and the Egyptians had learned the art, which in itself, is not only to be approved, but is also most useful, and contains not only the most delightful speculations, but ought to contribute much toward exciting in the hearts of men a high reverence for God.[13]

Elsewhere Calvin granted that the Chaldeans, although they pursued the false judicial astrology, were also "skilled in the true and genuine knowledge of the stars. They observed the course of the stars, as there was no region of the world so full of them and none possessed so extensive an horizon on all sides."[14] He refused to apply taunts or mockery to the astronomers whose very difficult labors to unravel the secrets of heaven "cannot be praised highly enough" because "their science both glorifies God and serves human purposes."[15]

In a host of passages, however, Calvin complained that the Chaldeans were not content with practicing this legitimate and eminently praiseworthy science. Instead, they also resorted to augurs and conjecturers "who not only discoursed on the course, distances, and orders of the stars, and the peculiarities of each, but wished to predict futurity from the course of the stars."[16] The Chaldeans had corrupted true and natural astrology, and, sadly, they went about with the name of astronomy to cloak their wicked curiosity, and in so doing, they defamed a science that was both useful and praiseworthy.[17]

The prophet Isaiah had formerly spoken about the uselessness of judicial astrology. In analyzing Isaiah's comments, Calvin said that the Babylonians were the authors of this "science." To observe the opposition of the stars is not itself sinful, he asserted, but the Babylonian astrologers had carried it farther than is proper because they drew conclusions regarding doubtful events and, in effect, extinguished all divine predictions because they attached a fatal necessity to the stars.[18] Because "the minds of men are inclined to vain and foolish curiosity" when people are "not content with legitimate science," then they fall into "foolish and perverse imaginations." What fortunetellers predict of any one's destiny he regarded as merely "foolish fanaticism."[19]

Calvin condemned judicial astrology at great length in his commentary on Isaiah 44:25, a verse that refers to Yahweh as the one who made the heavens and "who foils the signs of false prophets and makes fools of diviners." From such people "sprung that bastard Astrology which is called Judicial, by which even now many persons of great abilities are led astray," he fulminated. These astrologers "assumed the name of Mathematicians, in order to recommend themselves more to the approbation of the people." Although the Egyptians boasted of being the authors of astrology, "the Babylonians practised that art from the very commencement and esteemed it highly." Isaiah merely condemned the "signs by means of which the Chaldeans prophesied, and imagined that they knew future events; for the Lord declares that they are absolutely worthless." Calvin suggested that "if any certain information could have been obtained from the position and aspect of the stars, the Lord undoubtedly would not thus have condemned that science. Since, therefore, he forbade it without exception, he showed that it contains nothing but absolute delusion, which all believers ought to detest."[20]

Judicial astrology came up again for criticism in the commentary on Acts 19:19, part of a record of the episode in Ephesus in which the practitioners of sorcery brought their scrolls to be burned publicly. Calvin wrote that

> Luke is speaking, not only about magic and its tricks, but about the frivolous and useless studies, of which the majority of men are usually far too fond. For he uses περιεργα, a word the Greeks use to describe whatever things do not contain any solid usefulness in themselves, but waste men's minds and efforts, diverting them through a variety of roundabout ways. Such is so-called judicial astrology, and all the divinations for the future that foolish men invent for themselves.[21]

The Christian should have nothing to do with judicial astrology.

The Structure of the Cosmos

Given that Calvin accepted astronomy as a legitimate form of astrology that was concerned with the structure of the cosmos, the determination of the positions of heavenly bodies, their sizes, the distances to them, and the mechanisms by which the cosmos runs, we may now ask what was his understanding of the cosmos. There is no doubt that he entertained a medieval conception of the universe. He adhered to the idea of an immobile Earth at the center of the cosmos, and he adhered to the idea that the heavenly bodies revolve about the Earth in a series of concentric nested spheres, for Calvin lived and moved and had his being in a fundamentally Aristotelian cosmos, although he took issue with Aristotle at a couple of points as we will discover later.

That Calvin believed that the Earth is at the center of the cosmos is abundantly plain. Two examples suffice to establish the point. The most straightforward statement occurs in the Argument to the *Commentary on Genesis* where he wrote that "we are indeed not ignorant, that the circuit of the heavens is finite, and that the earth, like a little globe, is placed in the centre."[22] The statement in Psalm 93:1 that "the world is firmly established; it cannot be moved," elicited the comment that

> the Psalmist proves that God will not neglect or abandon the world, from the fact that he created it. A simple survey of the world should of itself suffice to attest a Divine Providence. The heavens revolve daily, and, immense as is their fabric, and inconceivable the rapidity of their revolutions, we experience no concussion—no disturbance in the harmony of their motion. The sun, though varying its course every diurnal revolution, returns annually to the same point. The planets, in all their wanderings, maintain their respective positions. How could the earth hang suspended in the air were it not upheld by God's hand? By what means could it maintain itself unmoved, while the heavens above are in constant rapid motion, did not its Divine Maker fix and establish it?[23]

As the quotation from the commentary on Psalm 93 indicates, Calvin believed that the terrestrial globe would naturally be unstable because it was surrounded by a whole series of rapidly revolving spheres. In Aristotle's view, the heavenly spheres were all linked together, but these linkages were operative down to the sphere of the Moon. As a result, the effect of the circular motions was transmitted only to the top of the atmosphere, not to the Earth itself, and natural motions in the sublunary sphere were up and down rather than circular. The central terrestrial globe, therefore, would be unaffected by the whirling of the heavens. But Calvin, making no explicit mention of Aristotle's explanation, sensed that the Earth would be destabilized by the rest of the cosmic mechanism if nature were left to itself. As a result, he invoked God's providence to stabilize the Earth. As Kaiser summed up the issue:

> In other words, Calvin argued, the massive motion of the heavenly spheres would inevitably disturb the equilibrium of the earth if God did not act continuously to keep it stationary. As the text cited shows, the issue was an existential one for Calvin: the incredible stability of the earth in the midst of the swirling heavens was a sign that God had not left terrestrial affairs to follow their own course or made them entirely subordinate to stellar influences—a sign of God's particular providence even in the everyday course of nature.[24]

Even astronomers in Calvin's time were worried about the enormous rates at which objects in the outer spheres had to travel. Even though it was believed that the stars were relatively close to the Earth, calculations showed that outer spheres might be moving at several millions of miles per hour to get around the Earth in a single day. Growing observational evidence that stars might be farther away than previously suspected would mean that the universe was larger than generally accepted and, as a result, the most distant stars would be traveling at unimaginable rates of speed.

There are several reasons for Calvin's acceptance of the geocentric universe. His predecessors and contemporaries were nearly unanimous in acceptance of the geocentric worldview and the accompanying explanations of the mechanics of the universe. Face-value readings of many scriptural texts such as Psalm 93:1 or the story of the long day of Joshua are consistent with the notions of the mobility of the heavens and the immobility of the Earth, corollaries of the geocentric view. Common sense visual experience made it obvious that the Earth is stationary and that the Sun and the rest of the heavens move around us every day. Finally, the alternative heliocentric view, newly proposed by Copernicus, was still being debated. Copernicanism had some support in the mid-sixteenth century, but no theologian would be likely to adopt a cosmology that had not even received the full endorsement of the community of astronomers.

In line with the cosmology of the day, Calvin took for granted the idea that the cosmos comprises a series of concentric shells or "spheres" that are nested around the central Earth. He was one of those theologians who wanted to restrict God's use of the spheres to physical matters. In the *Institutes*, for example, he alluded to that approach when he said that, after learning that there is a Creator, faith must go on to infer that the Creator is also governor and preserver, not just in that he "drives the celestial frame as well as its several parts by a universal motion, but also in that he sustains, nourishes, and cares for everything he has made, even to the least sparrow."[25] Like his predecessors in theology, Calvin, too, "tried to prevent the Aristotelian account of the massive world machine from embracing all of life and to secure a preserve for the direct action of God in human affairs."[26]

Although Calvin elsewhere mentioned the cosmic spheres more explicitly, he never went into as much detail about their nature as Luther did.[27] He did not discuss their number, identify them, or talk about the harmony of the spheres, but merely alluded to the heavenly spheres on occasion. For example, he mentioned the fact that "astronomers make a distinction of spheres."[28] He referred briefly to the entire system of spheres where commenting on the ascension of Jesus. "I grant," he wrote, "that the word 'heaven' is taken in various ways: sometimes for the air, sometimes for the whole system of the spheres."[29] His brief mention of the *primum mobile* did not appear in comments regarding the stars or the Sun but in reference to the curse on the ground that God addressed to the newly guilty Adam. Of that tragic moment, he said that "as the *primum mobile* rolls all the celestial spheres along with it, so the ruin of man drives headlong all those creatures which were formed for his sake."[30] In writing about the ascent of Christ higher than the heavens (Ephesians 4:10), Calvin observed that "when Christ is said to be in heaven, we must not take it that He dwells among the spheres and numbers the stars. Heaven denotes a place higher than all the spheres, which was appointed to the Son of God after his resurrection."[31] Such remarks suggest that he may have envisioned the heavens in which the resurrected Son of God dwells as a physical place located beyond the outermost cosmic sphere.

The Revolution of the Heavens

The common experience of humanity has been that the Sun, the Moon, planets, stars, and other heavenly objects appear to revolve around the Earth on a daily basis, rising in the east and setting in the west. Throughout the first millennium and a half of the Christian era, the belief was that all these objects were attached to revolving, transparent spheres. As noted, Calvin was tremendously impressed that such an enormous structure whirled around the Earth each day. This awe-inspiring daily revolution provided compelling evidence for the mighty power of God, who kept the entire cosmos intact despite its immense size.

Calvin mentioned the revolution of the heavens in several contexts. The prophecy of Zechariah presents an oracle in which the Lord, the one who stretches out the heavens, lays the foundations of the Earth, and forms the spirit of a man within him, declared that he would make Jerusalem an immovable rock when all the nations were gathered against her. Calvin commented that the heavens are in continual motion, and "they yet retain their positions, and do not fall into disorder."[32] Isaiah 48:13, likewise, mentions the Lord as laying the foundations of the Earth and his right hand spreading out the heavens. Calvin's translation of the text incorporated the idea of God "measuring" the heavens. He thought that the word "measure" denoted "God's amazing wisdom in having adjusted on all sides, with such exact proportion, the vast extent of the heavens, so that it is neither nearer to the earth nor farther from it than is advantageous for preserving order. In this prodigious expanse there is nothing jarring or unseemly." Even if one preferred to use the term "uphold" rather than "measure," he said, it would still be "an extraordinary commendation of the wisdom and power of God, in 'upholding' the huge mass of the heavens in continual motion, so that it neither totters nor leans more to one side than to another."[33] The reference in Isaiah 40:26 to God's creating the heavens, bringing out the starry hosts one by one and calling each by name prompted Calvin to marvel that "it is not by chance that each of the stars has had its place assigned to it, nor is it at random that they advance uniformly with so great rapidity, and amidst numerous windings move straight forwards, so that they do not deviate a hairbreadth from the path which God has marked out for them." He regarded these motions as a "wonderful arrangement."[34] Jeremiah's linkage of God's covenant with the day and night to his covenant with David led Calvin to write that

> unceasing are the progresses of the sun, moon, and stars; continual is the succession of day and night. This settled state of things is so fixed, that in so great and so multiplied a variety there is no change. We have rain, then fair weather, and we have various changes in the seasons; but the sun still continues its daily course, the moon is new every month, and the revolving of day and night, which God has appointed, never ceases; and this unbroken order declares, as it is said is Psalm 19, the wonderful wisdom of God. The Prophet then sets before us here the order of nature.[35]

A couple of Calvin's sermons on Job also contain lengthy remarks on the revolving heavens. He likened the revolution of the sky to the wheels and axle of a speeding chariot. In his first sermon on Job 26, for example, he preached that

> the sky turns about upon the pole that is there. For like as in the wheels of a chariot, there is an extree [axle] that runs through the middle of them, and the wheels turn round about the extree by reason of the holes that are in the naves [hub of the wheel] of them; even so is it in the skies. It is manifestly seen; that is to say, they that are well acquainted with the course of the firmament, do see that the sky turns so about. For on the north side there is a star apparent to our eye [no doubt a reference to Polaris, the North Star], which is as it were the extree that runs through the nave of the wheel about the which the skies are seen to turn. There is another pole hidden under us, which we cannot perceive, and that is called the Antarctic. And why? Because the sky turns about that also, as though one extree were put through both the wheels, as has been said afore. When I speak of this course of the heaven, I mean not the daily course of the sun that we see; for the sun has a peculiar moving by itself; but this is a universal moving for the whole cope of heaven. And the said two stars are as it were fastened to those places, so as they do not remove nor stir.[36]

The same general thought was expressed more briefly in the second sermon on Job 9 where Calvin preached that "like as we see the wheels of a chariot turn about because there is an extree [axle] overthwart, whereupon are the two naves by means whereof the wheels go; even so God has set these two stars to be as naves in the wheel of a chariot, about the which the sun is seen to turn."[37] It is undeniable that Calvin was fully immersed in the medieval geocentric worldview. There is no hint of Copernicanism here.

The Motions of Individual Bodies

The changes in position of the planets like Venus and Jupiter relative to the positions of the fixed stars, the fact that the Moon rises later each night, and the changes in position of the Sun and of the entire set of fixed stars relative to the horizon during the course of a year indicated to the ancients and to medieval scholars that additional motions are superimposed on the daily revolution of the heavens. To make matters more complex and perplexing, the planets occasionally reverse direction. Therefore, individual objects in the sky have their own distinctive motions to which Calvin referred in the sermons on Job and in the commentaries. For example, he remarked on the reference to God's work of creation in Jeremiah 10 that

> the sun performs its daily course; that it changes its track daily; that the planets have two motions; that they appear in different parts; and that the sun seems now to ascend and then to descend. In short, Jeremiah here extols all the se-

crets of astrology, when he says, that the heavens have been expanded by God, and expanded with singular and incomparable wisdom.[38]

In the context of the warnings of Deuteronomy 4 not to be enticed into worshiping and bowing down to the Sun, the Moon, and stars, he observed that in these ordinary circumstances

> God's admirable providence is fitly commended in respect to their varied position, and course, and different offices; for the sun does not enlighten and warm all lands at the same moment; and, again, it now retires from us, and now approaches us more closely; the moon has her circuits; the stars rise and set as the heaven revolves. I pass over the slower movement of the planets; but according to the aspects of the stars, one climate is moister, another drier, one feels more heat another more cold.[39]

Calvin was puzzled that some of these motions seemed to work at odds with one another. That these apparently opposed motions did not interfere with the smooth operation of the whole universe again impressed him as another amazing evidence of God's power in upholding the cosmos. By way of example, in writing on that part of Paul's address in the synagogue of Antioch of Pisidia in which he mentioned the failure of the rulers and people of Jerusalem to recognize who Jesus is as well as their condemnation of him, Calvin alluded to these celestial motions. "Just as with wonderful skill," he wrote, "God controls movements in the sun and the other planets that are contrary and in conflict with each other, so by his secret influence, He directs the perverse efforts of the ungodly towards a different end than they thought and intended."[40] He also expressed amazement at the power of God in controlling the motions of the heavenly bodies in his second sermon on Job 9:

> We see well that the sun keeps one circuit every day, that after he is risen he goes down again, and that he turns about the earth as well beneath as above. Men see this. Also we see how the sun has another clean contrary course. How? whereof comes winter, whereof comes summer, but of the sun's approaching to us, or of his retiring away from us, and of his keeping of a higher or lower gate in respect of us? For according as he goes further from us draws he nearer to us; thereafter makes he the diversities of seasons. We see this, I say even the rudest and most ignorant of us all. True it is that they perceive not how the sun walks a clean contrary course to that which he makes in keeping his daily course; but the experience thereof is known by the effect. For we have neither winter nor summer but by the sun.[41]

Finally, in regard to the "long day" of Joshua, Calvin remarked that solar and lunar motions are subject to the will of God who "opens his mouth and tells the sun and the moon to deviate from the perpetual law of nature." As a kindness to the human race, God divided "the day from the night by the daily course of the sun and constantly whirls the immense orb with indefatigable swiftness" but

at the time of Joshua's long day he was also "pleased that it should halt for a
short time till the enemies of Israel were destroyed."[42]

Now that we have caught a glimpse of the role that medieval cosmology
played in Calvin's thought world, it is appropriate to ask how and when he became acquainted with that cosmology. Kaiser maintained that the earliest indications of Calvin's detailed interest in Aristotle's cosmology appeared in the
Commentary on Genesis. Calvin began work on the commentary in 1550, and it
was published in 1554. Kaiser suggested that it is in the Genesis commentary
that we find the first surviving discussion of the celestial spheres. As to the stability of the Earth, Calvin first dealt with that issue in his *Commentary on the
Psalms* and in sermons on the same book during the mid-1550s. Kaiser argued
that the appearance of those passages on Aristotle's cosmology in the early
1550s was probably fortuitous. Because the sermons were not systematically
recorded until the late 1540s, and because Calvin did not begin his sustained
work on the Old Testament commentaries until then, Kaiser suspected that his
natural philosophy probably had its origins earlier in his career. He speculated
that Calvin originally became informed about natural philosophy during his college days in Paris, and that his interest could have been further stimulated by his
study of Seneca and by reading Basil's *Hexameron* and Luther's *Lectures on
Genesis* (1544). The fact that Calvin's texts did "not give detailed evidence of
this interest until the early 1550s is merely the result of his adopted schedule of
preaching and writing."[43]

Distances to Stars

Apart from larger cosmological issues, Calvin had some familiarity with
specific astronomical discoveries such as the distance from the Earth to various
heavenly bodies or the sizes of stars. In his second sermon on Job 9, he preached
that it is one of the tasks of astronomy to determine "what distance there is in
highness and lowness" of the stars and planets. He said that we know that not all
heavenly objects are the same distance away because of our "experience that the
sun is higher than the moon." As to how we know that, Calvin responded that "it
is because that when the moon comes full between our sight and the sun, behold
there is made an eclipse, whereby I say we perceive that the moon is the lower."
He suggested that our perception of the true sizes of heavenly bodies may be
affected by their distances from us. The Moon is not bigger than the other stars
or planets, he said,

> for it is certain that there are stars in the sky which are bigger than the moon.
> And why cannot we see them so greater? Because of their far distance from us.
> For they are exceeding high in respect of us, insomuch that they seem not so
> great as they be, by reason of the great distance that is between the skies and
> us.[44]

In the second sermon on Job 38, he expressed the thought that we should all be "abashed" when we behold the "great and far distance" between the Earth and clouds and the Earth and the sky "where the stars and planets are."[45] In Psalm 90, Moses asked God to "teach us to number our days aright, that we may gain a heart of wisdom." Calvin used this text as an occasion to scold the human race. It is monstrous, he said, that we are unable to "number threescore and ten years" wisely and properly whereas "men can measure all distances without themselves." He knew that men had measured "how many feet the moon is distant from the center of the earth," the distances between the different planets, and, in short, "all the dimensions both of heaven and earth."[46]

In *A Warning against Judiciary Astrology*, Calvin also mentioned that the knowledge of the distance of one star from another is a legitimate concern of astronomy. He then repeated the widely held misperception [to this day!] that "the sun is farther from us in winter than in summer."[47]

Sizes of Stars

In ancient Greece and Rome when the stars and other objects in the sky were considered to be rather close to the Earth, it was assumed that these objects were not very large. Many philosophers believed that the Sun was approximately the size of a shield! By Calvin's day it was recognized that some of the objects were much larger than that.

Calvin also considered determination of the size of the heavenly bodies as another legitimate task of astronomy. On various occasions, he mentioned that the relative sizes of the Sun, the Moon, the Earth, and Saturn had been determined by the philosophers although he never named any specific individuals who may have made such determinations. In his lectures on the first verse of Ezekiel, where we read that the heavens were opened and that Ezekiel saw visions of God, Calvin observed that "the sun appears small to us, yet it far exceeds the earth in size. Then the other planets, except the moon, are all like small sparks, and so are the stars."[48] In the Genesis commentary, he stressed that the planet Saturn, despite appearances, is larger than the Moon.[49] And in his second sermon on Job 9 he remarked that "it is certain that there are stars in the sky which are bigger than the moon."[50] He even understood that "the dimension of the earth is also conjectured" by the philosophers.[51]

Even though the size of the entire cosmos was unknown, Calvin believed that its size had been determined and adjusted by God's amazing wisdom. God had "adjusted on all sides, with such exact proportion, the vast extent of the heavens, so that it is neither nearer to the earth nor farther from it than is advantageous for preserving order."[52]

Celestial Phenomena

As noted above, Calvin pointed out that solar eclipses provide one line of evidence that the Sun is farther from the Earth than is the Moon. It was one thing to "perceive such things" as eclipses; it was another to understand "the reason how it comes to pass that the moon passes so between the sun and us."[53] He returned to that point in writing about Matthew's account of the darkness coming over the land between the sixth and ninth hours during the crucifixion of Jesus. Although considering the darkness as a miraculous phenomenon, he attributed a physical cause to it, namely, a solar eclipse. Calvin asked about the reason for a solar eclipse. He rejected as fiction the view expressed in the tragedies of the ancient poets that the light of the sun is "withdrawn from the earth when any foul crime is committed." He also rejected the opinion that the putative eclipse of the Sun at the crucifixion extended to every quarter of the world. "If the eclipse had been common to the whole world," he reasoned, "men would more easily have missed its significance. While the sun shone elsewhere, Judaea was plunged into shades; this made the prodigy more notable."[54] This comment suggests that Calvin may have thought that ordinary, non-miraculous solar eclipses affected the entire globe. Given that total solar eclipses darken only a portion of the Earth's surface at any one time, it is ironic that he regarded an eclipse with local effects as more miraculous than an eclipse that would be visible everywhere. Not inclined to associate eclipses with portents and omens, he generally considered them as natural phenomena that "have no signification, unless one counts the fact that they produce rain, wind, whirlwinds, or other such things."[55]

Calvin did regard the signs of the Zodiac as genuine signs. "There are in the firmament," he said, "twelve signs by which astrologers especially make their calculations. These signs are not the vain fictions of men but what God has created and appointed."[56] Perhaps he believed that the positions of these constellations bore some relation to weather patterns and agricultural practice.

The Influences of Stars on Earth

Given Calvin's hostility toward judicial astrology with its penchant for fortune-telling and claims that earthly events are determined by the positions of heavenly bodies, it may come as a surprise that he was far more likely to acknowledge significant stellar influences on terrestrial processes and events than are contemporary Christians. Calvin's ideas on this score were perfectly in line with his decidedly medieval outlook on the cosmos. We know, of course, the obvious effect of the Sun in heating the Earth's surface in the daytime, in stirring up winds at sunrise and sunset, on promoting the growth of plants, and on the nature of the four seasons. We know, too, that the tides are caused by the position of the Moon relative to the Earth. For people in the Middle Ages, however, the heavens were thought to exert far greater effects on the Earth than we think today. After all, the heavens were understood to be much closer to the Earth than we know now. Moreover, medieval thinkers conceived that God influenced affairs on the Earth indirectly by means of the revolving spheres. The positions and distances of the stars from the Earth were thought to produce considerable effects on physical phenomena and on human affairs. The constellations of the Zodiac were, to be sure, associated with the passage of the seasons, but beyond that, it was felt that the constellations in part caused the seasons. The stars influenced birth and death and the growth of vegetation. Fossils, interpreted by our scientific culture as the petrified remains of once living plants and animals that were entombed in sediment, were regarded by many medieval thinkers as *lusus naturae* (sports of nature) that grew in place in the rocks under stellar influences in imitation of living things. Exhalations stimulated within the Earth by stellar influence were thought to produce ore deposits.[57] The thirteenth-century Italian scholar Ristoro d'Arezzo maintained that the stars exerted an influence on the elevations of mountains much as a magnet attracts iron filings. In his view, terrestrial topography mimicked the positions of the stars in such a way that the highest mountains lay below the most distant, that is, "highest" stars and the valleys lay beneath the closest stars.[58]

Some of these beliefs were also entertained by Calvin. In regard to Deuteronomy 4:19, a text in which Moses warned the children of Israel not to worship things that God had created for human benefit, he wrote that

> God's admirable providence is fitly commended in respect to their varied position, and course, and different offices; for the sun does not enlighten and warm all lands at the same moment; and, again, it now retires from us, and now approaches us more closely; the moon has her circuits; the stars rise and set as the heaven revolves. I pass over the slower movement of the planets; but, according to the aspect of the stars, one climate is moister, another drier; one feels more heat, another more cold.[59]

He did not attribute climatic conditions or temperature changes solely to the Sun's position with respect to the Earth, for he also envisioned the entire set of stars as contributing its influence.

Calvin's view that the positions of the stars and the Sun had significant effects on the terrestrial seasons was spelled out even more thoroughly where he wrote pertaining to Jeremiah 10:1-2 that

> when the sun is in Cancer it has not the same power and influence as when it is in Virgo, and it differs as to the other signs. In short, as to the order of nature, the stars, the planets, as well as the fixed stars, are to us for signs. We number the years by the solar course, and the months by the lunar; and then the sun, with respect to the twelve signs, introduces the spring, then the summer, then the autumn, and lastly the winter. . . . In this way we account for sterilities, and pestilences, and other things of this kind. When the air seems temperate, pestilence prevails, the year is less fruitful, and men are famished, and no cause appears. Then this diversity in nature itself shews that God has not resigned his

power to the stars, but that he so works by them, that he still holds the reigns of government, and that he, according to his own will, rules the world in a way different from what even the acutest can divine by the stars. Yet this is no reason why we should deny to them the office which I have mentioned.[60]

It is not just that the stars happen to be in certain positions in the sky when the seasons roll by. God "works by" the stars to bring the seasons to pass.

When Moses blessed the tribe of Joseph just before his death, he asked God to bless Joseph's land with dew from heaven above and with deep waters from below, and with the best that the Sun and the Moon could yield. Of this text Calvin confessed that he was unable to tell "whether there are any grounds for assigning, as some do, to the sun the produce which springs from seed and the vintage; and to the moon, cucumbers and gourds; nor do I attempt to decide whether their idea is more correct who suppose the latter to be flowers or fruits which appear every month."[61] This comment lets us know that he had not ruled out the possibility that the influences of the Sun and the Moon were apportioned to the production of different kinds of vegetables.

Calvin believed that the course of some diseases was influenced by the Moon. He said that "they are called lunatics who during the waning of the moon, suffer from epilepsy or are tormented with dizziness. . . . For sure experience teaches us that those increase or decline according to the course of the moon."[62]

The Old Testament refers to specific stars or groups of stars, although the identity of these astronomical features is uncertain. Even Calvin wrote in regard to Amos 5:8 that "the Jews, ignorant of the liberal sciences, cannot at this day certainly determine what stars are meant." The various translations and commentators have commonly identified them as the Pleiades (the nebulous star cluster located between the constellations Perseus and Taurus) and Orion (Job 9:9, 38:31; Amos 5:8) and Arcturus or "the bear" (Job 9:9, 38:32). Some commentators believe that Aldebaran and the Hyades are possibilities.

The precise meaning of Job 38:31 has been difficult to ascertain. Modern commentators and translations maintain that the idea of binding the heavenly bodies is in view. Hence the New International Version translates: "Can you bind the beautiful Pleiades? Can you loose the cords of Orion?" and the New American Standard Bible translates: "Can you bind the chains of the Pleiades, or loose the cords of Orion?" In contrast, the King James (Authorized) Version, translated the first part of this text as "the sweet influences of the Pleiades," quite possibly an indication that the medieval belief in stellar influences on the Earth was still in vogue in 1611. We should not be surprised, then, at the extent of Calvin's acceptance of stellar influence in his treatment of these texts.

The reference in Amos 5:8 to God being the one "who made the Pleiades (or the seven stars) and Orion, who turns the blackness into dawn and darkens day into night" elicited one of Calvin's most intriguing discussions of astronomy. Being a shepherd, Amos never learned the niceties of astronomy, and, therefore, he spoke about the stars "according to the common notions of his age." Amos, Calvin opined, selected two stars of an opposite influence. The Pleiades (which are also called the seven stars) are, we know, mild; for when they rise, they moderate the rigor of the cold, and also bring with them the vernal rain. But Orion is a fiercer star, and ever excites grievous and turbulent commotions both at its rising and set-ting.[63]

This selection makes clear that Calvin, like his contemporaries, thought that stellar positions caused seasonal and climatic changes on the Earth. Calvin called Orion a star, whereas we regard Orion as the name of a constellation, the great hunter. Was he thinking of Rigel or Betelguese, the two dominant stars of Orion, or was he thinking of a different star that is nowhere near what we call the constellation Orion?

Calvin also mentioned the Pleiades in his fourth sermon on Job 38. After noting that it is God who commanded the stars to rise and set and had "given them their influences from heaven," he asked as to the cause "that the earth is fresh in the springtime." The reason is "because the Pleiades reign then." Of course, this did not mean that God does not reign. After all, "although he had given the celestial signs their influences, yet do they not anything of their own peculiar motion."[64]

Calvin's most detailed comments about the effects of heavenly bodies occur in *A Warning against Judiciary Astrology*. Although expostulating at length what the stars cannot do and excoriating the abuses and distortions by astrology, he devoted a surprising amount of space to those influences that he thought the heavens might exert. He seemed to believe that the Moon has significant effects on the growth of organisms, maintaining that "natural astrology will indeed be able to demonstrate to us that bodies here below receive some influence from the moon, because it will note that oysters become full or empty as the moon waxes and wanes, as does the marrow in bones."[65]

The heavens may affect human health, and knowledge of the heavens may be an aid in the practice of medicine, Calvin thought. Thus, he stated that "from the true science of astrology doctors draw their judgments concerning the appropriate time to order blood-lettings, infusions, pills, or other medical necessities. Therefore we must admit that there is some correspondence between the stars and planets and the dispositions of human bodies."[66] Later in the book he repeated that "although the stars are signs which show us the season to plant or to sow, to heal or to give medicine, to cut wood, etc., this does not mean that they are signs which tell us whether or not we should wear new clothes."[67] Even some human physical characteristics might be partly attributable to the stars. Calvin granted "that as for the complexions of men and especially their affections, which participate in the qualities of their bodies, these do depend in part upon the stars."[68] He downplayed the effect, however, saying that "the stars do indeed have some concurrence in forming our complexion and especially influence those things which have to do with the body. But I deny that they are the chief cause of such things."[69] The physical features of twins also made him suspicious about the influence of the stars. He noted that some twins have different features, and he especially wondered why there should be boy and girl twins if the stars had such potent effects on the way people look. He rightly suspected that the seed of the parents had a "virtue" that was a hundred times more powerful than that of all the stars together.[70]

Whatever effects the stars might have on physical attributes, Calvin denied that they had any control over events. "At the most, the stars are able to imprint people with certain qualities," he conceded, but "they cannot make this or that happen to them besides."[71] He complained that "this bastard astrology, not content with determining the character and complexion of men, extends the limits of its powers of forecasting even further: it even foretells what will happen to people throughout their lives and when and how they will die."[72]

As in his sermons and commentaries, Calvin maintained that climatic phenomena and famines might well be affected by the stars. He wrote that

> insofar as the terrestrial bodies have some correspondence with the heavens, one can indeed note certain causes in the stars for the things which happen here below. Just as the influence of the heavens often causes tempests, whirlwinds, changes in the weather, and continual rain, so it consequently brings about barrenness or sterility. Inasmuch, therefore, as one sees an order and a sort of "liaison" between the higher and the lower, I will not forbid anyone to search the celestial bodies for the origin of the accidents we observe here in the world. I understand the word "origin" not as the first and principal cause, but rather as a means which is inferior to the will of God and which he uses in preparing the accomplishment of his work (just as he has determined it in his eternal counsel). All the same, we need not altogether deny that there is sometimes a certain correspondence between a plague which we see here and a constellation which astrologers point out in the sky. Nevertheless, a general rule cannot be made out of this.[73]

Calvin apparently wished to limit the negative influences of the heavens to correlations with human sinfulness, because he suggested that "neither famines, nor plagues, nor wars ever occur because of the position of the stars" unless it is because "God wants to let his anger against the malice of men be known." On the other hand, he ruled out some positive influences as well. "The abundance of goods, health, and peace," he wrote, "do not proceed from the influence of the stars, but from the blessing of God."[74]

Calvin seriously questioned whether the stars could affect the hour of birth; anyway, he thought, the hour of conception of a child is much more important than the time of birth. He argued against horoscopes on the grounds that people with very diverse natures can have the same horoscope.

It is clear, despite some acceptance of a role for stellar influences, that there was reticence on Calvin's part in accepting all astrological claims. Although he was very open to granting influence to the heavens, he was prone to downplay the power and importance of those influences lest the power of God be infringed. As a case in point, he wrote regarding the severe famine that was predicted for the entire Roman world by the prophet Agabus that famine can sometimes be predicted from the disposition of the stars, but there is nothing certain in predictions of that kind, sometimes on account of conflicting combinations; sometimes, in particular, because God directs earthly affairs according to His will differently from what one has deduced from the stars. . . . Finally, even if these predictions have a standing of their own, yet the prophesies of the Sprit far surpass them.[75]

Calvin's commitment to biblical theology served to temper his acceptance of medieval cosmology and to curb its potential metaphysical excesses.

Stars Are Not Divine

Despite the fact that the stars might produce impressive effects on the Earth, Calvin insisted that stars lack divinity. They are, after all, only creatures of the living God who alone is worthy of worship. He repeatedly argued that when God forbade the worship of the Sun and stars in his law, he put forward as a reason for that prohibition that the whole celestial host was created for our use. Because the Sun is our servant and the Moon is our handmaid, and because the stars were created to serve us, "it is preposterous to depart from the divinely ordained order, that the sun which was given us to spend his time in our service should be to us a god."[76] Moses reproved the "absurdity of transferring the worship of God to the stars, which, by God's appointment, are to minister to us." Moses' teaching that "God hath divided them unto all nations" implied the subjection of the heavenly bodies to us "as if he had said that the sun was our minister, and the moon, together with all the stars, our handmaid."[77]

Calvin and Copernicus

Now that we have assembled the fundamental elements of Calvin's physical cosmology, we will devote some attention to the question that has most greatly exercised students of Calvin who have inquired into his scientific views: "What was Calvin's attitude toward Copernicus?" Inasmuch as Calvin died in 1564, several decades before the work of Galileo, Kepler, and Newton that firmly established the heliocentric conception of the solar system and dethroned the prevailing geocentric universe of the medieval era, it is asking too much of Calvin to display in his sermons and commentaries strong support for the heliocentric conception of the cosmos. Nevertheless, he was well into his thirties when Copernicus published his revolutionary work in 1543 on the workings of the solar system. We might at least look for signs that he knew about Copernicus' work to see if he had any opinion on it. Would Calvin look with any favor on the new order or would he insist on retaining the old medieval geocentric view?

The question is especially germane in light of the presumed negative attitudes of some of the other Reformers about the revolutionary astronomer. In notes taken of his *Table Talk* of June 4, 1539, Martin Luther (1483-1546) is reported to have commented, in reference to "a certain new astrologer," presumably Copernicus, "who wanted to prove that the earth moves and not the sky, the sun, and the moon," that

> whoever wants to be clever must agree with nothing that others esteem. He must do something of his own. This is what that fellow does who wishes to turn the whole of astronomy upside down. Even in these things that are thrown into disorder I believe the Holy Scriptures, for Joshua commanded the sun to stand still and not the earth.[78]

Kenneth Howell has cautioned that, assuming their historical accuracy, Luther's objections might simply reflect an antipathy toward novel, audacious claims to explain the heavens rather than informed opposition.[79] On the other hand, there is no doubt that "Luther's lieutenant," Philipp Melanchthon (1497-1560), opposed the Copernican hypothesis. Melanchthon was a strong advocate of the liberal arts including mathematics and sciences, particularly at the University of Wittenberg, and actually contributed to the dispersal of Copernican astronomy throughout Europe. Although he accepted the superior mathematical data collected by Copernicus, Melanchthon rejected his cosmology because he did not think that there were sufficiently convincing physical proofs to compel acceptance. As Howell put it, the "mathematical astronomy" of Copernicus at best saved the appearances. And "since compelling physical arguments for the earth's motion were lacking in the 1540s, Melanchthon no doubt felt his physical conclusions confirmed by Scripture."[80] But what about Calvin?

In the nineteenth century, the prominent English churchman Frederic Farrar (1831-1903), variously canon and archdeacon of Westminster Abbey, dean of Canterbury, and chaplain of the House of Commons and Queen Victoria, delivered the Bampton Lectures for 1885 in which he made the following statement: "'Who,' asks Calvin, 'will venture to place the authority of Copernicus above that of the Holy Spirit?'"[81] Unfortunately, Farrar did not inform his readers as to the source of the alleged quotation from Calvin. Just a few years prior to Farrar's comment, Charles Woodruff Shields (1825-1904), a professor of the harmony of science and revealed religion at the College of New Jersey, later to become Princeton University, wrote in the first edition of his *Philosophia Ultima* that "Calvin introduced his *Commentary on Genesis* by stigmatizing as utter reprobates those who would deny that the circuit of the heavens is finite and the earth placed like a little globe at the center."[82]

Thus was laid the foundation for a widely held belief that John Calvin was a bitter opponent of Copernicanism and even an opponent of scientific progress. Ever on the lookout for signs of antipathy on the part of theologians toward the sciences, Andrew Dickson White (1832-1918), the first president of Cornell University, quite probably had read both Farrar and Shields (but probably not Calvin) when he wrote in his landmark two-volume *History of the Warfare of Science with Theology in Christendom* and in earlier articles that

Calvin took the lead, in his Commentary on Genesis, by condemning all who asserted that the earth is not at the center of the universe. He clinched the matter by the usual reference to the first verse of Psalm 93, and asked, "Who will venture to place the authority of Copernicus above that of the Holy Spirit?"[83]

White's very influential book did much to promulgate the now discredited warfare hypothesis regarding the relationship between science and religion. Many readers of White, picking up on the alleged Calvin quotation, perpetuated the belief that Calvin vigorously opposed Copernicus and heliocentricity. For example, we find such claims in the writings of Bertrand Russell, Paul Kocher, Thomas Kuhn, and Timothy Ferris. British logician Bertrand Russell (1872-1970) wrote in his *A History of Western Philosophy* that "Calvin, similarly, demolished Copernicus with the text: 'The world also is stablished, that it cannot be moved' (Ps. 93:1), and exclaimed: 'Who will venture to place the authority of Copernicus above that of the Holy Spirit?'"[84] In his book, *Science and Religion in Elizabethan England*, Elizabethan literature scholar Paul Kocher (1907-1998) claimed that Luther, Calvin, and Melanchthon all condemned Copernicanism as contrary to Scripture.[85] Philosopher of science Thomas Kuhn (1922-1996), writing on the assimilation of Copernican astronomy in *The Copernican Revolution*, claimed that Martin Luther and Philip Melanchthon made use of Scripture in repudiating the Copernican hypothesis. He went on to say that some other Protestant leaders soon participated in rejecting Copernicus. According to Kuhn, Calvin cited Psalm 93:1 in his *Commentary on Genesis* and demanded, "Who will venture to place the authority of Copernicus above that of the Holy Spirit?"[86] As his source for these assertions about Calvin, Kuhn cited A. D. White. He did not cite Calvin, however. Kuhn carried matters even farther. Just after mentioning that Luther, Calvin, and their followers wanted to restore to the church to at a state of pristine Christianity, Kuhn maintained that Protestant leaders vigorously objected to the intricate metaphorical and allegorical interpretations of the Bible. Allegedly, the literal adherence of these Reformers to Scripture when it came to the business of cosmology was without parallel since the time of Lactantius, Basil, and Kosmas. Kuhn thought that perhaps they viewed Copernicus as a prime example of someone putting forward one of these convoluted re-interpretations of the biblical text that had put a wedge between the Christian believers of the Middle Ages and the original basis of their faith. As a result the "violence of the thunder" directed against Copernicus by so-called "official Protestantism" almost appeared a natural consequence in Kuhn's judgment. He charged that Luther, Calvin, and Melanchthon not only took the lead in leveling biblical passages against Copernicus but also in urging that Copernicans be repressed. Of course, the repressive measures of the Protestants were rather ineffective in comparison with those subsequently applied by the Catholics inasmuch as the Protestants lacked the kind of "police apparatus" that was available to the Roman Catholic Church. Besides, these repressive measures were ultimately abandoned after the evidence favoring the Copernican hypothesis eventually became overwhelming. Nonetheless, Kuhn maintained, it was the Protestants who launched the "first effective institutionalized opposition" to the Copernican worldview. Kuhn provided no evidence whatever of Calvin's literal adherence to the Bible in matters of cosmology, no evidence of violent thunder directed against Copernicus by official Protestantism, no evidence of Calvin's urging of the repression of Copernicans, and no evidence of official institutionalized opposition apart from the opposition to Copernicanism at the University of Wittenberg. Most recently, popular science writer and astronomer Timothy Ferris, treating the reluctance of Copernicus to publish his book for fear of "censure by the religious authorities," thought that Protestants were no more likely "to kiss the heliocentric hem" than the Roman Catholic Church. Having discovered the infamous quotation in Russell's book, Ferris wrote " 'Who will venture to place the authority of Copernicus above that of the Holy Spirit?' thundered Calvin."[88]

Even enthusiastic Calvinistic theologians fell into the trap of accusing Calvin of anti-Copernicanism! James Orr (1844-1913), a professor of apologetics and systematic theology in the United Free Church College in Glasgow, Scotland, perpetuated the erroneous conception in his book, *The Bible Under Trial*. In a section dealing with "Oppositions of Science," Orr addressed alleged objections to Christianity coming from the field of astronomy. Remarking that some people think the Copernican system is fatal to the Christian worldview, Orr observed that this objection was "keenly felt at first by believers in the old Ptolemaic astronomy, which made the earth to be the center of the universe. Luther, Melanchthon, Calvin, John Owen, John Wesley even, all opposed the new doctrine as contrary to Scripture. They were mistaken."[89] So was James Orr.

This unfortunate mishandling of historical sources has been detailed by historian of science Reijer Hooykaas (1906-1994) of the Free University of Amsterdam and by Copernicus scholar Edward Rosen.[90] The fact is that no one has ever found Farrar's alleged quotation about Copernicus and the Holy Spirit in any of Calvin's writings. So far as we know he never made the statement. On the other hand, Shields distorted what Calvin actually said in his Argument to the Genesis commentary. In the Argument, Calvin did make a reference to geocentricity as we saw earlier in this chapter. He said that "we indeed are not ignorant, that the circuit of the heavens is finite, and that the earth, like a little globe, is placed in the center." This sentence does occur in a passage in which Calvin was quite critical of certain individuals. For example, he castigated those "who will not deign to behold him [i.e., God] thus magnificently arrayed in the incomparable vesture of the heavens and the earth" and said that they would afterwards "suffer the just punishment of their proud contempt in their own ravings." Might those individuals who failed to appreciate the glory of God displayed in the heavens perhaps be the "utter reprobates" of Shields' quote? Calvin also referred to the impiety of those who ridiculed Moses for saying that so little time had elapsed since the creation of the world and who wondered why it took so long for God to get around to the business of creating the world. To such folk he retorted that "by sporting with sacred things they exercise their ingenuity to their own destruction" and also that "they who now so freely exult in finding fault with the inactivity of God will find, to their own great cost, that his power has been infinite in preparing hell for them."[91] Therefore, although the clause about the Earth being at the center of the cosmos is located in this section of the Argument, Calvin simply did not condemn anyone who did not hold to the idea that the Earth is the center.

After surveying the relevant data, Rosen concluded that Calvin never "demolished, condemned, rejected, opposed, or stigmatized as an utter reprobate the quiet thinker who founded modern astronomy." In fact, Rosen said, he had no attitude at all toward Copernicus, because he had never heard of him.[92] In a brief reply, Joseph Ratner (1901-1979), although appreciating Rosen's uncovering of the shoddy checking of sources by Farrar, Shields, and the others, found it "incredible that Calvin 'never heard' of Copernicus."[93] He argued that because traffic between Wittenberg and Geneva was "constant and heavy," knowledge of Copernicus' work certainly would have reached Geneva in the twenty years or so after his death. Rosen replied to Ratner that the "complete silence about Copernicanism in every one of Calvin's numerous discussions of astronomical topics provided the best evidence" for his conclusions about Calvin's ignorance.[94]

In 1971, the debate took a major turn. Calvin scholar Richard Stauffer reported that he had uncovered a passage in the eighth sermon on I Corinthians 10-11 that seemed to reject the concept of the motion of the Earth around an unmoving Sun. Kaiser translated the crucial passage as follows:

> Let us not be like these madmen who have a spirit of such venomous contradiction, contriving to gainsay everything and perverting the very order of nature. We shall find some who are so stark raving mad, not only in matters of religion but showing their monstrous nature in all things, that they will even say that the sun does not budge, and that it is the earth that bestirs itself and that turns around. When we come across such individuals we must really say that the devil has possessed them and that God placed them before us as mirrors in order to make us stay within the fold of those who fear him. So it is with those who debate with unquestionable malice and who think nothing of being contemptuous. When you tell them, "That is hot": "Not at all!" they will say. "It is obviously cold!" If you show them something black, they will say that it is white! Or it could be the other way around, as in the case of the man who said that snow was black, for in spite of the fact that its whiteness is clearly visible, as everyone well knows, still he wished to dispute it openly. But that's the way it is. There are madmen around who would change the very order of nature and would even try to dazzle people's eyes and stupefy their senses.[95]

Although this sermon passage appears on the surface to reject the Copernican hypothesis, Copernicus is not mentioned. Reflecting on Stauffer's discovery, Hooykaas, who earlier had claimed that Calvin showed "not the slightest indication of hostility toward Copernicanism" inasmuch as he had simply ignored the issue, now conceded that "we cannot maintain any longer than Calvin never mentioned the doctrine of the earth's motion, and we should not rashly say that

Copernicus' name was unknown to him."[96] Hooykaas, moreover, regarded the passage as an indication that Calvin rejected the Copernican system.

A book-length article by French theologian Pierre Marcel on Calvin and Copernicus, as well as an extract translated into English, appeared in 1980-81. Marcel argued that because Calvin had tremendous respect for scientific astronomy, referring to it even as "the alphabet of theology," he thought it proper to leave astronomy free from theology to do its own work and draw its own conclusions. According to Marcel, he kept "theology and the church far from partisan squabbles and demonstrates the peaceful relationships that science and the Christian faith have in common if each remains on its own territory." We should not regard him as a disciple of Copernicus, however, because he "lacked the competence to appraise the mathematical 'proofs' of Copernicus and it was not possible for him to involve himself in or commit himself to a scientific battle."[97] Marcel saw Calvin's silence regarding Copernicus as a sign of respect for the labors of the practicing astronomers.

Around the same time, Robert White reviewed the question in light of Stauffer's discovery. Although granting that the passage indicated that Calvin rejected the hypothesis of solar stability, White nevertheless insisted that he did not reject that view because it was a denial of the Bible, "but because it is a denial of rationality; it is rejected, not as an impious doctrine unworthy of the Christian, but as an aberrant philosophy unworthy of the thinking man." Therefore, he concluded that although it is false to claim that Calvin condemned Copernicus as contrary to Scripture, it was clear that Calvin "had acquired at least an elementary understanding of the heliocentric hypothesis, and on at least one occasion dismissed it as a delusion."[98]

Christopher Kaiser, however, did not think that Calvin was rejecting Copernicanism. From a detailed analysis of the critical passage from the sermon, Kaiser concluded that Calvin may have been paraphrasing several statements from Cicero's *Academica*. In support of this contention, he quoted a passage from *Academica* that refers to the view that the Earth is in motion and that all the heavenly bodies are stationary. He noted, too, a reference in *Academica* to a Greek philosopher who reasoned that snow is black, another assertion mentioned in Calvin's passage. But why would Calvin have been paraphrasing Cicero? Just who was it that he had in mind in bringing up this passage? Kaiser argued at length that Calvin was attempting to undercut the views of Sebastien Caastalion (Castellio) (1513-1563), a former friend and supporter who had drifted away and become excessive in his advocacy of religious tolerance. Kaiser suggested that

> in the context of Calvin's theological and political struggles of the time (around 1556), we can assume that the allusion to the *Academica* was aimed at Castellio and his followers and was intended to substantiate Calvin's claim that tolerance in matters of religion would lead to skepticism in natural philosophy as well as anarchy in civil affairs. Calvin's anti-geodynamic remark was anti-Castellian (or anti-Bellianist), not anti-Copernican.

Kaiser judged, too, that Calvin's remark should be viewed as anti-geodynamic, not necessarily anti-heliocentric. In other words, Calvin purportedly opposed the idea that the Earth moves rather than the idea that the Sun is at the center of the cosmos. Kaiser further granted that there still existed the possibility that Calvin was aware of the work of Copernicus and even critical of it, but insisted that the situation remained pretty much as Rosen had described it, namely, that "we have no clear evidence that Calvin ever commented on or even knew of the work of Copernicus."[99]

In his biography of Calvin, Bernard Cottret alluded to the sermon passage in question. Apparently unaware of Kaiser's article, inasmuch as he made neither reference to it nor effort to refute it, he simply assumed that Calvin was decidedly anti-Copernican.[100]

I suggest that Calvin probably did know of the Copernican hypothesis but that, in light of his admiration for the work of the astronomers, his profound appreciation of science generally, and his frequent application of the principle of accommodation in conjunction with "scientific" matters, he took no definitive stand on the issue for at least three reasons. In the first place, Calvin was generally very cautious about deriving scientific conclusions from biblical statements, something Luther was more likely to do. Secondly, as a theologian and biblical exegete, he would leave the pronouncements on issues of astronomy to experts in the field, and lastly, the outcome of the debate over the Copernican hypothesis lay a century in the future. On the assumption that he was aware of the debate, Calvin may have thought it proper to wait until the astronomers had settled the issue before forming his own settled opinion. The fact that Calvin issued no unequivocal condemnation of Copernicus by name speaks volumes about the way in which he approached the interface between theology and science.

NOTES

1.   For Plato's cosmology, see Plato, *Timaeus*, trans. H. D. P. Lee (Baltimore: Penguin Books, 1965).
2.   Aristotle's cosmology is found primarily in three works, Aristotle, *On the Heavens*, trans. W. K. C. Guthrie (Cambridge, Mass.: Harvard University Press, 1939); Aristotle, *On Coming-to-Be and Passing-Away*, trans. E. S. Forster (Cambridge, Mass.: Harvard University Press, 1955); and Aristotle, *Meteorologica*, trans. H. D. P. Lee (Cambridge, Mass.: Harvard University Press, 1952).
3.   C. B. Kaiser, *Creational Theoloy and the History of Physical Science*, 27.
4.   Christopher B. Kaiser, "Calvin's Understanding of Aristotelian Natural Philosophy: its Extent and Possible Origins," in *Calviniana: Ideas and Influence of Jean Calvin*, ed. R. V. Schnucker (Kirksville, Mo.: Sixteenth Century Journal Publishers, Inc., 1988), 82-83.
5.   On medieval Christian ideas about the structure of the cosmos, see N. Max Wildiers, *The Theologian and His Universe: Theology and Cosmology from the Middle Ages to the Present* (New York: Seabury Press, 1982).
6.   C. B. Kaiser, *Creational Theology and the History of Physical Science*, 102.
7.   Howell, *God's Two Books*. Howell's work provides an excellent analysis of the early reception of the heliocentric hypothesis of Copernicus. Not only did Howell address the reactions of such great astronomers as Tycho Brahe, Giordano Bruno, Galileo Galilei, and Johannes Kepler to the ideas of Copernicus, but he also discussed attitudes toward Copernicanism on the part of Luther, Calvin, and their successors.
8.   Christine M. Probes, "Calvin on Astrology," *Westminster Theological Journal* 37, (1974): 24-33.
9.   Calvin's booklet on astrology was first published in French in 1549. For a new English translation of *Advertisement contre Astrologie*, see John Calvin, "A Warning against Judiciary Astrology and other Prevalent Curiosities," trans. Mary Potter, *Calvin Theological Journal*, 18, (1983): 157-89.
10.   See again note 8 in Chapter 1.
11.   Calvin, "A Warning against Judiciary Astrology," 180.
12.   Commentary on Isaiah 44:25.
13.   Commentary on Jeremiah 10:1-2.
14.   Commentary on Daniel 1:4.
15.   Calvin, "A Warning against Judiciary Astrology," 174.
16.   Commentary on Daniel 4:19.
17.   Commentary on Acts 1:26.
18.   Commentary on Isaiah 47:14.
19.   Commentary on Daniel 1:4.
20.   Commentary on Isaiah 44:25.
21.   Commentary on Acts 19:19.
22.   Commentary on Genesis, Argument.
23.   Commentary on Psalm 93:1. Ironically, Psalm 96:10 also speaks of the world being established, but in that context Calvin interpreted that establishment in terms of restoration of stability from a state of confusion and disorder brought about by ungodliness. In Psalm 96 Calvin envisioned establishment in spiritual terms whereas he interpreted Psalm 93 in physical terms.
24.   Kaiser, "Calvin's Understanding of Aristotelian Natural Philosophy," 86.
25.   Institutes, 1. 16. 1.

26. Kaiser, "Calvin's Understanding of Aristotelian Natural Philosophy," 84-85.
27. Jaroslav Pelikan, ed., *Luther's Works*, vol. 1, *Lectures in Genesis* (St. Louis: Concordia Publishing House, 1960). This and all subsequent quotations from this source are excerpts from Luther's Works Vol. 1 © 1960 Concordia Publishing House. Used with permission. Al rights reserved.
28. Commentary on Genesis 1:16.
29. Commentary on Acts 1:11.
30. Commentary on Genesis 3:17.
31. Commentary on Ephesians 4:10.
32. Commentary on Zechariah 12:3.
33. Commentary on Isaiah 48:13.
34. Commentary on Isaiah 40:26.
35. Commentary on Jeremiah 33:19-20.
36. First Sermon on Job 26.
37. Second Sermon on Job 9.
38. Commentary on Jeremiah 10:12-13.
39. Commentary on Deuteronomy 4:19.
40. Commentary on Acts 13:27.
41. Second Sermon on Job 9.
42. Commentary on Joshua 10:12.
43. Kaiser, "Calvin's Understanding of Aristotelian Natural Philosophy," 90-92.
44. Second Sermon on Job 9.
45. Second Sermon on Job 38.
46. Commentary on Psalm 90:12.
47. Calvin, "A Warning against Judiciary Astrology," 165.
48. Commentary on Ezekiel 1:1.
49. Commentary on Genesis 1:16.
50. Second Sermon on Job 9.
51. Commentary on Jeremiah 31:37.
52. Commentary on Isaiah 48:13.
53. Second Sermon on Job 9.
54. Commentary on Matthew 27:45.
55. Calvin, "A Warning against Judiciary Astrology," 183.
56. Commentary on Jeremiah 10:1-2.
57. See discussions by Frank Dawson Adams, *The Birth and Development of the Geological Sciences* (New York: Dover Publications, 1954) and Martin J. S. Rudwick, *The Meaning of Fossils*, 2nd ed. (Chicago: University of Chicago Press, 1976) for additional information about medieval views on fossils and ore deposits.
58. On Ristoro d'Arezzo's ideas, see Adams, *The Birth and Development of the Geological Sciences*.
59. Commentary on Deuteronomy 4:19.
60. Commentary on Jeremiah 10:1-2.
61. Commentary on Deuteronomy 33:13.
62. Commentary on Matthew 17:17.
63. Commentary on Amos 5:8.
64. Fourth Sermon on Job 38.
65. Calvin, "A Warning against Judiciary Astrology," 166-67.
66. Ibid., 167.
67. Ibid., 174.
68. Ibid., 168.

69. Ibid., 169-70.

70. Ibid., 169.

71. Ibid., 171.

72. Ibid.

73. Ibid., 174-75.

74. Ibid., 176.

75. Commentary on Acts 11:28.

76. Commentary on Ezekiel 8:16.

77. Commentary on Deuteronomy 4:19.

78. Helmut T. Lehman, ed., *Luther's Works*, vol. 54, *Table Talk* (Philadelphia: Fortress Press, 1967), 358-59. The quotation is from Luther's Table Talk of June 4, 1539 and was transcribed by Anthony Lautenbach (1502-1569), a protégé of Luther who was said by Luther's wife to have taken more notes at the Reformer's table than anyone else. A month after recording Luther's comments on Copernicus, Lautenbach became pastor in Pirna, a few kilometers southeast of Dresden, where he remained until his death. For a sympathetic examination of Luther's thoughts about Copernicus, see Donald H. Kobe, "Copernicus and Martin Luther: an Encounter between Science and Religion," *American Journal of Physics* 66, (1998): 190-96.

79. Howell, *God's Two Books*, 40.

80. Ibid., 57.

81. Frederic W. Farrar, *History of Interpretation: Eight Lectures Preached before the University of Oxford in the Year MDCCCLXXXV* (New York: E. P. Dutton, 1886), xviii.

82. Charles Woodruff Shields, *The Final Philosophy* (New York: Scribner, Armstrong and Co., 1877), 60.

83. Andrew Dickson White, *A History of the Warfare of Science with Theology in Christendom*. vol. 1. (New York: D. Appleton, 1896), 127.

84. Bertrand Russell, *A History of Western Philosophy and Its Connection with Political and Social Circumstances from the Earliest Times to the Present Day* (New York: Simon and Schuster, 1945), 528.

85. Paul H. Kocher, *Science and Religion in Elizabethan England* (New York: Octagon Books, 1969), 191.

86. Thomas S. Kuhn, *The Copernican Revolution: Planetary Astronomy in the Development of Western Thought* (Cambridge, MA: Harvard University Press, 1957), 192.

87. Ibid., 195-96.

88. Timothy Ferris, *Coming of Age in the Milky Way* (New York: HarperCollins, 2003), 67.

89. James Orr, *The Bible under Trial: Apologetic Papers in View of Present-Day Assaults on Holy Scripture* (London: Marshall Brothers, 1907).

90. The error of A. D. White in falsely attributing anti-Copernican statements to Calvin was pointed out by Reijer Hooykaas, "Thomas Digges' Puritanism," *Archives Internationale d'Histoire des Sciences* 8, (1955):151. For a more thorough treatment of the misattributions of anti-Copernican quotations to Calvin see Edward Rosen, "Calvin's Attitude toward Copernicus," *Journal of the History of Ideas* 21, (1960): 431-41.

91. Commentary on Genesis, Argument

92. Rosen, "Calvin's Attitude toward Copernicus," 441.

93. Joseph Ratner, "Some Comments on Rosen's 'Calvin's Attitude toward Copernicus,'" *Journal of the History of Ideas* 22, (1961): 382.

94. Edward Rosen, "A Reply to Dr. Ratner," *Journal of the History of Ideas* 22, (1961): 386.

95. Richard Stauffer, "Calvin et Copernic," *Annales Musee Guinet., Rev. Hist. D. Religions* 179, (1971): 31-40. The quotation is from Christopher B. Kaiser, "Calvin, Copernicus, and Castellio," *Calvin Theological Journal* 21, (1986): 16-17.
96. Reijer Hooykaas, "Calvin and Copernicus," *Organon* 10, (1974), 144.
97. Pierre C. Marcel, "Calvin and Copernicus," *Philosophia Reformata* 46, (1981): 14-36.
98. Robert White, "Calvin and Copernicus: The Problem Reconsidered," *Calvin Theological Journal* 15, (1980): 233-43.
99. Kaiser, "Calvin, Copernicus, and Castellio," 31.
100. Cottret, "Calvin," 285-86.

CHAPTER 3

CALVIN ON PHYSICS
AND THE ATMOSPHERE

Just as Calvin inherited a view of the cosmos that had been profoundly shaped by Aristotle, so, too, he was an heir to an essentially Aristotelian conception of the "physics" of the sub-lunary world.[1] Objects below the sphere of the Moon were commonly interpreted in terms of Aristotle's theories of the elements and of natural places. The early phases of the Greek philosophical enterprise, initiated by Thales (624-548 B. C.), were concerned with the problem of substance. Thales and subsequent Ionian philosophers asked, "What is the fundamental substance of the world?" Upon observation and reflection, Thales concluded that water is the basic stuff of which the world is made. Anaximenes (588-524 B. C.) argued instead that the basic substance is air, a logical choice, he thought, because air could be converted into other substances by expanding or compressing it. Moreover, owing to its invisibility, air is a material substance that also comes very close to being an immaterial, spiritual kind of entity. Still later, Heraclitus (535-475 B. C.), impressed by the fact that everything is constantly changing, maintained that fire, with its flickering behavior, is the substance that most closely reflects the changing nature of things. Ultimately, Empedocles of Agrigentum (495-435 B. C.) proposed that there are four basic substances: fire, air, water, and earth. Transformations in nature were said to occur as a result of the action of two opposing principles, love and strife, on these four elements. Plato (428-347 B. C.) subsequently incorporated the notion of four elements into his cosmology, although he conceived of the elements as qualities or properties rather than substances. He also suggested that each element was composed of tiny particles having a specific geometrical shape. Thus, he said, the element earth is composed of cubes, water is composed of icosahedra (solids having 20 triangular faces), air is composed of octahedra (solids having eight sides, each of which is an equilateral triangle), and fire is composed of pyramids.

Aristotle (384-322 B. C.) further developed the conception of four fundamental elements. He believed that each element is a continuous substance. In other words, there is no empty space and there are no atoms. In this respect he differed from Plato and the atomist philosophers Leucippus of Miletus (c. 480-c. 420 B. C.) and Democritus of Abdera (c. 460-c. 370 B. C.). Aristotle taught, particularly in his work *De Generatione et Corruptione*, that the four elements result from combinations of four primary qualities that act on raw matter: hot, cold, wet, and dry.[2] The element, fire, is produced by the combination of hot and dry. Air is produced by the combination of hot and moist. Water is produced by cold and moist, and earth is produced by cold and dry. Fire and earth are pure elements, whereas water and air are intermediate in character. Aristotle further explained how the elements could be transformed into one another. For example, water can be transformed into air if the cold is overpowered by the hot. Likewise, fire can be transformed into air if the dry is overpowered by the moist.

The medieval scholars who adopted and modified this theory of the elements knew nothing of the modern conception of chemical elements like calcium, copper, zinc, and fluorine that are composed of atoms that differ from one another in terms of their masses and proton contents. Instead, the medieval world and Calvin's contemporaries had inherited a long-lived tradition of alchemy. Long before the time of Christ, peoples in ancient cultures around the world discovered that many materials serve some useful purpose. The ancients found that melted sand could be converted into glass from which to fashion art objects or drinking vessels. Ancient civilizations recognized that the addition of small quantities of various substances to the melt could impart different colors to the glass. They also learned that a variety of metals such as copper, silver, gold, mercury, and iron could be extracted from particular rocks upon intense heating and used for jewelry, weapons of war, tools, or utensils.

Various substances that were extracted from plants or animals were found to be useful in the manufacture of inks, dyes, paints, salves, medicinal potions, perfumes, aphrodisiacs, and much else. In China, Egypt, Mesopotamia, and Greece, experience with these substances and procedures for producing them, such as primitive forms of distillation, commonly became intertwined with elaborate rituals and incantations. Such was the nature of alchemy, a long-lived set of arts whose practitioners became fascinated by the problem of transformation of materials. Alchemists concentrated on efforts to transform substances to higher states of perfection. In the case of mineral substances, that generally meant transformation into gold. But alchemy was also concerned with a more interior form of transformation involving the human person. In the case of human beings, attainment of longevity or even immortality was in view. Transformations might be brought about with the aid of a material substance, some sort of potion, or a revelation.

In Greece, alchemical practice was given theoretical underpinnings in terms of the four sub-lunary elements. The alchemical arts were passed on to the medieval Christian world by way of the Arabs, who introduced the instrumentality of the philosopher's stone and the elixir of life. Improvements in the extraction, purification, and manufacture of metals and a variety of other substances, both liquid and solid, continued throughout the Middle Ages up to the sixteenth century when belief in the four fundamental elements and in alchemy continued to hold sway.[3] Consequently, it is not surprising that Calvin assumed the general validity of the theory of four elements that was accepted by his contemporaries and medieval predecessors. On the other hand, his attitude toward alchemy is not clear. I have not found any explicit reference to alchemy or alchemical practices in his writings, although he did mention that "the philosophers" knew about the "transmutations" that occur in nature.[4] The lack of allusions to alchemy is curious given the close links between alchemical procedures and the practice of magic throughout the Middle Ages and into Calvin's era. One would assume that he had some suspicions about aspects of alchemy.

The Aristotelian theory of four elements was intimately connected to the theory of natural places. As we saw, Aristotle taught that things in the sub-lunary realm tend to move in an essentially straight-line manner, rather than in circular motion as the heavenly spheres do. In Aristotelian physics, then, the elements move up or down in accordance with their relative weights, and earth, the heaviest element, tends to move downward toward its natural place at the center of the universe. Because water is also heavy but not so heavy as earth, it, too, tends to move toward the center but not as efficiently as earth. Therefore, water tends to accumulate in a spherical shell that surrounds earth. In contrast, air, being light, tends toward its natural place above the water where it forms a spherical envelope encircling the water sphere. And fire, the lightest element of all, tends to rise even above the air toward its natural place. Flickering flames clearly strive upward. If all the elements were able to move completely unimpeded, then ideally each element would arrive at its natural place, and the cosmos would consist of a series of concentric spheres with earth at the center, superseded by a sphere of water, then a sphere of air, and then a sphere of fire up to the outer limits of the lower region of the cosmos where the sphere of the Moon is located. This has not happened completely, however, because of the possible transformations of elements into one another. Calvin also generally accepted this theory of natural places, but as we will see, he did have some reservations about Aristotle's version.

Although Calvin's conceptions of the theories of the four elements and of natural places are closely intertwined, we will look first at texts that refer to the four elements and then at those bearing on his ideas about natural places. We will recognize that he was quite aware of deviations from the supposed natural order of things. Calvin viewed these deviations as evidences that the world is not just an autonomous natural order governed by inexorable law but that God operated in the world to produce these deviations from an otherwise monotonous unyielding order, especially in regard to the distinction between land and sea. He viewed the existence of oceans that were kept separate from the land areas as a perpetual miracle of major proportions.

Four Elements

In Calvin's references to the four sub-lunary elements, he was constantly seeking ways to treat them as creatures directly subject to the will of God rather than just as parts in an inexorable natural machine. "How can we account for the fact that the air which is so thin doesn't consume itself by blowing incessantly? How can we account for the fact that the waters don't waste away by flowing," he asked in writing about the passage in Psalm 119:91 that says that God's "laws endure to this day for all things serve you." In answer he appealed to "the principle that the elements obey the secret command of God."[5] Likewise, where discussing God's creation of the sand as an everlasting boundary that the waters of the sea cannot cross, he observed that "the inanimate elements obey his bidding."[6]

Although explicit references to "four elements" are rare in Calvin's works, they are not altogether lacking. The reference to "waters above the skies" in Psalm 148:4 provided him with the perfect opportunity to reject the notion of several theologians that there is a sphere of waters in the upper region of the cosmos beyond the Moon and the stellar firmament. Such a viewpoint would have run counter to Aristotle's scheme in which water belongs to the lower sub-lunary region as a mutable element. Calvin evidently was sufficiently comfortable with Aristotelianism that he wanted to confine water to the sub-lunary region, and so he affirmed that there is no foundation for the conjecture "that there are waters deposited above the four elements."[7] He was inclined to view biblical references to waters above the heavens as allusions to the clouds. He went on to say that "it is adhering too strictly to the letter of the words employed, to conceive as if there were some sea up in the heavens, where the waters were permanently deposited" on the grounds that Moses and the Prophets ordinarily spoke in a popular style that was "suited to the lowest apprehension."[8]

That Calvin accepted four elements is also clear from the fact that he mentioned earth, water, air, and fire individually as elements and never mentioned anything else as an element. Thus, he referred to "the two elements, water and earth."[9] He stated that the "moon is placed above the element of fire." The Moon, therefore, must necessarily be a fiery body, a quality that accounts for its luminosity.[10] The birds "come nearer the sun and the element of fire."[11] The air is one of the elements that "obey the secret command of God."[12]

Following Aristotle, Calvin also believed that the elements were essentially circular (spherical) envelopes continuously filled with matter. Regarding water, he stated that "being an element, it must be circular."[13] He noted elsewhere that "natural philosophers are compelled to admit, and it is even one of their first principles, that the water is circular."[14] He wrote that "the sea and the other elements are spherical. Just as the earth is round so is the element of water, not to mention air and fire."[15] In reference to the Earth and its waters, he stated that "these elements are of spherical form."[16] His allusions to water or earth as spherical elements must be understood as a reference to a series of nested, concentric spheres.

The Theory of Natural Places

Calvin, too, accepted Aristotle's basic theory of natural places, but, as we shall see, with some reservations. In line with the standard theory, Calvin placed the element earth at the center of the universe. This location, of course, posed a major problem because the Earth seemed to be suspended in air or in free space. How could that be? Calvin faced the problem when he analyzed Psalm 104:5, the text that asserts that God founded the Earth on foundations so that it could never be moved. Interestingly, he did not appeal solely to the miraculous power of God to explain how the Earth could just hang in space. He attempted to give a scientific explanation, believing that the problem could be solved "on natural principles." The explanation sounds almost tautological: "the earth, as it occupies the lowest place, being the centre of the world naturally settles down there." Of course, "the wonderful power of God" is displayed in this "contrivance."[17] In his commentary on Psalm 75, Calvin wrote that "the earth occupies the lowest place in the celestial sphere" even though it seems to be suspended in air.[18] But why does the element earth naturally settle down at the center? Why does it occupy the lowest place in the celestial sphere? His answer was that "the philosophers maintain that the solid earth stands naturally in the middle of creation because it is the heaviest element. The reason they give that the earth is suspended in mid-air is that the center of the world attracts what is most heavy."[19] So density, or "heaviness" played a critical role in the theory of natural places.

Following the philosophers, Calvin assumed that the sphere of earth was in turn surrounded by envelopes of water, air, and fire. Immediately above the sphere of earth was that of water. "The element of earth, it is true, in so far as it occupies the lowest place in the order of the sphere, is beneath the waters."[20] "Philosophers allow that the natural position of the waters was to cover the whole earth, as Moses declares they did in the beginning," wrote Calvin.[21] After all, water is heavier than air and lighter than earth. The element of earth is "grosser and denser" and more firm than the other elements, "but the waters, though lighter than the earth, approach it nearest."[22] Water also "occupies the region intermediate between the earth and the air."[23] Moreover, consistent with the idea that water rather than earth occupies the sphere adjacent to that of air is the comment that "water has greater affinity with the air than earth does."[24] This comment was introduced in reference to the creation of birds from the waters rather than from earth after the manner of vegetation.

Above water was the sphere of air. The element of air rises "on account of its being light." Last comes the element of fire "nearer to what heaven is."[25] In his second sermon on Job 26, Calvin summed up his conception of the natural places of the four elements:

> if a man ask the philosophers and such as search the whole order of nature, they will confess that if the elements had their full scope throughout according to their nature, the earth should be hidden under the water: and in good sooth, experience shows it to be so. For why is the earth in the middle of the world, but because it is firm and substantially by reason of his weight. For the waters are lighter, and therewithal they sheede, so as they are not so firm. Consequently the air is above the waters; and the fire is also above the air. We see then that the elements are distinguished according to their properties. Seeing that the air environs the whole earth as we see the waters also ought to go around between them both, that is to say, between the earth and the air. For that is their proper place and situation.[26]

These four elements, then, take us up to the realm of the Moon which was placed above the element of fire and said by Calvin necessarily to be a "fiery body."[27]

Calvin recognized that deviations from the natural order of elements proposed by Aristotle existed. On the theory of natural places, water should form a spherical shell that is sandwiched between the sphere of earth beneath and the sphere of air above. Obviously that has not happened, and a good thing, too, for unless earth at least locally rises above the water, human life would be impossible.

So, the position of the waters in the oceans posed a major puzzle for Calvin in view of his allegiance to the theory of natural places. The biblical creation story points out that, on the third day of creation, God caused the dry land to appear out of the waters below the firmament. God separated the dry land from the gathered waters which he called "seas." Calvin, of course, had no difficulty accepting the biblical teaching, but he was mightily perplexed by the resulting phenomenon. Given the nature of water and earth in the theory of natural places, what was the cause for the dry land, composed of the element earth, being higher than the ocean, composed of the element water? What prevented the water, whose natural place was thought to be higher than earth, from overflowing and destroying the dry land? "If the waters are higher than the earth, because they are lighter, why do they not cover the whole earth round about?" he asked. The only solution that he thought acceptable was that "the natural tendency of the water to do so is counteracted by the providence of God, that a dwelling-place might be provided for man."[28] After all, he maintained, "the waters, if not kept within their limits, would naturally cover the earth, were it not that God has seen fit to secure a place of habitation for the human family."[29]

Calvin pondered the puzzle in some detail at various points. He returned again and again to the issue. In his commentary on Psalm 24:2, he asked:

> How is it that the earth appears above the water, but because God purposely intended to prepare a habitation for men? Philosophers themselves admit, that as

the element of the water is higher than the earth, it is contrary to the nature of the two elements, for any part of the earth to continue uncovered with the waters, and habitable. Accordingly Job extols, in magnificent terms, that signal miracle by which God restrains the violent and tempestuous ragings of the sea, that it may not overwhelm the earth, which, if not thus restrained, it would immediately do, and produce horrible confusion. Nor does Moses forget to mention this in the history of the creation. After having narrated that the waters were spread abroad so as to cover the whole earth, he adds, that by an express command of God they retired into one place, in order to leave empty space for the living creatures which were afterwards to be created. . . . The element of earth, it is true, in so far as it occupies the lowest place in the order of the sphere, is beneath the waters; but the habitable part of the earth is above the water, and how can we account for it, that this separation of the water from the earth remains stable, but because God has put the waters underneath, as it were for a foundation?[30]

Calvin returned to the same problem in the second sermon on Job 26. After summarizing the theory of natural places, he preached as follows:

And like as the fire overspreads all; so also would the waters not leave one foot of dry ground: the very mountains, yea even the highest of them should be covered under them. But now we see low and hollow places abide dry, and yet the sea mounts above them. . . . For when we consider what a thing the sea is specially when it rises aloft; it is a wonder that the earth is not overwhelmed by it. . . . The sea is so violent a thing, as there seems to be no means to hold it in; and yet for all that, it is barred within lists. The sea seems to threaten to drown the earth, and it seems that the earth should be swallowed up at the rushing forth of every wave. Yet notwithstanding, God does always restrain the sea from winning any further than it pleases him to threaten men withal, to the end they should learn to humble themselves and to walk in greater wariness. . . . If any man allege that not only the sea but also the rivers do some times get the upper hand and so pass their bounds as they tear up all things before them so that both houses and vineyards are overwhelmed and exceeding great and excessive breaches are made by violence of the sea; the answer thereunto is that yet notwithstanding God ceases not to preserve the world in general and his suffering of the sea to pass his bounds in that wise is to make us to think upon his power which is showed us here. . . . How are we here upon earth. Surely even as in a grave. For behold the sea and the waters are over us. And of whom is it long that they swallow us not up but of God who holds his hand between them and us? But we be so far off from marking this, that we become like swine, filling our bellies and pampering our selves with God's benefits, and not thinking one whit upon the things which he shows us to the eye; that is to wit, that we cannot live one minute of an hour, but by miracle. For it is he that bridleth the sea in such wise.[31]

In this amazing passage, Calvin plainly attributed the present arrangement to a miracle by which God restrains the sea from overflowing the land. In fact, he even suggested that the ocean actually is higher than the land. Much the same thought was also expressed at length in the commentary on Jeremiah:

Now if any inquire how it can be that the earth is above the sea, it must be confessed as a miracle that can't be accounted for. After all the sea and the other elements are spherical. Just as the earth is round so is the element of water, not to mention air and fire. Since its form is spherical we must know that it isn't lower than the earth. Since it is lighter than earth it must stand above it. But water is a liquid and should overflow the earth. It can't stand in one place unless it is retained by some secret power of God.

Now the word of God, though it is not heard by us, nor resounds in the air, is yet heard by the sea; for the sea is confined within its own limits. Were the sea tranquil, it would still be a wonderful work of God, as he has given the earth to be the habitation of men; but when it is moved, as I have said, by a tempest, and heaven and earth seem to blend together, there is no one, being nigh such a sight, who does not feel dread.

It is indeed true that the sea sometimes overflows its limits; for many cities, we know, have been swallowed up by a flood; but still it is rightly said, that it is a perpetual ordinance or decree, that God confines the sea within its own limits. For whenever the sea overflows a small portion of land, we hence learn what it might do without that restraint, mentioned here by Jeremiah and in the book of Job. We hence learn that there is nothing to hinder the sea from overflowing the whole earth but the command of God which it obeys. In the meantime the perpetuity of which the prophet speaks remains generally the same; for though many storms arise every year, yet the fury of the seas still quieted, but not otherwise than by the command of God. True then is this that the sea has prescribed limits, over which its waves are not permitted to pass.[32]

One of the most striking passages that considers the problem of the position of the sea occurs in the second sermon on Job 38. In this sermon Calvin alluded to Jeremiah 5, a text that speaks of God having set the bounds of the sea. These bounds are absolutely necessary because "the Sea is above us." It is not just that the sea ought to overflow the land; the sea, in effect, is piled up on either side of the land not unlike the piling up of the Red Sea when the children of Israel passed through on dry land. Calvin maintained that people do not even begin to realize the danger that is posed by the sea.

The simple and ignorant perceive not that the sea overbeareth us and that it is higher than the earth: but they suppose that the water is under the earth and far beneath it. But this is clean contrary. And when we be near the sea, we see and perceive even by the eyesight, that it is higher than the earth.[33]

The same sentiments were expressed in his analysis of Psalm 104:9. Here Calvin averred that "it is entirely owing to the providence of God, that a part of the earth remains dry and fit for the habitation of men." Mariners were said to have "the most satisfactory evidence" of this fact. Indeed, the evidence is so obvious that "were even the rudest and most stupid of our race only to open their eyes, they would behold in the sea mountains of water elevated far above the level of the land." This situation is such that "no banks, and even no iron gates, could make the waters, which in their own nature are fluid and unstable, keep together and in one place." In support of his contention that the sea should naturally overflow the land apart from a "counteracting law" established by God keeping the sea within bounds, Calvin referred to a major inundation of the Flemish lowlands by the Baltic Sea. This episode, he said, served as a warning of what could happen if God removed the restraints that hold back the sea.[34]

These remarkable comments about the sea being visibly higher than the land raises the question as to whether Calvin had ever been to the sea. Had he visited the Mediterranean Sea, the English Channel, or the Atlantic Ocean? Was he basing his assertion on the opinion of someone who had been to the sea? Did he base his assertion on his own observation while standing on the shore of Lake Leman at Geneva? If one sits on the beach and looks straight out at the ocean it is possible to convince oneself that the water does slope gently toward the land, but with a glance to the side, the horizontality of the surface of the sea becomes evident, and the appearance of a gentle landward slope vanishes. Calvin's conception, of course, poses the additional difficulty that a sailing ship heading out to sea must literally be sailing uphill and then sailing downhill as it returned to port.

Calvin's other major question mark with the theory of natural places concerned the presence of water in the air. Aristotelian physics taught that the natural place of water is below that of air. The natural tendency, therefore, would be for water to fall through the air as it does when it rains. Even common sense seems to tell us that water, being heavier than air, should not accumulate high in the sky in the form of clouds. Calvin faced this issue in his second sermon on Job 26. He considered it amazing that "the waters should hang in the air and bide fast there." "The air is so fine and thin as it continually gives place" to flowing waters. And "the waters of their own nature are heavier than the air. Therefore the waters ought to fall down according to reason. But they are held there as it were in tubs." Calvin figured that we really ought to be drowned by all the water held in the air. The "clouds and the waters enclosed in them, therefore, are because God stretched out his hand," he concluded.[35] Likewise in dealing with Psalm 148, he observed of the masses of water in the sky that "it seems contrary to nature that they should mount aloft, and also, that though fluid they should hang in vacant space." Unable to find a reasonable physical explanation why the heavier element should remain suspended in the lighter, Calvin again envisioned the miraculous, stressing "the marvelous fact that God holds the waters suspended in the air."[36]

By assuming the general validity of the theory of natural places, Calvin adopted the scientific theory of his day. Nevertheless, he observed phenomena that did not seem to him (or others) to be consonant with that theory. He had no strictly physical explanation to account for the anomalous phenomena that might make sense in terms of the reigning theory. Despite his deep awareness of these "violations" of the theory of natural places, it never occurred to him, or to almost everyone else, that the entire theory might be fundamentally flawed. To account for the supposedly anomalous behavior of water, Calvin simply invoked an ongoing providential miracle. He adopted what would today be regarded as a "God-of-the-gaps" explanation, a strategy that attributes to the direct agency of God a phenomenon that cannot be accounted for in terms of current scientific theory. To be sure, Calvin allowed that God probably uses second causes in the formation of clouds, but these causes still did not "fit" the prevailing conception of the order of nature. Calvin, of course, did not see anything improper in introducing a miraculous action of God to complement otherwise natural behavior. Many of his scientifically-minded predecessors, e.g., Henry of Langenstein (c. 1325-1397), a professor at the University of Paris who refuted astrological superstitions about comets, also resorted to miracle to account for what they perceived as anomalies in the Aristotelian worldview they inherited.[37] What is striking is that whereas Calvin envisioned God as establishing the natural order (as interpreted by Aristotle) in the first place, he seems never to have questioned why God needed to counteract that natural order for the benefit of man. In other words, why did not God simply create a natural order in the first place that was perfectly suited for human habitation without the necessity of resorting to "tinkering" or "fine tuning?" One can only speculate as to why Calvin did not think of dry land above the sea and water suspended in air as "natural" aspects of the world as God created it rather than deviations from that natural order that had to be propped up by special providential action.

Exhalation Theory

John Calvin was also strongly influenced by the theory of exhalations that was developed by Aristotle in *Meteorologica*. Aristotle invoked a comprehensive exhalation theory to account for a wide range of phenomena in the atmosphere and the subsurface. In the next chapter, we will consider exhalation theory in regard to earthquakes. For now, let's see how the theory was applied to the atmosphere.

Aristotle claimed that there two sorts of exhalation—moist and dry."[38] The moist exhalation, he said, is called vapor and the dry exhalation is a kind of smoke. The heat of the Sun, as it approaches the Earth, draws up the moist exhalation. The idea that the Earth exhaled vapors came naturally enough from the observation that mists rise above lakes and land in the morning. But the Sun also heats the Earth and produces a dry exhalation of which the winds are made. When the Sun recedes, the vapor is condensed by cold into water. The Sun and the warmth in the Earth produce both kinds of exhalations. Air is a composite of a wet and cold exhalation and of a dry and warm exhalation. Because exhalations are constantly both increasing and decreasing and expanding and contracting, clouds and winds are always being produced. Sometimes vaporous exhalation predominates and sometimes the dry, smoky one does.

Although winds blow horizontally, the exhalations rise vertically. But the circular motion of the heavens is imparted to the spherical body of air and causes lateral wind motions.[39] By the same token, on Aristotle's view, exhalations were received back into the Earth. For Aristotle the stirring of the wind in the morning and evening resulted from the exhalation arising out of the Earth and then returning to it.

In step with the thought of his age, Calvin accepted the exhalation theory of moisture and wind. He envisioned exhaled vapors arising from the Earth as causing a whole catalog of atmospheric phenomena such as thunder, lightning, rain, wind, hail, snow, and frost. In *Secret Providence* he referred to the "mists which the earth exhales" sometimes being sufficiently thick as to obscure the Sun.[40] Amos 5:8 refers to Yahweh as the one "who calls for the waters of the sea and pours them out over the face of the land." Of this verse Calvin observed that the philosophers "say that vapors are drawn up both from the earth and the sea by the heat of the sun." He claimed that, although natural causes could be assigned to the formation of clouds and darkening of the sky by means of the vapors, God still controlled the element of water and the timing of the drawing up of the water. Vapor, he said, is "gross air, or air condensed" and these "vapors arise from the hollow places of the earth as well as from the sea."[41] Regarding Psalm 147:7-8 he noted that "gross vapors are exhaled from earth and sea."[42] The idea of God calling for the waters of the sea is repeated in Amos 9:6, a text that elicited the observation that rains are formed predominantly by vapors from the Earth. Calvin also granted that "vapors arise from the sea."[43]

Calvin's most extensive discussion of exhalations appears in the commentary on Jeremiah 10:12-13. He wrote that "we see that vapours arise from the earth and ascend upwards." He granted that the philosophers had shown how this took place, but he insisted that the power of God was not thereby excluded "when we say that anything is done according to nature." Calvin observed that the winds originate in the caverns of the Earth: "the earth, where it is hollow, generates winds." He further granted that the philosophers had found out the cause why the winds arise from the Earth. "The sun," he said,

> attracts vapours and exhalations; from vapours are formed clouds, snows, and rains, according to the fixed order of the middle region of the air. From the exhalations also are formed the thunders, lightnings, the comets also, and the winds, for the exhalations differ from the vapours only in their lightness and rarity, the vapours being thicker and heavier. Then from vapour arises rain; but the exhalation is lighter, and not so thick; hence the exhalations generate thunders as well as winds, according to the heat they contain. How, then, is it that the same exhalation now breaks forth into wind, then into lightnings: It is according to the measure of its heat; when it is dense it rises into the air; but the winds vanish and thus disturb the lower part of the world.[44]

The Sun can even breathe out deadly exhalations.[45] Calvin talked not only in general terms about exhalations and vapors, but he also discussed in greater detail individual aspects of weather such as winds, rain, rainbows, hail, thunder, lightning, and the like.

Winds

Now we will look at how Calvin understood specific atmospheric phenomena in terms of the theories of exhalations and natural places. As noted above, he related winds to exhalations. Jeremiah 49:36 refers to God scattering the Elamites to the four winds. Calvin commented that "though the winds arise from the earth, yet their blowing is not perceived until they ascend into mid air: and though sometimes they seem to be formed above the clouds, they yet arise from the earth; for the origin of the wind is cold and dry exhalation."[46] A couple of chapters later, Jeremiah 51:16-17 mentions that God makes clouds to arise from the ends of the Earth and also that God "brings out the wind from his store-houses." Calvin wrote that "winds arise from the earth, even because exhalations proceed from it."[47] God, of course, was the sole author and creator of these exhalations.

A number of passages indicate that Calvin knew that winds blowing from specific directions have distinctive characteristics. The reference in Daniel's night vision to the four winds of heaven led him to note that "philosophers enumerate more than four winds when they desire to treat of the number with precision, although four winds is the common phrase."[48] Mention in Isaiah of God's "fierce blast" and "a day the east wind blows" induced him to write that "each country has its own particular wind that is injurious to it." In some countries it is the north wind, in others it is the south wind, and in still others it is the east or equinoctial wind. These various winds occasion "great damage, throwing down the corn, scorching or spoiling all the fruits, blasting the trees, and scarcely leaving anything in the fields uninjured."[49] Some biblical texts refer to the east wind. Hosea 12:1 states that "Ephraim feeds on the wind; he pursues the east wind all day and multiplies lies and violence." Calvin observed that "the east wind is in Judea a dry and often stormy wind. Other winds either bring rain or some other advantage, but this wind brings nothing but drought and storms."[50] He made similar comments on Habakkuk 1:9, a verse that refers to the Babylonians as those whose "hordes advance like a desert wind and gather prisoners like sand." Here Calvin wrote that "the east wind was very injurious to the land of Judea. It dried up vegetation and consumed the whole produce of the earth. The violence of that wind was also very great."[51] Lastly, in the oracle concerning the desert by the sea in Isaiah 21, the first verse refers to an invader coming from the desert, from a land of terror, and sweeping through the southland like whirlwinds. Calvin commented that the prophet says

from the south, because that wind is tempestuous, and produces storms and whirlwinds. When he adds that "it cometh from the desert," this tends to heighten the picture; for if any storm arise in a habitable and populous region, it excites less terror than those which spring up in deserts. In order to express the shocking nature of this calamity, he compares it to storms, which begin in the desert, and afterwards take a more impetuous course, and rush with greater violence.[52]

When all is said and done, Calvin the theologian was eager to maintain that, whatever natural causes and general characteristics may be assigned to wind, it is still God who ultimately controls those winds. He rejected the notion that wind, like all other occurrences in the natural world, can be accounted for *purely and solely* in terms of natural, or secondary, causes. For example, regarding Psalm 104:4 where Scripture says that God "makes the winds his messengers, flames of fire his servants," he commented that "God rides on the clouds, and is carried upon the wings of the wind, inasmuch as he drives about the winds and clouds at his pleasure, and by sending them hither and thither as swiftly as he pleases, shows thereby the signs of his presence." He insisted that the winds did not blow by chance. Instead, it is God who sovereignly rules and controls "all the agitation and disturbances of the atmosphere." Moreover, he continued, "if at any time noxious winds arise, if the south wind corrupt the air, or if the north wind scorch the corn, and not only tear up trees by the root, but overthrow houses, and if other winds destroy the fruits of the earth, we ought to tremble under these scourges of Providence." Then, too, God might also "moderate the excessive heat by a gentle cooling breeze...purify the polluted atmosphere by the north wind...or moisten the parched ground by south winds."[53]

Divine control of the winds is a theme that appears in a variety of contexts. The discussion of Jeremiah 49:36 conveys the same understanding of divine providence operating in conjunction with natural causes. "The air is in a moment put in motion whenever it pleases God," wrote Calvin,

> and when Scripture extols the power of God it does not without reason refer to the winds. For it is not a small miracle when the whole world is on a sudden put in motion. It is now tranquil and then in half an hour the winds rise and conflict together in mid air. And God alludes to what is usual in nature; as then he suddenly rouses up winds which make, as it were, the whole world to shake and tremble; so he says he would raise up winds from the four ends of the world.[54]

The same general thoughts were also expressed in comments on the tenth chapter of Ezekiel, in which the prophet saw a vision of the glory of God departing from the temple. Ezekiel 10:2 says that God told a man clothed in linen to "go in among the wheels beneath the cherubim." In what seems like one of his most unpredictable utterances, Calvin wrote about this verse that

> when the wind rises, when the sky is covered with clouds and mists, when the rain descends, and the air is disturbed by lightnings, we think, when all these things happen, that such motions and agitations take place naturally. But before this God wished to teach us that great agitations are not blind, but are directed by secret instinct, and hence the notion or inspiration of the angels, always exists.[55]

For Calvin, there is a "secret instinct" by which motion in nature occurs. The somewhat unpredictable comment about motion and secret instincts driven by angels in relation to this text becomes more understandable when it is understood that this idea was introduced in the very beginning of the commentary on Ezekiel and recurs throughout. In the very first vision in Ezekiel the cherubim (living creatures) and their wheels are introduced with these words: "I looked, and I saw a windstorm coming out of the north—an immense cloud with flashing lightning and surrounded by brilliant light. The center of the fire looked like glowing metal and in the fire was what looked like four living creatures" (Ezekiel 1:4-5). A few verses later, the vision introduces the wheels to which the living creatures were attached. Calvin understood the wheels in reference to motion and change. He observed that "no creature moves by itself, but that all motions are by the secret instinct of God." There is no fixed condition in the world but continual change. What is striking about Calvin's comments on Ezekiel 1:4, however, is a reference to the role of angels in the motion of the air, and, indeed, in any kind of motion. He continued his argument by asserting that no changes occur by chance, but depend upon the agency of angels. It is not that angels move things by their inherent power, but because they act as God's hands. All motion depends upon the angels, but God guides the angels according to his will.[56] This discussion formed the background for Calvin's reference to the activity of angels in respect to wind, rain, and the like.

We encounter similar ideas in Calvin's review of Ezekiel 10:13:

> Not even the slightest motion happens without that secret instinct. When the air is serene and calm, we do not think that God's voice reigns there, but we imagine some natural cause: so also when the sky is clouded, when it rains, when storms rise, when other changes happen, in some way or other we exclude God from these actions. . . . But there was a certain hidden inclination by which all creatures obey his command.[57]

The angelic control of winds also found expression in Calvin's thoughts on Psalm 18:10 when he wrote that "the very violence of the winds is governed by angels as God has ordained."[58] Winds originate from exhalations by natural causes and yet at the same time they are controlled by God through the instrumentality of his angels.

Finally, we should note that Calvin believed that God has winds stored up for use on any occasion in opposition to natural means. The Lord does not need to rely on the action of winds that can be "explained" in terms of secondary causes to accomplish his ends and purposes.[59]

Rain

For Calvin, rain in the appropriate amounts was one of God's greatest blessings to the human race. Rain is a gift from the creator. He repeatedly expressed this thought. Even in discussing the extensive portion of Deuteronomy 28 that enumerates all manner of curses that might be inflicted on Israel because of its disobedience, Calvin took the opportunity to remind his readers that not just rain in general comes from God, but that "not even a drop of rain falls to the earth except distilled by God, and that whenever it rains, the earth is irrigated as if by his hand."[60] This is but one of a number of places in which he took pains to stress God's intimate providential involvement with the smallest details of nature and history.

As we noted earlier, Calvin regarded the presence of water in the air as something of a miracle. In his second sermon on Job 26, for example, he marveled:

> is it not a miracle that the waters should hang after that sort in the air, and bide fast there? We see that the waters do flow, yea and that the air is so fine and thin, as it gives place continually to them, and the waters are of their own nature heavier than the air. And therefore the waters ought of reason to fall down.

But obviously the waters don't always fall down as they are supposed to. They are, after all, stored in the clouds. Calvin continued that "as oft as the clouds gather in the air and we see the waters inclosed in them, and yet the earth is not drowned by them; that cometh to pass because God stretched out his hand."[61] He alluded again to the miraculous character of the fact that rainwater is suspended in air in his fifth sermon on Job 36. He marveled that "there are a hundred millions of drops in one little cloud," and that even though each one of those drops is by nature "ready to fall away and to disperse all the rest of the body," the drops are all held together. We would never believe such a thing about water in the sky "if we knew it not and perceived it not." Given the amazing suspension of water in the skies, Calvin proclaimed that we must acknowledge an infinite power in God when we see things that are unbelievable.[62]

Despite this repeated insistence that rain owed its origin to the hand of God, Calvin clearly believed that rain was also formed by natural causes and that an accounting of the formation of rain was possible. In the same sermon on Job 36, he specifically addressed that question. He asserted that rain is engendered when vapor, which by itself would not rise up from the "steams" that are contained in the hills of the Earth, rises up "by the drawing of the sun, which sucketh up the moisture to hale it up on high," a process that works counter to the downward natural tendency of water. Even though the plain countryman cannot discuss such matters, Calvin went on, the philosophers know "how the rain is engendered by drawing up of the vapours or steams, insomuch that when the sun strikes upon the earth, forasmuch as the earth is full of holes, and not so close shut but that there are little veins in it."[63] Calvin envisioned a kind of porous Earth thoroughly penetrated by water, so much so in fact, that he marveled that the Earth didn't get dissolved. The sermon continued with the observation that "the sun draws up the vapors aloft, and by little and little they become thick, and when they are in the midst of the air, there they engender rain. By that means the moistures are drawn up little by little, until all of them grow ripe to give us rain."[64]

Even though God essentially performed miracles in bringing water into the sky and keeping it suspended against its natural tendency until such time as it rains, Calvin seemed to sense that God worked these miracles in a regular fashion by means of the same natural cause. He recognized that God regularly employs the action of the Sun to suck up moisture from the Earth and to draw it into the sky to form the rain clouds.

Drought

If Calvin reflected Scripture by preaching that rain comes down as a blessing from God, then he also reflected the witness of Scripture in maintaining that drought is instigated at divine initiative in response to human sin. A representative specimen of his understanding of drought appears in his reflections on Jeremiah 14:3, part of a passage that deals with drought in the land of Judah. The weeping prophet observed that "the nobles send their servants for water; they go to the cisterns but find no water. They return with their jars unfilled; dismayed and despairing, they cover their heads." Calvin wrote that

> droughts indeed often happen when there are no waters in most places; but when no well supplies any water, when there is not a drop of water to be found in the most favorable places, then indeed it ought to be concluded that God's curse is on the people, who find nothing to drink; for in nothing does God deal more bountifully with the world than in the supply of water.[65]

Calvin did not attempt to work out a natural explanation for the occurrence of droughts

Hail

Calvin discussed hail several times. In some of the biblical episodes in which hail played a part, the hail appeared to be of such miraculous nature that it was not generated by natural causes as far as he was concerned. Examples included the Egyptian exodus plague of hail and the hail at the long-day battle in the Valley of Aijalon. Writing of the plague of hail, Calvin maintained that Egypt was stricken with the worst hailstorm in its history, a storm in which crops were flattened and livestock destroyed, whereas the land of Goshen, in which the children of Israel lived, experienced no hail. The atmosphere, Calvin said, was manifestly armed by God for battle. He saw several indications in the text that the hail of the seventh plague did not arise from natural causes. One indication was that the time of the storm was announced by Moses before the face of Pharaoh. What astronomer or philosopher could "thus measure the moments for storms and tempests?" he inquired. He was also impressed by the fact that the unusual violence of the storm, "such as had never been seen before," had been appointed. The extent of the storm from one side of Egypt to the other indicated the unusual nature of the hailstorm. Scarcely once in twenty years would such a storm prevail so widely. The distinction between Goshen and the rest of Egypt also compelled Calvin to conclude that "this hail was not produced by an accidental impulse, but made to fall by God's hand; in a word, that it was not the drops of moisture frozen in mid air, but a portent which transcended the bounds of nature."[66]

Calvin also claimed that the hailstorm associated with Joshua's victory over the Amorites at the battle of Gibeon was not an ordinary occurrence. "This was not common hail, such as is wont to fall during storms," he claimed. Instead, "God threw down great stones of hail from heaven: For the meaning is that they fell with extraordinary force, and were far above the ordinary size."[67] Obviously Calvin had not heard the Weather Channel reports of golf-ball-sized or grape-fruit-sized hail falling on Kansas or Oklahoma!

On the other hand, Calvin understood that hail is generally a phenomenon that is produced by natural causes. He had certainly seen hailstorms in France and Geneva. In the fifth sermon on Job 36, Calvin had preached about hail as well as rain. Here he talked about the distribution of heat in the atmosphere. He said that the country folk did not understand why it is not so hot in the middle of the atmosphere even though it is nearer to the Sun. He then informed his Geneva congregation that the cause of this thermal phenomenon is that "the heat sets itself here upon the earth as upon a hearth, whereas in the air it spreads abroad inasmuch wise as it cannot rest there. That is the cause why hail is engendered there." Evidently the dissipation of solar heat in the atmosphere led to the lower temperatures that would allow for hail production. He acknowledged that it was certainly strange that "the hail should thicken in the air" and that "we would hardly believe it if it were not a common thing among us."[68]

Calvin also referred to the formation of hail in his fourth sermon on Job 38. The snow is engendered in the "middle room" of the air, which is cold. When a great quantity of vapor has been drawn up to the middle part of the atmosphere, the vapor eventually comes together and freezes, and so snow is engendered. But "if the same stuff be more harder bound, then is hail engendered, because the thing is become more fast and substantial." This is what men were saying about the origin of hail, and so far as Calvin was concerned, that was true.[69]

Thunder

Like other atmospheric phenomena, Calvin thought that "thunder is not produced merely by chance or by natural causes, independent of the appointment and will of God." Despite being a work of God, thunder functions in accord with natural causes which the philosophers have worked out. Thunder occurs when "cold and humid vapors obstruct the dry and hot exhalations in their upward course." As a result, "a collision takes place which produces the rumbling along with the noise of clouds colliding." As ever, the Creator is the supreme governor who "penetrates into the hidden veins of the earth, and draws forth exhalations and divides them into different sorts and disperses them through the air and collects the vapor and sets them in conflict with subtile and dry heats. Thunder seems to proceed from his own mouth."[70] Some of Calvin's reflections on the natural causes of thunder appear in his discussion of the words "my heart grew hot within me" in Psalm 39:3. Perhaps Calvin envisioned the human body as something of a small-scale analog of the larger cosmos. He stated that "in the summertime the sun causes the dry and hot exhalations to arise. If nothing occurs in the atmosphere to obstruct their progress, they would rise into the air without commotion. But when clouds intervene to prevent their free ascent, there is a conflict which produces the thunders."[71] Such an event, he said, is not unlike when the godly lift up their hearts to God.

Lightning

Calvin was understandably impressed by lightning. Here was yet another remarkable and arresting atmospheric phenomenon that had its origins in God, that could be attributed to natural causes, and yet that seemed to be a contradiction, an impossibility whose surprising occurrence should lead us to worship and wonder before God. In the case of lightning, the contradiction came in that "lightnings are mixed with rain, things quite opposite in their nature one from another. Did not custom make us familiar with the spectacle, we would pronounce this mixture of fire and water to be a phenomenon altogether incredible."[72] In the first place, neither the element of fire or of water that combined to make lightning was located in its natural place during the process. And, of course, Calvin knew that a fire could be extinguished by dousing with water. So why wasn't the fire of lightning quenched by the rain associated with it? Like other atmospheric phenomena, lightning was ultimately viewed as a product of exhalations. Thus, in discussing the bright light from heaven that Paul experienced on the road to Damascus, Calvin wrote that "often at night lightning flashes out, produced from the hot vapours of the earth."[73]

The flashing splendor and terror of lightning make it easy to understand why Calvin would feel that, if nothing else could persuade us to believe in the existence of God, lightning certainly leaves us without excuse. In the first sermon on Job 37, he proclaimed that

> the lightnings do as it were cleave asunder the skies, and we see such a brightness, as God shows himself sufficiently, yea even to take all covert from us, that no man might flatter himself in his hypocrisy nor go about to justify himself, as though we had known nothing of God. For the lightning is enough to show us the glory that is in him.[74]

Calvin would undoubtedly have appreciated the spectacular summertime lightning shows of the Arizona desert.

Rainbows

Calvin assumed that the colors of the rainbow are the effect of natural causes and that we should not "contend with philosophers respecting the rainbow" in their attempts to explain them.[75] The philosophers taught that the colors do not have any substance but are formed when the rays of the Sun are reflected on a hollow cloud.[76]

In reference to the rainbow that appeared at the end of the great deluge, Calvin insisted that people "act profanely who attempt to deprive God of the right and authority which he has over his creatures."[77] In contrast to Luther, Calvin doubted that rainbows were features created for the first time at the conclusion of the deluge. He was persuaded that the rainbow is an originally created phenomenon of God. In his commentary on the end of the flood account that describes God setting the rainbow in the sky, he said:

> From these words certain eminent theologians have been induced to deny, that there was any rainbow before the deluge: which is frivolous. For the words of Moses do not signify, that a bow was then formed, which did not previously exist; but that a mark was engraven upon it, which should give a sign of the divine favour towards men.

> For, as it pleases the Lord to employ earthly elements, as vehicles for raising the minds of men on high, so I think the celestial arch which had before existed naturally, is here consecrated into a sign and pledge; as many falsely suppose, but because God wished to stir up our hope with that symbol, as often as thick vapours cloud the heavens.[78]

The same view was posited in his commentary on Ezekiel 1:28, a verse in which the glory of the Lord was likened to the appearance of the rainbow in the cloud on a rainy day. Calvin wrote that in "Scripture calls it the bow of God, not because it was created after the Deluge, as many falsely suppose but because God wishes to stir up our hope with that symbol, as often as thick vapors cloud the heavens." Shortly thereafter, he further claimed that "some distort this as if the bow was not in existence before; but there is no doubt that God wishes to inscribe a testimony of his favour on a thing by no means in accordance with it, as he freely uses all creatures according to his will."[79]

Comets

We conclude our review of Calvin's ideas about atmospheric phenomena, typically related to exhalations, with a glance at the reformer's thoughts on comets. We now know that comets are objects that orbit the Sun far removed from the Earth's atmosphere. Having no conception of the distance of comets from the Earth, however, Calvin considered them to be atmospheric or meteorological phenomena. In this respect he was again influenced by Aristotle, although he may not have been fully conversant with the great philosopher's theory of comets.

Unlike Anaxagoras (c. 499-428 B. C.) and Democritus, Aristotle rejected the notion that "comets are a conjunction of planets, when they appear to touch each other because of their nearness." And he disagreed with the Pythagoreans that a comet is one of the planets. Nor did Aristotle like the view of Hippocrates that the tail of a comet does not actually belong to the comet but is acquired when the comet draws up moisture as it travels through space.[80] Aristotle reminded his readers that the outer part of the terrestrial world, that which lies beneath the celestial revolutions, is composed of a hot, dry exhalation. The circular motion of this exhalation and most of the air beneath it causes ignition of substance of appropriate composition, thus producing shooting stars. Should a fiery principle that is neither too strong nor too weak interact with a suitable condensation as a result of such motion, a comet is produced provided that another exhalation of appropriate consistency and extent is also available from below.[81] Aristotle also taught that if an exhalation is formed by the movement of a fixed star or a planet, then one of them becomes a comet. The tail of the comet, he said, is not attached to the star itself but is something like a stellar halo, not unlike the haloes that surround the Sun or the Moon when they move, and these haloes are formed by the condensation of the air beneath these bodies. The fact that comets are fiery bodies, Aristotle went on, is proved by the observation that whenever comets appear in substantial numbers, that is a sign of coming wind and drought, because hot exhalations dissolve moist evaporation and make the air drier. When comets appear frequently and in considerable numbers, the years are notoriously dry and windy.[82]

So what did Calvin think? Well, he rarely mentioned comets, and when he did he said very little. One important reference occurs in *A Warning against Judiciary Astrology* where he maintained that comets "are inflammations which occur not according to fixed terms of birth, but according to God's good pleasure. In noting this we can already see how comets differ from the stars; since they produce themselves from accidental causes."[83] Elsewhere, he commented that comets are formed from exhalations from the Earth along with thunder, lightning, and wind.[84]

In conclusion, we find that Calvin was just as indebted to the Aristotelian worldview in regard to the notion of four fundamental elements, the theory of natural places, and the effects of wet and dry exhalations on atmospheric phenomena as he was in regard to the structure of the cosmos. However, he did not hesitate to find weak spots in the prevailing theories that he was altogether willing to consider as points at which God could display his providential care in miraculous fashion. And, as ever, he was insistent that, no matter how convincingly one could account for the phenomena of nature in terms of natural or second causes, such phenomena ultimately owed their existence and character to the sovereign will of God.

NOTES

1.   For a synopsis of Aristotle's conception of the four elements and the theory of natural places, see David C. Lindberg, *The Beginnings of Western Science: The European Scientific Tradition in Philosophical, Religious, and Institutional Context, 600 B. C. to A. D. 1450* (Chicago: University of Chicago Press, 1992) and also Kaiser, "Calvin's Understanding of Aristotelian Natural Philosophy."

2.   For the most detailed discussion of the theory of four elements, see Book II of Aristotle, *On Coming-to-Be and Passing-Away.*

3.   For detailed discussion of alchemy in particular and the development of other chemical concepts more generally, see William H. Brock, *The Chemical Tree: A History of Chemistry* (New York: W. W. Norton, 2000) and Cathy Cobb and Harold Goldwhite, *Creations of Fire: Chemistry's Lively History from Alchemy to the Atomic Age* (New York: Plenum Press, 1995). For a very comprehensive, but somewhat dated history of chemical concepts see James R. Partington, *A History of Chemistry,* 4 vol. (New York: St. Martin's Press, 1961).

4.   Commentary on Exodus 7:8-13.

5.   Commentary on Psalm 119:91.

6.   Commentary on Jeremiah 5:22.

7.   Commentary on Psalm 148:3-10.

8.   Ibid.

9.   Commentary on Psalm 24:2.

10. Commentary on Genesis 1:15.

11. Commentary on Jeremiah 8:7.

12. Commentary on Psalm 119:91.

13. Commentary on Genesis 1:9.

14. Commentary on Psalm 104:9.

15. Commentary on Jeremiah 5:22.

16. Commentary on Psalm 136:4.

17. Commentary on Psalm 104:5.

18. Commentary on Psalm 75:3.

19. Commentary on Jeremiah 10:12-13.

20. Commentary on Psalm 24:2.

21. Commentary on Genesis 1:9.

22. Commentary on Amos 9:6

23. Commentary on Psalm 104:9.

24. Commentary on Genesis 1:20.

25. Commentary on Amos 9:6.

26. Second Sermon on Job 26.

27. Commentary on Genesis 1:15.

28. Commentary on Psalm 104:5.

29. Commentary on Psalm 136:4.

30. Commentary on Psalm 24:2.

31. Second Sermon on Job 26.

32. Commentary on Jeremiah 5:22.

33. Second Sermon on Job 38.

34. Commentary on Psalm 104:9.

35. Second Sermon on Job 26.

36. Commentary on Psalm 148:3-10.

37. On Henry of Langenstein and the "God-of-the-gaps" methodology often employed by medieval Christian thinkers, see Kaiser, *Creational Theology*, 110-11.

38. Aristotle, *Meteorologica*, II.4.

39. Ibid.

40. John Calvin, *The Secret Providence of God*, trans. Henry Cole (Grand Rapids, Mich.: Reformed Free Publishing Association, 1987), 250.

41. Commentary on Amos 5:8.

42. Commentary on Psalm 147:7-8.

43. Commentary on Amos 9:6.

44. Commentary on Jeremiah 10:12-13.

45. Commentary on Psalm 69:22.

46. Commentary on Jeremiah 49:36.

47. Commentary on Jeremiah 51:16-17.

48. Commentary on Daniel 7:2.

49. Commentary on Isaiah 27:8.

50. Commentary on Hosea 12:1.

51. Commentary on Habakkuk 1:9.

52. Commentary on Isaiah 21:1.

53. Commentary on Psalm 104:4.

54. Commentary on Jeremiah 49:36.

55. Commentary on Ezekiel 10:2.

56. Commentary on Ezekiel 1:4.

57. Commentary on Ezekiel 10:13.

58. Commentary on Psalm 18:10.

59. Commentary on Hosea 13:15.

60. Commentary on Deuteronomy 28:21-23.

61. Second Sermon on Job 26.

62. Fifth Sermon on Job 36.

63. Fifth Sermon on Job 36.

64. Fifth Sermon on Job 36.

65. Commentary on Jeremiah 14:3.

66. Commentary on Exodus 9:13-26.

67. Commentary on Joshua 10:10-13.

68. Fifth Sermon on Job 36.

69. Fourth Sermon on Job 38.

70. Commentary on Psalm 18:13.

71. Commentary on Psalm 39:3.

72. Commentary on Psalm 135:7.

73. Commentary on Acts 22:6.

74. First Sermon on Job 37.

75. Commentary on Genesis 9:13.

76. Commentary on Ezekiel 1:28.

77. Commentary on Genesis 9:13.

78. Ibid.

79. Commentary on Ezekiel 1:28.

80. Aristotle, *Meteorologica*, 39-41.

81. Ibid., 51.

82. Ibid., 53-55.

83. Calvin, "A Warning against Judiciary Astrology," 183.

84. Commentary on Jeremiah 10:12-13.

CHAPTER 4

CALVIN ON THE EARTH

Geology is the science that is concerned with the composition, structure, physical behavior, and historical development of the Earth and its component parts. Among those component parts are the various minerals, rocks, and fossils exposed at the surface. I have often thought that geologists in the field must seem rather odd to passersby. Envision, if you will, a group of geologists on a field trip, kneeling on a rock outcrop, bent over with their faces a couple of inches from the rock, and holding hand lenses to get an even better look at the rock. That posture is one of the more frequent postures adopted by practitioners of geology. As a professional geologist, then, I found it amusing to read the following passage from Calvin's commentary on Isaiah 40:26:

> For while God formed other animals to look downwards for pasture, he made man alone erect, and bade him look at what may be regarded as his own habitation. . . . The Prophet therefore points out the wickedness of men who do not acknowledge what is openly placed before their eyes concerning God, but, like cattle, fix their snout in the earth; for, whenever we raise our eyes upwards, with any degree of attention it is impossible for our senses not to be struck with the majesty of God.[1]

Much as the description seems to fit geologists, I suspect that Calvin was not thinking about them when he wrote about people who "fix their snout in the earth." The reason is simple: apart from those involved in mining, very few people were engaged in systematic study of the Earth. Geology as a science did not yet exist. Chief among Calvin's contemporaries in the study of the Earth was Georg Bauer (1494-1555), better known as Agricola, a student of mines and mining. Agricola slowly began to advance our understanding of Earth materials beyond the conceptions of Aristotle and the Middle Ages. The Calvinist, Conrad Gesner (1516-1565), arguably the most highly regarded naturalist of his era, contributed to increased understanding of the nature of fossils. There was, how- ever, no grasp of the fundamental principles of stratigraphy, magmatic activity, rock deformation, earthquake activity, or metamorphism. There was no concep- tion of the antiquity of the globe. No one yet perceived that the Earth contains a record of its own history. There were no geological surveys and no professors of geology. Geologic maps had not yet been invented. The term "geology" had not been coined. Significant developments in the scientific investigation of the Earth lay at least a century, and, in most cases, at least two centuries in the fu- ture.

The Bible does mention many features of geological interest: mountains, earthquakes, veins, smoking mountains, pillars of salt, pitch, brimstone, gem- stones, floods, and other aspects of the hydrologic cycle (Ecclesiastes 1:7). Cal- vin did comment on some of these features and gave very faint glimmers of in- sight into "geological" conceptions of his day, but, regrettably, he said far less about geological matters than about astronomical matters. This reticence may be traced to the fact that the study of the Earth was not as advanced as that of the heavens, and, for the most part, it lacked scholarly practitioners who were of equivalent ability and stature to astronomers like da Cusa, Copernicus, or Rheticus. Calvin never commended the study of the Earth as enthusiastically and as directly as he did the study of the stars. Intellectuals had not yet developed fruitful procedures and methods for studying the Earth and extracting meaning- ful information from it. Now let's see what Calvin had to say about the Earth.

The Shape of the Earth

In ancient civilizations such as those of Mesopotamia and Egypt, the Earth was regarded as a flat disk surrounded by an ocean and covered by a hemi- spherical dome containing the heavenly bodies. The fact that the Earth is a globe was established by the Greeks. Aristotle taught that the Earth is a globe, and two centuries before the birth of Christ, the director of the great library at Alexan- dria, Eratosthenes (276-194 B. C.), measured the circumference and radius of the globe with remarkable accuracy by means of brilliant geometrical reasoning. What may surprise many readers is how much of the globe was known to in- habitants of the Roman Empire at the time of Christ. During the sixth and fifth centuries B. C., Persian navigators like Sataspes and Scylax and Carthaginian sailors like Hanno and Himilcon had sailed along much of the west coast of Af- rica, along the Atlantic coast of Europe, along the east coast of Africa, and from the Red Sea to the Indus River in India. Aristotle's pupil, Alexander the Great (356-323 B. C.), extended his empire all the way to the Indus River in the fourth century B. C. During the same century, Pytheas (c. 380-c. 310 B. C.) sailed into the North and Baltic Seas and encountered the sea ice of the Arctic. And the

Roman Empire extended all throughout Europe to the British Isles, throughout the Middle East, and across the northern part of Africa.

The invasions of the Roman Empire by Goths and other foreign tribes during the early Christian centuries introduced knowledge of the Asiatic interior to the inhabitants of Mediterranean region. Early in the second millennium of the Christian era, the travels of William of Rubruck (c. 1210-c. 1270), Odoric of Pordenone (c. 1286-1331), and Marco Polo (1254-c. 1323) greatly increased Europe's knowledge of Asia and fostered trade with the Far East, which, in turn, promoted the development of faster, safer, more efficient ways of reaching China, and led to the era of spectacular navigational achievements during the fifteenth and sixteenth centuries.

Prince Henry of Portugal (1394-1460), often called Henry the Navigator, established an "oceanographic" institution at Cape St. Vincent in Portugal. His avid promotion of exploration led to expeditions to the Azores, Madeira, and the Canary Islands, and along the west coast of Africa. After Henry's death, Portuguese exploration of the African coastline continued and culminated in the epochal voyages of Bartolomeu Dias (c. 1450-1500) around the Cape of Good Hope in 1488 and of Vasco da Gama (1469-1524) around the Cape to the west coast of India by 1498. Between 1492 and 1514, Christopher Columbus (1451-1506) completed four expeditions across the Atlantic Ocean where he explored the Caribbean islands and northern coast of South America, although he remained persuaded that he had found India. In time, Columbus' discoveries confirmed that a vast uncharted territory lay between Europe and China and that the globe had a much larger diameter than was thought by some Renaissance scholars like the Chancellor of the University of Paris, Bishop of Cambrai, and highly influential Cardinal, Pierre d'Ailly (1350-1420), and by Columbus himself. If anything, the voyages to the New World confirmed the essential correctness of Eratosthenes' calculation of the dimensions of the Earth a millennium and a half earlier. Several additional expeditions to the Caribbean region took place after those of Columbus, John Cabot (c. 1455-1498) explored Newfoundland in 1497, and Amerigo Vespucci (1454-1512) participated in a 1499 Spanish expedition to the "New World," a term that he originated, and later returned to explore the east coast of South America in 1501 and 1503. The 1507 world map of Martin Waldseemüller (1470-1518) labeled the newly discovered southern hemisphere continent America in honor of Vespucci. Soon thereafter, maps and globes distinguished North and South America. In 1513, Vasco Núñez de Balboa (1475-1519) crossed the isthmus of Panama and laid eyes on the Pacific Ocean.

A series of Portuguese voyages around Africa arrived in the Moluccas (East Indies) and China by 1514. Navigators likely also encountered Australia shortly thereafter. Before long, Ferdinand Magellan (c. 1481-1521) circumnavigated the globe from 1519 to 1522, while Giovanni da Verrazzano (1485-1528) cautiously sailed along the eastern coastline of North America in 1524 in search for a possible passageway that would ultimately lead to China. Jacques Cartier (1491-1557) explored the St. Lawrence River in 1524-1525 for much the same reason. Mexico and South America yielded many of their secrets to Europe when the

Spanish explorer Hernando Cortés (1485-1547) subjugated the Aztecs of Mexico in 1521, and Francisco Pizarro (c. 1475-1541) conquered the Incas in Peru in 1533.[2]

Much of this frenzy of world exploration was taking place just before Calvin was born and during the early years of his life. Europe of the sixteenth century, which sponsored all these expeditions, possessed a rapidly expanding fund of knowledge about global geography. But what did John Calvin know about world geography? Had he heard about any or all of these expeditions and did he know anything about their results?

Calvin mentioned the globular nature of the Earth only a few times. Unquestionably he accepted what educated people had already believed for centuries, and there is little reason to doubt that he was instructed in his youth that the Earth is a globe. So, we find no indication in his writings that the voyages of Columbus led him to adopt the idea that the Earth is a globe. I have found no mention whatever of either Columbus or the discovery of the New World in any of his writings. Calvin's failure to refer to Columbus or, for that matter, to any of the other great fifteenth and sixteenth century explorers like Dias, da Gama, or Magellan or to the results of their expeditions raises the question of the extent of Calvin's awareness of the great explorations of the Far East and of the Americas. One would expect that his education would have included some reference to these revolutionary voyages.

Calvin referred to the Earth as a globe in the Argument to his commentary on Genesis. As we have noted he wrote that he was not ignorant that "the circuit of the heavens is finite, and that the earth, like a little globe, is placed in the centre."[3] Then, in his discussion of the Garden of Eden, Calvin took issue with people who claimed that "the surface of the globe may have been changed by the deluge," a clear indication that he knew that the Earth is a globe.[4] In the second sermon on Job 38, he remarked about the great size of the Earth. But, he said, if we compare the size of the Earth to the greatness of the heavens we are forced to "confess with the philosophers that it is but a little ball."[5] The final reference to the shape of the Earth comes in the comments on Daniel 7:2. In his dream of the four beasts, Daniel saw "the four winds of heaven churning up the great sea." Of this verse, Calvin wrote that it was "the common phrase to speak of four winds blowing from the four quarters or regions of the globe."[6] Calvin obviously assumed that the Earth is a globe.

The Age of the Earth

The western world into which Calvin was born had been dominated for centuries by Catholic thought and practice. The church fathers had generally maintained on biblical grounds that creation occurred less than 6000 years ago. For example, Theophilus, Bishop of Antioch (second century A. D.) calculated that 5698 years had elapsed from the creation of the world to his own day, and Clement, Bishop of Alexandria (d. c. 215) figured on 5590 years between the creation of Adam and the birth of Jesus Christ. Catholic scholars up through the Middle Ages continued adherence to the same conviction. The Protestant Reformers inherited the common Catholic tradition regarding the approximate date of creation. They had no reason to quarrel with that belief.[7] Neither Luther, Melanchthon, Calvin, nor their immediate successors were exceptions to that rule. Luther, for example, believed that the Earth was not yet 6000 years old. There is not a scintilla of evidence to indicate that Calvin interpreted either the days of creation or the genealogical tables in the Old Testament in anything other than a literal manner. Adherence to these opinions would virtually guarantee acceptance of a very young Earth, and, indeed, there is no evidence to indicate that he thought that the Earth or the cosmos as a whole might be older than about 6000 years. Nor is there any hint that he was even open to the *possibility* that the world might be more than 6000 years in age. That possibility could not be seriously entertained in the first half of the sixteenth century. By that time, the astronomers had developed neither instruments such as the telescope nor conceptual tools that would ultimately lead to the discovery of the great antiquity of the cosmos. Even individuals like Agricola who pondered the nature of the Earth had not yet recognized that the planet contains a record of its own history within the layers of sedimentary rock. That intellectual breakthrough would not occur until a century later. As a result, there was no convincing evidence emerging from study of the physical creation that might even have raised the question of a universe older than 6000 years for Calvin and his contemporaries.

Calvin did refer to the age of the world in some of his writings, although he never attempted a precise calculation of the age of the Earth as did several Catholic and Protestant contemporaries and successors. The exact value proposed by these different writers depended on variations in calculations based on genealogical data in the Old Testament. Interestingly, Calvin made no reference to the age of the Earth in his comments on the creation account of Genesis 1. He did, however, mention the age of the world in off-hand fashion in sermons, in commentaries, and in the *Institutes*.

In the second sermon on Job 38, Calvin nowhere mentioned the age of the Earth, but he did observe that God's creation of the world was not characterized by "long continuance of time." Moreover, he proclaimed, God "did quickly finish all this goodly workmanship that is seen in heaven and earth."[8] Although no number was given, the comments are consistent both with the prevailing view of a relatively short terrestrial lifetime and with his own statements elsewhere.

Calvin wrote in similar general terms about the age of the world in discussing Psalm 102:25, a text that speaks of the creation of the Earth and the heavens. Here he simply remarked about how long the heavens had continued to exist in comparison with the swiftly fleeting human life span and the endless generations, but he did not specifically state how old he thought the world to be.[9] He also remained vague about the age of the world in his comments about the heavens declaring the glory of God in Psalm 19:1. At that point he wrote that Scripture "makes known to us the time and manner of the creation,"[10] but he did not explicitly state when that time of creation was. Calvin did give a sense of how he thought one might arrive at a date for creation in discussing Daniel 9:25, a text that speaks prophetically of the restoration of Jerusalem and the coming prince. He remarked that the Reformer Johannes Heusegen (1482-1531), widely known as Oecolampadius, admonished that computations about future events should start at the beginning of the world. "For until the ruin of the Temple and the destruction of the city," Calvin wrote, "we can gather with certainty the number of years which have elapsed since the creation of the world: here there is no room for error."[11] But again, he did not state how many years he thought that was.

Calvin also rejected the claims of heathen cultures for an excessive global antiquity. The book of Nahum is a prophecy directed against the ancient Assyrian city of Nineveh. Calvin remarked in respect to Nahum 2:8 that the common opinion was that Nineveh had no beginning. Ancient cultures seemed to be plagued by such fables. Egypt, too, had "fabled respecting their antiquity; they imagined that their kingdom was five thousand years before the world was made; that is, in numbering their ages they went back nearly five thousand years before the creation."[12] Calvin still did not express his view of the age of the Earth.

Where we do find Calvin's opinion about the age of the Earth is in a passage reflecting on Exodus 33:19, a verse that deals with the revelation of God's goodness to Moses while he was hidden in the cleft of the rock. In this context, he talked about the disputatiousness of men in their quarrels with God. He singled out the foolishness of those who wondered why God had taken so long to get around to creating the world and what he was doing with himself before that. He observed that it seemed absurd to such folk that God should be idle for so many ages. According to Calvin, they asked, in ridiculing fashion, why it finally entered God's mind to make the world "which has not yet reached its sixth millennium?"[13] If nothing else, these comments make it clear at the very least that Calvin's contemporaries believed that the world was not quite 6000 years old. Calvin was not obviously bothered by contemporary belief about the age of the world and made no effort to correct that idea, but he was intensely bothered by the attitude of the critics of God.

There are also two references in Book I of the *Institutes* that pertain to the age of the world. These are the most explicit references on the subject in all his writings. Here Calvin wrote again regarding these impious folk who wondered why it didn't enter God's mind sooner to create the world but idled away an immeasurable time, albeit "the duration of the world . . . has not yet attained six thousand years." Again, one might argue that Calvin simply reported the view of the critics of God that the world is not quite six millennia without endorsing that view himself. Later in the same section of the *Institutes*, however, it becomes perfectly plain that Calvin himself accepted the 6000-year age when he exclaimed: "As if within six thousand years God has not shown evidences enough on which to exercise our minds in earnest meditation!"[14] Without question, he believed that the world was only around 6000 years in age, in complete accord with the prevailing opinion of his time.

Earthquakes

Knowledge of earthquakes and volcanoes in Calvin's time had changed very little since the days of Aristotle. Greek and Roman scholars such as Seneca (c. 2 B. C.-A. D. 65), Strabo (63 B. C.-A. D. 21), and Vitruvius (d. 25 B. C.) speculated about the nature of volcanoes, and Pliny the Younger (A. D. 61-114) left a striking account of the cataclysmic eruption of Mount Vesuvius in A. D. 70 in which his uncle, Pliny the Elder, the author of an extended natural history, perished.[15] More detailed study of volcanoes did not really begin until the work of Sir William Hamilton (1731-1803) and Louis Spallanzani (1729-1799) at the end of the eighteenth century.[16] Modern approaches to the study of earthquake activity were stimulated largely by the catastrophic 1755 Lisbon earthquake and the subsequent work of John Michell (1724-1793).

Aristotle's theory of exhalations provided the theoretical framework within which people thought about earthquakes and volcanoes for centuries. In his mind, earthquakes are a necessary result of the existence of the moist and dry exhalations. The cause of tremors, he argued, is the wind that is produced when an external exhalation flows into the Earth. The majority of earthquakes, therefore, occur during calm weather after the wind has already flowed inside the Earth. Some less violent earthquakes could take place as the wind is plunging into the Earth. Because the dry windy exhalation returns to the Earth as the Sun retreats, most large earthquakes occur at night, although some also occur at midday, the calmest time of day. Aristotle further maintained that severe earthquakes occur in places where the sea is full of currents and the Earth is porous and hollow. Porous regions can be shaken more violently because they are capable of absorbing larger amounts of wind. The most severe shocks occur when a large amount of wind cannot get through constricted pore spaces underground. Where a violent wind arises the inflowing sea drives the wind back into the Earth when otherwise it would be naturally exhaled. The violent wind, in effect, is trapped in the restricted space of porous Earth and causes shaking.[17]

Aristotle wrote that earthquakes occur most frequently in spring and fall or during times of rain and drought because these are the windiest times. In times of rain, for example, exhalation is produced in greater amounts within the Earth. When that increased amount of exhalation is trapped in a constricted space underground and forcibly compressed by incoming water, the impact of the trapped wind stream creates a severe shock. Earthquakes are something like the tremors and throbbings in our bodies that are caused by the force of the pent up wind within. Little had changed in the understanding of earthquakes by the sixteenth century.

The geographic setting in which much of the redemptive history of the Bible took place is seismically very active. The Sea of Galilee, the Jordan River, the Dead Sea, and the Gulf of Aqaba are aligned along a prominent trench that is the topographic expression of the Dead Sea rift, a major left-lateral strike-slip fault zone that separates the Arabian tectonic plate from the Eurasian tectonic plate. The plate containing Israel is slowly moving in a southerly direction relative to the plate east of the rift that contains the Arabian Peninsula and Jordan. Earthquakes are to be expected in such a region. It should come as no surprise to read in the Bible of earthquakes such as the one that occurred during the reign of King Uzziah (Amos 1:1; Zechariah 14:5) and those that accompanied the crucifixion and resurrection of Christ (Matthew 27:57; 28:2). Greece is also part of a seismically active region in which Africa and the Mediterranean seafloor are slowly migrating in a northerly direction toward southern Europe, and the Mediterranean seafloor is descending beneath the Eurasian tectonic plate. The Pyrenees, the Apennines, the Alps, and the Dinarides are manifestations of the collisions between these plates. Given the geological context of the Mediterranean basin, Greece is earthquake prone. And so we read in Acts 16:26 about an earthquake that released Paul and Silas from prison at Philippi. Prophetic warnings of earthquakes throughout the book of Revelation would have made a strong impression on people who lived in a part of the world that is susceptible to seismic tremors. Given the biblical references to earthquakes, Calvin was bound to give some opinion of them. Being located in Geneva in the Alpine mountain belt, he may even have experienced minor earthquakes.

Calvin conveyed the impression that earthquakes are more frequent in the plains than they are in the mountains, presumably because mountains are "stronger" than the plains. He expressed this view in discussing biblical passages that refer to the shaking of the mountains. "Mountains," he wrote in his commentary on Isaiah, "are very strong, and earthquakes do not so frequently take place in them as in plains."[18] He used this presumed strength, durability, and earthquake-resistant quality of the mountains to emphasize God's covenant faithfulness in a biblical text affirming that "though the mountains be shaken and the hills be removed, yet my unfailing love for you will not be shaken, nor my covenant of peace be removed."

Habakkuk 3:6 says that God "stood, and shook the earth; he looked, and made the nations tremble. The ancient mountains crumbled and the age-old hills collapsed." Calvin opined that "if an earthquake happens on a plain, it seems less wonderful," implying that an earthquake in the plains was not as unusual as one occurring in the mountains.[19] His language suggests that it was recognized even in the sixteenth century that the violent effects of earthquakes are felt much more intensely in broad alluvial plains that are underlain by poorly consolidated sediments than they are in areas that are underlain by solid bedrock. As an example of this phenomenon, consider that the damage caused by the famed April 18, 1906, San Francisco earthquake was considerably greater in those areas of the city that were constructed on mud that had been excavated from San Francisco Bay in comparison to the damage near Twin Peaks, an area in the center of the city that is underlain by bedrock. This phenomenon results from the fact that earthquake waves are transmitted much more intensely through unconsolidated sediments, especially those that are wet.

The only place in which Calvin alluded to an earthquake mechanism is in his commentary on Habakkuk 3:6. After observing that an earthquake on the plains is "less wonderful," he acknowledged that, in some cases, mountains can be damaged by tremors. As an explanation, he suggested that "if any of those mountains cleave, which are not so firmly fixed, it may be on account of some hollow places; for when the winds fill the caverns, they are forced to burst, and they cleave the mountains and the earth."[20] This explanation of the cause of earthquakes can again be traced to Aristotle. Calvin's opinion here provides another indication that he was conversant with, and acquiescent to, Aristotle's theory of exhalations.

The earthquakes that occurred at the crucifixion and resurrection of Jesus Christ were noted in passing by Calvin, but he made no comments of a scientific nature. The earthquake that split the rocks during the crucifixion bore testimony to the creator and witnessed against the hard-heartedness of a perverse nation. The earthquake during which the stone that blocked the entrance to Jesus' tomb was rolled away at the time of the resurrection was an event by which divine power might be perceived. The earthquake was a "portent" that would cause the women "to expect nothing now of human or earthly sort, and should lift up their minds to a new and unexpected work of God."[21] Likewise the earthquake that took place when Paul and Silas were in the Philippian jail was considered as another visible sign of the Lord's provision for his servants that they might know that their prayers were answered. The earthquake also proved to be an "example of His power" that should be of profit for all the ages.[22]

Mountains

In view of the fact that Calvin spent several years in Geneva in very close proximity to magnificent alpine peaks with massive Mont Blanc, the highest peak in Europe, plainly visible from locations northeast of the city, it is mildly baffling that he said relatively little about mountains. Unlike today's travelers, who rave about the awe-inspiring and spectacular beauty of mountains, he said little by way of appreciation for these landforms. He did not wax eloquent about the beauty or majesty of mountains as he typically did in regard to the stars. Although he unequivocally attributed every feature of the world to the work of the Creator, he never made mountains the *prime* exhibit in his parade of evidence for the power and divinity of God. Perhaps Calvin shared some of the suspicions about mountains that were entertained by those who looked upon them as little more than impassable piles of jagged rocks and sheer precipices mantled by frozen glaciers, inhospitable wastes, and endless forests full of frightening creatures.[23] Perhaps the dark, brooding aspect of mountains tempered any sense of wonder that might have lurked in his breast. The most enthusiastic that he became in regard to mountains was in his second sermon on Job 38 where he preached about the greatness of the heavens in relation to the small size of the Earth. The heavens render us "abashed," he exclaimed, such that one might wonder "what is the earth in comparison with the heavens?" Nevertheless, he argued, "if we but look upon the mountains that are on the earth, we shall find even there whereat to marvel, and wherefore to glorify the work master that made all."[24]

In only a few places did Calvin comment on mountains at any length. We touched above on his impression that mountains are very strong and much less prone to earthquakes than are the plains. His comments on Habakkuk 3:6 indicate that he envisioned mountains as almost immutable, hence, to him, the remarkable nature of the fact that the mountains could crumble. "The Prophet relates an unusual thing," he opined, "and wholly different from the ordinary course of nature—that the mountains of eternity, which had been from the beginning, and had remained without any change, were thus demolished and bowed down."[25] For Calvin, the strength and immutability of mountains was part of the "ordinary course of nature." Lacking our present notion of a long-lived dynamic Earth, he had no conception that mountains are formed by the uplift of thick accumulations of sedimentary rocks that have been intensely folded, fractured, faulted, metamorphosed, and injected by magmas. Nor did he have a strong sense of the fact that mountains are constantly being worn down by the forces of erosion.

In comments on Deuteronomy 33:15 where we read that Moses pronounced a blessing on the tribe of Joseph "with the choicest gifts of the ancient mountains and the fruitfulness of the everlasting hills," Calvin said that "we know that the tops of mountains are generally arid and uncultivated, or at any rate bear nothing but trees that have no fruit."[26] Elsewhere he wrote about Isaiah 30:25, which says that "in the day of great slaughter, when the towers fall, streams of water will flow on every high mountain and every lofty hill." This text prompted him to say that "water is not plentiful on the peaks of mountains, which are exceedingly dry; the valleys are indeed well moistened and abound in water; but it is very uncommon for water to flow abundantly on the tops of the mountains."[27] Calvin's belief in the dryness of mountains also appeared in his reflections on Psalm 104:13, a verse that refers to God watering the mountains from his chambers. Here he mentioned that mountains "seem to be condemned to perpetual drought." In spite of that presumed condition and the fact that mountains are, as it were "suspended in the air," the mountains nevertheless "abound in pastures." So remarkable did Calvin regard this situation that he treated it as "no ordinary miracle." With the psalmist, he held that the montane "fruitfulness proceeds from nothing else but the agency of God, who is their secret cultivator."[28]

In light of Calvin's situation in Alpine Europe, we can understand why he might say that the tops of mountains are uncultivated, and surely he must have been aware that high peaks have timber lines above which no trees grow at all owing to the perpetual cold. But it is curious that he would refer to mountaintops as exceedingly dry when he could look out on his own surroundings and observe the abundant snow and ice, and even vast glaciers, on the higher elevations. He must have known that the "well moistened" valleys obtained their water from the melted snow and ice pack. And surely he had seen, or heard reports of, rushing high mountains streams. Was he simply thinking of a general lack of rain because of the snow-producing cold high up on mountains?

Calvin made his most interesting comments about mountains in the second sermon on Job 38 in which he marveled at the steadiness of the Earth, a phenomenon that he believed should "ravish us into wonderment." As we saw earlier, he thought that the torquing effect of the rapidly revolving heavenly spheres should have bowled the Earth over or set it in motion in some fashion. Hence, all the more remarkable is the Earth's stability. He was impressed that, even though there is great variety in the Earth, it always remains in its place. One would think that the great contrasts in topography brought about by the "high mountains which do as it were emboss the earth, and the unlevelness of the places" would effectively destabilize and overturn the Earth. He suspected that mountains posed a threat to the stability of the Earth, but he also sensed that the Earth and the mountains were laid out in perfect balance. Although it seemed to him that the mountains should "oversway" the Earth, nonetheless he saw that the various mountains are "answerable to another as the counterpoise abides always steadfast." In some way, the Earth itself served as a counterweight to balance the destabilizing effects of the mountains. The Earth always stands steadfast, Calvin reasoned, by the "proportionable and even-leveled counterpoise of itself." What an incredible testimony to God's handiwork that the Earth remains stable even though "environed" with water and decorated with "huge mountains that advance themselves as it were to tumble it into the sea." By the great height and looming character of mountains, perhaps they appeared to him like giant waves on the verge of collapse, but the Earth itself served as a counter-balance to preserve stability.[29]

Gemstones

Unquestionably, knowledge about the nature of our planet lagged far behind knowledge of the heavens in the early Christian era. The fault did not lie with the Greeks, for they were remarkable observers of geological processes. Greek thinkers like Aristotle, Strabo and Herodotus (c. 484-c. 425 B. C.), for example, were well aware of some of the processes of sedimentation.[30] They also recognized that shells are commonly found in layers of sediment far inland from the sea, and they took it for granted that these shells represented remnants of once living organisms. From their observations, they concluded that the sea had been more extensive in the past, and they developed elementary theories of the interchange of land and sea resulting either from rise or fall in sea level or uplift or subsidence of the land. Unconstrained by any preconceptions about the antiquity of the Earth, they seemed to sense that processes of sedimentation, sea level change, and land elevation might require long periods of time. Some of the early Greek ideas about minerals, too, had a strong observational basis and emphasis on the physical properties of the minerals.

During the Christian era, however, geological objects and processes were increasingly thought to be influenced by heavenly bodies. As a result, Christian thinkers debated about the nature and origin of objects dug out of the ground. During the Middle Ages, all such objects, including what we call rocks and minerals today, were considered "fossils." Some of these fossils bore a striking resemblance to living organisms or to parts of organisms. These organic-looking objects, which later became known as "formed stones," engendered the greatest amount of controversy. Nowadays, geologists restrict the term "fossil" to the remains of animals or plants that have been preserved in sediment that was subsequently converted into rock. Some scholars even before Calvin's time, such as the great Italian artist and inventor, Leonardo da Vinci (1452-1519), adopted the viewpoint, now universally accepted, that these types of "fossils" represent the remains of organisms that had once been alive. Somehow the remains had become entombed in sediment layers or in rocks. Several individuals who held that view further assumed that the fossils had been formed when the organisms were destroyed in the great flood of Noah, but da Vinci discounted that interpretation. The most widely held conception about these curiously shaped objects throughout the Middle Ages was that fossils are sports of nature.[31]

Why should there have been so much disagreement about the nature of these objects? For one thing, the distinction that we draw today between organic and inorganic realms was not so clear in the Middle Ages. The phenomenon of growth, for example, is not restricted to animals and plants, for growth occurs in strictly inorganic features such as hot spring deposits, stalactites in caves, and crystals. In that sense, these inorganic features resemble living things. In addition, crystals are not just found in rocks. Organisms are capable of secreting crystals. Gallstones and kidney stones grow inside of human organs. Oysters grow pearls by secreting thin films of calcium carbonate around grains of sand. Corals, clams, and a host of other marine invertebrates secrete hard parts composed of calcium carbonate. On the surfaces of some rocks, one may find branching, tree-like deposits of black material that we now call "dendrites." They look superficially like plants but are composed of manganese dioxide. Many of the shelly objects found in limestone and shale strongly resemble parts of organisms, but to the medieval mind they were simply mimics. Most nature-minded individuals rightly recognized that, although a lot of these shelly objects might resemble modern shells, they definitely are not identical to them. In most cases, organic-looking objects embedded in rock are not the same as the parts belonging to any known living creature. In addition, the "shells" commonly are not composed of the same material as the shells of living clams, but consist of the same substance as the enclosing rock.

A very persuasive reason for not regarding these kinds of fossils as remains of once living organisms was the frightening prospect that, if they were parts of animals, then, clearly, many kinds of creatures had become extinct. But the principle of plenitude held a strong grip on people's thinking. The idea behind the principle of plenitude was that God had created a well-ordered, perfectly integrated, beautifully functioning world. This finely tuned world required that all its parts interact harmoniously. Should any part fail, the world would be thrown out of kilter. The extinction of an animal species was, therefore, regarded as utterly incompatible with the notion of God's harmonious creation. Accustomed as we are to the reality of extinction and of the severe threats to numerous existing species, we may find it difficult to appreciate just how compelling the notion of the impossibility of extinction was to folks in Calvin's day.

Another very persuasive reason for doubting the organic origin of many fossils concerned their location. Fossil shells are commonly found embedded in rock layers that are exposed at high elevations in the hills and mountains, hundreds if not thousands of feet above sea level. To make matters worse, many fossil shells occur vast distances inland from the sea. In the Middle Ages, the location of shells far removed from the sea raised the obvious question of how they got there. No one had any conception of the uplift of the land by thousands of feet. Nor did they have ideas about mountain building or about the advance and retreat of the ocean in relation to landmasses. The most satisfactory explanation for most thinkers was that these shell-like objects were merely striking resemblances that naturally grew in place within the rocks, very likely as a result of the influences of the heavenly bodies upon earth.

Even a century and a half after Calvin's death, some of the greatest students of fossils continued to deny their organic origin. The British naturalists Martin Lister (1639-1712), Robert Plot (1640-1696), and Edward Lhwyd (1660-1709), for example, steadfastly maintained that fossils were generated in rocks in one way or another even at a time when a growing number of voices, among them Robert Hooke (1635-1703) and Niels Stensen (1638-1686), were developing a very persuasive case for their organic origin. John Ray (1627-1705), arguably the outstanding British naturalist prior to Darwin, wrote a lengthy discourse on the origin of fossils. He reasoned persuasively and in detail in favor of fossils as remains of once-living creatures, demolishing the counter arguments along the way. But then he turned about face and argued persuasively for the opposite side of the question, raising especially the problems of location and extinction. In the end, Ray confessed perplexity, not certain what to make of it all. He clearly thought the evidence in favor of an organic origin was compelling, but he was unable to follow through because he was not prepared to accept the idea of extinction and not quite willing, at least in print, to concede that the world might be a lot older than everyone thought.[32]

I have alluded to the fact that fossils, whatever their origin, resemble parts of living creatures. In fact, during the Middle Ages fascination with resemblances (or "signatures" and "correspondences") was widespread.[33] A number of plants, for example, were known to show strong resemblances to other organisms such as scorpions or hands. Resemblances were thought to provide keys to the purposes and uses of objects. A prominent example is provided by male and female stones, so designated because of their distinctive shapes. A male stone might be what would today be called a "concretion" in the shape of a phallus. Among the female stones were objects that today we call "geodes." A geode is a somewhat spherical or ovoid rock that has a hollow interior that may be lined with crystals of quartz or calcite or lined with banded agate.[34] In the Middle Ages, geodes were thought to resemble a womb and the crystals were regarded as something like embryos growing within their rock-womb. This resemblance to the womb led to the belief by some people that geodes might be used as aids in childbirth. It was also surmised that large birds of prey carried these stones into their nests to assist in the laying and hatching of eggs.

The analogy between stones and the organic world was carried even farther because some clear crystals of quartz, for example, contain small fluid inclusions or needles of other minerals such as tourmaline or rutile. These inclusions reminded many people of internal organs that might have participated in the growth of the crystals.

Throughout the Middle Ages a variety of authors published lists of stones called "lapidaries."[35] These compilations typically incorporated some mention of the characteristics and uses of these stones. The concept of resemblances played an important role in assessing the "virtues" of some of these objects. Among the authors of lapidaries were individuals such as the historian of early English Christianity, the Venerable Bede (c. 672-735), Bishop Isidore of Seville (c. 560-636), and Marbodus (1035-1123), the Bishop of Rennes in France. The lapidary of Marbodus is particularly interesting because of the various alleged virtues or occult properties of stones that he listed. For example, he mentioned that certain kinds of stones provide a good speaking voice, give success in battle, stop flows of blood, instigate evil visions, detect whether a spouse has been unfaithful, or grant success in prayer.

Not until the notion of heavenly influences on the growth of stones was dispelled and not until greater attention was paid to physical properties such as hardness, color, and density, was much real progress made in understanding geological objects. Theophrastus (c. 371-c. 287 B. C.), a successor of Aristotle at the Lyceum, had made a promising beginning in describing the physical properties of minerals, but during the Christian era, attention was diverted from such study and interest in the alleged occult virtues of stones increased. Albertus Magnus made some headway in returning to a more fruitful, scientific study of stones, but it was primarily Calvin's contemporary, Agricola, who was very skeptical of the medieval approach to geological materials. He carefully described the physical properties of dozens of gems, ores, and rocks, discussed the details of metallic ore deposits, and postulated that ores had been deposited from hot watery fluids percolating through fractures in rocks. He was not impressed by the medieval appeals to mystical "plastic virtues" in rocks that supposedly produced the shell-like objects that puzzled so many people. Later, we will discover whether Calvin was influenced by Agricola's more modern views, or if he still held onto medieval conceptions about the growth of organic mimics in rocks and about the virtues of stones.

The Bible contains an abundance of references to gemstones. The breastpiece to be worn by the high priest, beginning with Aaron, is described in Exodus 28 and again in Exodus 39. The breastpiece was adorned with four rows of precious stones with three stones in each row. These gems were all mounted in gold. According to the New International Version, these stones were ruby, topaz, beryl, turquoise, sapphire, emerald, jacinth, agate, amethyst, chrysolite, onyx, and jasper. Each of the twelve stones was engraved with the name of one of the twelve tribes of Israel. In Ezekiel 28, a passage that contains a prophecy against the king of Tyre, the king was described in rich imagery as one who lived in Eden, the very Garden of God, and was adorned with every precious stone: ruby, topaz, and emerald; chrysolite, onyx, and jasper; sapphire, turquoise, and beryl. The settings for all these stones were likewise made of gold. There is difficulty in determining the precise identity of some of these gemstones from the Hebrew terms, a situation reflected in the fact that the King James Version translated ruby as "sardius," turquoise, as "emerald," emerald as "diamond," jacinth as "ligure," and chrysolite as "beryl."

In the New Testament, Revelation 21 transforms the twelve stones representing the twelve tribes of Israel into the twelve foundations of the holy city of God representing the twelve apostles. This transformation is in line with the New Testament teaching that the church is founded on the testimony of the apostles and prophets. In Revelation both the twelve gates and the twelve foundations of the city of God bear the names of the twelve apostles of the Lamb. In John's apostolic vision the foundations are composed of jasper, sapphire, chalcedony, emerald, sardonyx, carnelian, chrysolite, beryl, topaz, chrysoprase, jacinth, and amethyst respectively. Each of the twelve gates is made of a single pearl, and the streets of the New Jerusalem are paved with gold that is as pure as glass. Here, too, the King James Version translated some of the gemstone names differently from the New International Version. Even in the throne room vision of Revelation 4, the one who sat on the throne had the appearance of jasper and carnelian, the rainbow encircling the throne resembled an emerald, and there was something like a sea of glass or crystal before the throne.

Clearly references to many precious stones are found throughout Scripture, and the stones bear symbolic significance. It would be interesting to know what opinions Calvin may have entertained about the nature and identity of these various stones. Would he have any ideas about where such stones are found and how they are formed? Unfortunately, the rock hounds, gemologists, and geologists among us are destined to be disappointed. Calvin wrote no commentary on Revelation and left no sermons on the book either. Because his lectures on Ezekiel stop at chapter 20, he never dealt with all the stones mentioned in chapter 28. That leaves us mainly with the two chapters in Exodus that describe the breastpiece of the high priest. Calvin wrote extremely little about Exodus 39 and said nothing whatever about the stones, perhaps because that chapter records the making of the ephod, breastpiece, and other priestly garments according to the specifications that had been spelled out in Exodus 28. So we are left with his thoughts on the list of stones in the breastpiece mentioned in Exodus 28. When we turn there we are disappointed again. Although he briefly discussed the breastpiece, he never talked about the stones individually or attempted to identify them. He said only that the twelve stones are stones of memorial. They were, he said, a "monument of the mutual agreement between God and them."[36]

One of the most "geological" passages in all of Scripture occurs within Job's final discourse. Throughout Job 28 we read of deposits of gold, silver, iron, and copper, of the mines that are excavated to extract the ore, and of the human wisdom that seeks out these valuable minerals. We read of the Earth being transformed as by fire. We read of flinty rock, the roots of mountains, the sources of rivers, and of sapphires. We read of onyx, jasper, rubies, topaz, and coral. If anywhere, it is here that we might anticipate that Calvin would have provided a glimpse of what he knew about these minerals and gems. But, as with the passages dealing with the bejeweled breastpiece of the high priest, we are again let down. In his first sermon on Job 28, Calvin preached about some of these matters but left us without a clue as to his "mineralogical" ideas. He referred very generally to the many secrets of nature and emphasized that God's wisdom is far higher than the human wisdom that may gain insight and understanding of all these secrets.

Calvin perceptively stated that it would profit his congregation very little to preach three or four sermons about seeking out the mines of gold and silver. We cannot all occupy ourselves in that trade, he said, but what suffices for the general believer is to recognize that God has put these secrets into nature so that he might be magnified by us. We ought to acknowledge God's infinite power and wisdom even in the least things of the world. How much more, then, should we acknowledge God's power and wisdom displayed in these secrets of nature that are strange to us, as is the case with gold and silver!

Later in his sermon Calvin observed that God had given abilities to both believers and unbelievers to understand and search out and judge "the things that are here beneath." Sometimes it is the wicked and the despisers of God who are the sharper witted and more skillful in such matters, he observed. Calvin wanted his congregation to grasp the point that although there are a great number of secrets in nature, it is still God who gives men the ability to figure out these secrets. He then posed a series of questions:

> How could men know where gold lies in the earth? How does it come to pass that men can make salt out of water? How can a man discern that gold or silver that is very finely distributed throughout earth so that you don't see its color is actually valuable? How can someone refine the gold or silver ore so that it becomes a precious metal and a means of trafficking between people?

Repeatedly, Calvin drove home the point that it is God who gives men the skill to solve these seemingly intractable problems. Even though men may "be dark at the first entrance," God has given "some capacity in men to comprehend natural things." He has given men the aids and means wherewith to "pass through" the world. Clearly he was impressed by the skill of those who could find valuable deposits, extract them from the Earth, and refine them for their profit and our benefit. But he did not even begin to speculate about how people do find the ore deposits nor did he share with his congregation even a guess along the lines of Aristotle regarding how these minerals might have formed.[37] Calvin's failure to elaborate on the science and technology of the day in regard to mining stands in stark contrast to the amount of time that he devoted in his sermons on Job to animals or the weather. Perhaps this omission in Calvin is a reflection of the very limited extent to which "geological" knowledge had penetrated the consciousness of ordinary citizens.

Other Geological Materials

A few other geological materials are briefly mentioned in Calvin's writings. Genesis 19 tells the story of the destruction of Sodom and Gomorrah by "fire and brimstone" or "burning sulfur," a situation that suggests the possibility of volcanic action.[38] Calvin was persuaded that "the Lord did not then cause it to rain, in the ordinary course of nature." Instead, he suggested that God had "fulminated in a manner to which he was not accustomed, for the purpose of making it sufficiently plain, that this rain of fire and brimstone was produced by no natural cause"[39] Believing that natural causes were not involved, Calvin saw no need to speculate about the possible roles of volcanoes, burning asphalt, or other geological processes in the destruction of these cities. Indeed, one gets the impression that he thought of this "rain" as one in which ordinary water drops were simply replaced by drops of fire and brimstone coming from high in the sky rather than from some alternative source.

Jeremiah 5:22 is one of a plethora of passages that refer to sand and the boundary between land and sea. "I made the sand a boundary for the sea, an everlasting barrier it cannot cross," God announced through the prophet. Calvin found it remarkable that God selected sand as a barrier. Moreover, he thought that it was much more "expressive" for the text to say that God had set the sand to be the boundary of the sea than to say merely that God had set boundaries to the sea without specifying the nature of the material that made up that boundary. The reason that the situation is so remarkable is that "the sand is movable and driven by a small breath of wind, and the sand is also penetrable." Calvin thought that if there were rocks along all the shores of the sea, it would not be such an amazing thing that the sea is kept at bay. Given his conviction that the sea is higher than the land and threatens to overwhelm it at every moment, his amazement that sand serves as a barrier becomes more understandable. "Had God then restrained the violence of the sea by firm and strong mounds," that is, rocks, then "the keeping of it within its limits might be ascribed to nature; but what firmness is there in sand? For a little water thrown on it will soon penetrate through it. How then is it, that the sea, when tossed by violent storms, does not remove the sand, which is so easily shifted?"[40] For Calvin, the fact that sand, rather than solid rock, serves as an effective boundary between land and sea, in spite of its porous nature, was an indication of divine establishment and control.

In his discussion of the burning coal that touched Isaiah's lips when God commissioned him to serve as a prophet, Calvin wrote that there is no reason to believe that the coal possessed any magical virtue or hidden power.[41] Although

Scripture mentions at one point or another a variety of rock types such as chalk-stone (Isaiah 27:9), flint (e.g., Deut. 8:15; 32:13; Isaiah 50:7), brimstone (e.g., Deut. 29:23; Job 18:15; Psalm 11:6; Ezek. 38:22), Calvin declined to take any special note of these rock types or their properties.

The Deluge

For at least the last three centuries, the biblical flood has played an important, if not central, role in geological theorizing.[42] During the late seventeenth and early eighteenth centuries, mainstream scientific thinkers such as Edmund Halley (1656-1742), Royal Astronomer at the Greenwich Observatory and discoverer of the famed comet that bears his name; John Woodward (1665-1722), a professor of physic (medicine) at Gresham College, London; William Whiston (1667-1752), Isaac Newton's successor in the chair of mathematics at Cambridge; and Alexander Catcott (1725-1779), Vicar of the Temple Church in Bristol, England, adopted the notion that the predominant agent of geological change during the history of the Earth was the flood. Many students of the Earth, particularly Woodward and Catcott, maintained that the Earth's fossil-bearing sedimentary strata had been deposited by the flood. The fossils were regarded as remains of organisms that had been obliterated and entombed in sediment during the cataclysm. During the latter eighteenth century, continued geological study cast doubt on the deluge hypothesis and uncovered evidence that rock strata had been deposited in various marine and terrestrial environments over long periods of time. That view became established among leading geologists well before the middle of the nineteenth century.

Despite the fact that an overwhelming amount of geological evidence continues to accumulate in support of the idea that the fossiliferous sedimentary strata were deposited in a wide variety of geological environments over several hundreds of millions of years, there still remain within Christian circles many individuals and groups who remain adamant that the biblical flood catastrophically deposited nearly all the stratified rocks of the planet within one year.[43] In view of the ongoing dispute between adherents of young-Earth "flood geology" and proponents of contemporary mainstream, professional old-earth geology, it would be interesting to know what ideas Calvin may have entertained in regard to the great deluge. Did Calvin have anything to say that might benefit the church of today in its struggle to understand the relationship between the biblical flood account and the geological record?

Without question, Calvin conceived of the flood as a global event. In this regard, he was in perfect accord with his predecessors and contemporaries in Europe. Although he did not explicitly argue for a global deluge in any systematic fashion, his view may be inferred from incidental comments. He admitted that he followed the common opinion that the ark landed in Armenia, "the mountains of which are declared, by ancient authors, almost with one consent, to be the highest."[44] He must have realized that such a flood would eventually cover the globe. Calvin's remarks about the landing site of the ark stand in striking contrast with those of Luther. In his *Lectures on Genesis*, Luther conceded that "it is the common opinion of almost everyone" that the mountains of Ararat referred to the mountains of Armenia near to the Caucasus and Taurus Mountains. In his view, however, the Bible was referring to "the foremost mountain of all, the Imaus, which divides India." Evidently Luther had the Himalaya range in mind. Other high mountains are like warts in comparison with those, he said. He envisioned the Caucasus, Taurus, and Lebanon ranges as something like the feet or roots of "Imaus" that were exposed as the floodwater receded long after the ark landing site was uncovered. Noah, he thought, was even able to see these lower mountains from his vantage point high atop the Imaus.[45] Calvin was more restrained in his deluge geography.

Calvin recognized that after the waters had covered the highest mountains, they rose yet another fifteen cubits.[46] He would also have understood the global implications of this arrangement. He also wrote about tigers, lions, and wolves entering the ark along with hares, oxen, and lambs.[47] Although lions and wolves may have been native to the Middle East at the time of the deluge, it is questionable whether tigers were. Presumably they would have had to migrate to the ark from some distance, indicating the likelihood that the flood would be global. If the flood were not global, then animals would not need to migrate to the ark from far distances in order to be preserved. It is possible, however, that Calvin assumed that all these animals were in the general vicinity of the ark to begin with and came to the ark prompted by the secret instinct of the Spirit of God. It is striking that Calvin made no mention of any of the animals that had been discovered in the New World in reference to entry into the ark. Did he fail to mention any of the animals that had been discovered across the Atlantic because he did not know about them, or because he thought they were not known to his readers, or because he did not think they were on board the ark? We can only imagine the reason. Perhaps he simply mentioned impressive animals most familiar to his readers. This lack of reference to American animals is just one facet of his larger omission of any acknowledgment in his writings of the voyages to the New World. It is very difficult to believe that Calvin was unaware of these expeditions and of the encounters with both people and strange animals across the sea. One cannot help wondering whether Calvin sensed some of the inconvenient problems that such discoveries posed for the idea of a global deluge and simply was not prepared to face those problems. We simply do not know.

Calvin was also rather restrained in discussing the general effects of the flood. Although he undoubtedly took it for granted that the flood was worldwide, he never breathed a word about the flood depositing sediments or being responsible for fossils. In contrast to Calvin, Luther said that the flood accounted for the discoveries of petrified wood and animal remains in the rocks encountered within mines.[48] Again, Calvin must have had some acquaintance with scholarly opinion about fossil remains, and it is remarkable that he said nothing about fossils as relics of the flood as Luther did. Conceivably Calvin thought that fossils were sports of nature in which case there would be no need to mention them in connection with the flood. In any case, his reticence to discuss scientific implications of the deluge underscores his more general reluctance to talk about scientific implications in the Bible unless they were explicitly stated in the text.

Calvin did refer to Noah's sending out the raven to see if it would be attracted by the stench of rotting carcasses exposed on dry ground. One particularly revealing comment occurs in the discussion of Genesis 2:10. Noting the difficulty pertaining to the description of the four rivers of the Garden of Eden, he observed that some people attempted to eliminate the difficulty by claiming that "the surface of the globe may have been changed by the deluge; and, therefore, they imagine it might have happened that the courses of the rivers were disturbed and changed and their springs transferred elsewhere."[49] Among adherents of this view was Luther, who again was less restrained than Calvin. After referring to Nicholas of Lyra's citation of authors who maintained that the flood wore away the entire surface of the Earth to a depth of three handbreadths, Luther asserted that "Paradise certainly was completely laid waste and ruined by the Flood." As a result, the Earth of today is "obviously more cursed" than the world before the flood.[50] Calvin was reticent to go that far. Although acknowledging that the Earth was "laid waste in many places by the deluge," he insisted that "it was the same earth which had been created in the beginning."[51] His discomfort with the idea that the courses of rivers had been changed by the flood is indicative of his view that the post-flood Earth was the "same earth." However Calvin may have conceived of the Genesis flood, his belief that the surface of the globe was fundamentally the same after the flood as before suggests that, had he known about "flood geology," he would not have looked favorably on that theory. "Flood geology," whether of the seventeenth, nineteenth, or twenty-first century variety, inevitably requires a complete change of the globe's surface because virtually the entire surface is being covered by thick deposits of sediment that would ultimately be converted into sedimentary rock like sandstone, shale, and limestone. Calvin's belief also suggests that he may have thought of the deluge as relatively placid and non-turbulent, and his statement that "the waters rose gradually by fresh additions" during the first forty days comports with that view.[52]

How did Calvin envision the source of water for the deluge? His extended discussion of Genesis 7:11 sheds some light on this question. In regard to the "fountains of the deep," he said that God, at the creation, "might have deposited, in certain channels or veins of the earth, as much water as would have sufficed for all the purposes of human life." But he also placed water above us as well as below us. Because these two sources of water threaten us with death, the hand of God restrained them from harming us. God "raised for men a theatre in the habitable region of the earth," and his secret power worked so that "the subterraneous waters should not break forth to overwhelm us, and the celestial waters should not conspire with them for that purpose." In other words, Calvin taught that God "designedly placed us between two graves lest, in fancied security we should despise that kindness on which our life depends." For Calvin, it was from these two sources or "graves" that the floodwaters originated. Nevertheless, he asserted that the expressions referring to the breaking up of the fountains of the deep and the opening of the cataracts of the heavens are metaphorical expressions indicating that, during the flood, the waters from below no longer flowed in their accustomed manner, and the waters from above no longer distilled from heaven in their accustomed manner. In effect, the distinction between the waters that had originally been established by God was now removed, and there were no longer any bars to restrain the violent eruption.[53]

Calvin's remarks indicate that he understood that regions of subterranean waters were established at creation, probably in underground channels or veins. A belief in the existence of vast reservoirs of underground water was widespread in the ancient Near Eastern world, in the Christendom of Calvin's day, and even in subsequent centuries within the western world. In the late seventeenth century, the numerous writers who developed elaborate theories of the history of the Earth in which the biblical deluge was the central formative event, such as Burnet, commonly derived the floodwaters from some sort of subterranean abyss. To this day, some Christians are persuaded that the Earth formerly housed vast subterranean reservoirs of water.[54]

NOTES

1. Commentary on Isaiah 40:26.
2. Information about world exploration can be found in Daniel J. Boorstin, *The Discoverers* (New York: Vintage Books, 1985); Jerry Brotton, *Trading Territories: Mapping the Early Modern World* (London: Reaktion Books, 1997); and J. H. Parry, *The Age of Reconnaissance: Discovery, Exploration, and Settlement 1450-1650* (Berkeley, Calif.: University of California Press, 1982).
3. Commentary on Genesis, Argument.
4. Commentary on Genesis 2:10.
5. Second Sermon on Job 38.
6. Commentary on Daniel 7:2.
7. On the history of ideas about the age of the Earth, see Francis C. Haber, *The Age of the World: Moses to Darwin* (Baltimore: Johns Hopkins Press, 1959); Claude C. Albritton, *The Abyss of Time: Changing Conceptions of the Earth's Antiquity after the Sixteenth Century* (San Francisco: Freeman, Cooper, 1980); Davis A. Young, *Christianity and the Age of the Earth* (Grand Rapids, Mich.: Zondervan, 1982); Stephen Jay Gould, *Time's Arrow, Time's Cycle: Myth and Metaphor in the Discovery of Geological Time* (Cambridge, Mass.: Harvard University Press, 1987); and especially Martin J. S. Rudwick, *Bursting the Limits of Time: The Reconstruction of Geohistory in the Age of Revolution* (Chicago: University of Chicago Press, 2005). For scientific evidence pertaining to the age of the Earth, see G. Brent Dalrymple, *The Age of the Earth* (Stanford, Calif.: Stanford University Press, 1990); G. Brent Dalrymple, *Ancient Earth, Ancient Skies: The Age of Earth and its Cosmic Surroundings* (Stanford, Calif.: Stanford University Press, 2004); Young, *Christianity and the Age of the Earth*, and Cherry L. E. Lewis and Simon J. Knell, eds., *The Age of the Earth: 4004 B.C. to 2002 A. D.* Geological Society Special Publication 190 (London: The Geological Society, 2001).
8. Second Sermon on Job 38.
9. Commentary on Psalm 102:25.
10. Commentary on Psalm 19:1.
11. Commentary on Daniel 9:25.
12. Commentary on Nahum 2:8.
13. Commentary on Exodus 33:19.
14. Institutes, 1.14.1.
15. For a discussion of Pliny the Younger's account of the eruption of Mount Vesuvius and the destruction of Pompeii and Herculaeum, see Haraldur Sigurdsson, *Melting the Earth* (New York: Oxford University Press, 1999).
16. For a history of early ideas about the nature of volcanoes see Davis A. Young, *Mind over Magma: The Story of Igneous Petrology* (Princeton, N.J.: Princeton University Press, 2003) and also H. Sigurdsson, *Melting the Earth*.
17. Aristotle, *Meteorologica*, II.7.
18. Commentary on Isaiah 54:10.
19. Commentary on Habakkuk 3:6.
20. Ibid.
21. Commentary on Matthew 28:2.
22. Commentary on Acts 16:26.
23. Marjorie Nicholson, *Mountain Gloom and Mountain Glory: the Development of the Aesthetics of the Infinite* (Ithaca, N.Y.: Cornell University Press, 1959).
24. Second Sermon on Job 38.

25. Commentary on Habakkuk 3:6.
26. Commentary on Deuteronomy 33:15.
27. Commentary on Isaiah 30:25.
28. Commentary on Psalm 104:13.
29. Second Sermon on Job 38.
30. Adrian J. Desmond, "The Discovery of Marine Transgression and the Explanation of Fossils in Antiquity," *American Journal of Science* 275, (1975): 692-707.
31. See Rudwick, *The Meaning of Fossils*, for a history of ideas about fossils. A briefer account is provided by Alan Cutler, *The Seashell on the Mountaintop: A Story of Science, Sainthood, and the Humble Genius Who Discovered a New History of the Earth* (New York: Dutton, 2003).
32. John Ray, *Three Physico-Theological Discourses* (New York: Arno Press, 1978). This volume is a reprint of the 3rd edition of Ray's book from 1713. Chapter 4 contains an extended discussion of Ray's ideas about the nature of fossil shells.
33. On signatures and correspondences see Adams, *The Birth and Development of the Geological Sciences*.
34. Geodes are formed as circulating ground water dissolves out cavities within limestone, a highly soluble rock composed of calcium carbonate. Crystals may precipitate onto the walls of the cavity from fluids that later fill or pass through it. Especially if the precipitated matter consists of very hard quartz or agate, an extremely finely crystalline variety of quartz, the cavity is rendered much more resistant to further chemical attack than the enclosing limestone. If weathering and erosion of a limestone layer with crystal-filled cavities persist over a very long period of time, the limestone may eventually be removed completely, leaving behind the far more resistant crystal-lined cavities. As a result, the geodes are commonly found on the ground in areas underlain by limestone.
35. For a discussion of lapidaries, see Adams, *The Birth and Development of the Geological Sciences*.
36. Commentary on Exodus 28:9.
37. First Sermon on Job 28.
38. For a recent discussion of the geology of the Sodom and Gomorrah event, see David Neev and Kenneth O. Emery, *The Destruction of Sodom, Gomorrah, and Jericho: Geological, Climatological, and Archaeological Background* (New York: Oxford University Press, 1995).
39. Commentary on Genesis 19:24.
40. Commentary on Jeremiah 5:22. Calvin was probably unaware that the sea is extremely efficient at moving sand in great quantities. Vast amounts of sand are moved parallel to shore lines around the world by means of the process of longshore drift. The reason that beaches do not disappear is that the sand at any given location is typically replenished by sand being moved in by the sea from another point along the shoreline. Storms also dramatically erode beaches, and huge quantities of sand are typically moved offshore as a result of major storms. When calm weather returns, the sand is gradually moved back toward the beach. Although a sandy beach may appear to be a permanent feature during the course of a human lifetime, it is an extremely fragile and dynamic "barrier" between land and sea.
41. Commentary on Isaiah 6:7.
42. For a historical overview of theories of the deluge, see Davis A. Young, *The Biblical Flood: A Case Study of the Church's Response to Extrabiblical Evidence* (Grand Rapids, Mich.: William B. Eerdmans, 1995). For a summary of flood theories, see Davis A. Young, "The Biblical Flood as a Geological Agent: a Review of Theories," *in The Evolution-Creation Controversy II: Perspectives on Science, Religion, and Geological Educa-*

tion, ed. Patricia H. Kelly, Jonathan R. Bryan, and Thor A. Hansen, The Paleontological Society Papers 5, (1999), 119-34.

43. For example, the Institute for Creation Research and the Creation Research Society are both committed to a very young Earth and a global deluge.

44. Commentary on Genesis 8:3.

45. Pelikan, *Luther's Works*, vol. 1, 107-8.

46. Commentary on Genesis 8:1.

47. Commentary on Genesis 6:22 and 7:8.

48. Pelikan, *Luther's Works*, vol. 1, 98.

49. Commentary on Genesis 2:10.

50. Pelikan, *Luther's Works*, 52.

51. Commentary on Genesis 2:10.

52. Commentary on Genesis 8:3.

53. Commentary on Genesis 7:11.

54. The hydroplate theory of Walt Brown entails the concept of a vast subterranean body of water that existed prior to the deluge. See Walt Brown, *In the Beginning: Compelling Evidence for Creation and the Flood*, 7th ed. (Phoenix: Center for Scientific Creation, 2001).

CHAPTER 5

CALVIN ON LIVING THINGS

The Bible is replete with references to animals and plants from beginning to end.[1] At the outset, Scripture informs us that seed-bearing plants, fruit-bearing trees, birds of the air, teeming water creatures, livestock, creeping things, and wild animals are all the result of God's omnipotent creative word. Upon his placement in the Garden of Eden, Adam was given the task of naming the various animals. He is given permission to eat from all the trees in the garden with the exception on one particular tree. A serpent makes its appearance in the garden to tempt Eve to eat fruit from the proscribed tree. The guilty Adam and Eve make fig leaves for themselves as clothing to hide their shame. In Genesis 4, their offspring Cain brings fruits of the soil as an offering to the Lord, and his brother Abel brings fat portions from his flocks. And so it continues all the way to the final chapter of the Bible where the Christ of the apocalypse says that those who wash their robes have access to the tree of life and that the dogs will be left outside the gates of the city. Because plants and animals are such an integral part of our environment, and because the Bible is so much a book about events that took place on the Earth, references to the biological milieu in which humans find themselves unavoidably pervade the whole of Scripture. Nor is the Bible content with vague, general allusions to fauna and flora. Dozens of specific domesticated and wild animals and plants well known to the inhabitants of the ancient Near Eastern world are mentioned again and again along with creatures such as *behemoth* and *leviathan* whose identity is not quite so certain. So it is inevitable that Bible commentators will leave clues as to their own ideas about plants and animals. It should be no different with Calvin, and it isn't.

But what was the status of biology in the times leading up to Calvin? Aristotle produced much valuable biological work by performing dissections of many creatures and examining specimens from many parts of the world that had been brought to him by his former student Alexander the Great. In the nine books of his *Historia Animalium*, Aristotle summarized a vast amount of knowledge of animals in comparative studies of the external parts, internal organs, reproductive habits, diet, diseases, and behavior of numerous animals and of humans.[2] Thanks in good measure to Aristotle's work and to the intrinsic awareness that people generally have of animals, knowledge of animal anatomy, behavior, and biogeography was relatively advanced in comparison with some of the other fields of natural knowledge before the time of Christ. In Roman times, Pliny the Elder (A. D. 23-79) wrote a voluminous work on natural phenomena.[3] In books VIII through XI of *Natural History*, Pliny compiled a wealth of information (along with an abundance of fantasy) about the appearance and behavior of a wide range of mammals, reptiles, fish, birds, and insects. He also described in detail the structure and function of numerous body parts, including internal organs. Pliny was strongly indebted to Aristotle.

Knowledge of the anatomy of several domesticated animals was furthered during the early Christian era as a result of dissections performed by the Roman physician, Galen of Pergamon (129-c. 216). Albertus Magnus summarized much knowledge about plants and animals during the Middle Ages. Scholars in Calvin's day were still greatly indebted to the classical writers. Unfortunately, as the Christian era progressed, much that was fanciful became intermixed with the wealth of accurate information about animals, including mention of mythical creatures and very inaccurate reports of the alleged behavior of animals. A lot of the misinformation was transmitted into the popular consciousness throughout the Middle Ages by means of bestiaries, namely, compilations of fact, fable, and moral lessons based on the purported behavior of animals.

Biological investigation began to improve just before and during Calvin's lifetime as experts in natural history like Guillaume Rondelet (1507-1566) and Conrad Gesner (1516-1565) learned much about marine life and about invertebrates in general. Moreover, numerous species of hitherto unrecognized plants and animals were discovered as a result of the many explorations of the New World in the latter fifteenth and early sixteenth centuries. Given this dramatic growth in knowledge about living things, what were Calvin's own beliefs about the organic world? How extensive and up-to-date was his knowledge of plants and animals? What kinds of animals might he have seen? Did he know anything at all about the strange new creatures that were being encountered across the Atlantic Ocean? And what was the source of his understanding of the organic world?

First, let's see what Calvin knew about animals. The most exhaustive compilation of animals in the Bible occurs in Leviticus 11. The passage even gives us a zoological classification. The animals are subdivided into the following categories: animals that have split hooves and chew cud, animals that chew cud without split hooves; animals that have split hooves but do not chew cud, water animals with fins and scales, water animals lacking fins and scales, unclean birds (meat, carrion, fish eaters), flying insects that walk on all fours except for those with jointed legs for ground hopping, animals that walk on their paws, and unclean animals that move on the ground. Not only is this classification provided (obviously in relation to which animals were to be considered unclean and which were not), but several examples from each category are mentioned. The text provides a sampling of those creatures very familiar to the Israelites. To our regret, Calvin did not take the opportunity to talk about any of these creatures in detail in his comments on Leviticus 11.[4] He acknowledged that, in this Levitical list, there was no ambiguity as to the identity of the tame animals or animals that are found everywhere. On the other hand, he recognized that many of the animals that were named were common in the east but were not known elsewhere. As a result, he saw little need to go into specifics and was content to take note of the specific characteristics of "clean animals" versus "unclean animals." Fortunately, he did give us a lot of insight into his views on many animals in dealing with other biblical passages.

Because Calvin had a lot to say about vertebrates and rather little about the invertebrates, we will concentrate primarily on his ideas about the vertebrates. When it came to vertebrate animals, he generally did not employ such terms as "mammal," "amphibian," or "vertebrate." He rarely used the term "reptile," but he did talk about "birds" and "fishes." For our purposes, we will examine Calvin's ideas about various animals belonging to what contemporary zoologists refer to as five informal categories of vertebrates: fishes, amphibians, reptiles, birds, and mammals.

Fishes

Inasmuch as Scripture contains several references to the fishes of the sea and, in some cases, fishes of the rivers, Calvin mentioned them at relevant junctures. The bulk of his references contains little of scientific interest and provides no insight into his ideas about the nature of various fishes. He did think that the diverse fishes received their final form on the fifth day of creation.[5] The most thorough comments about fishes occur in Calvin's reflections on the story of Jonah and the great fish. Jonah 1:17 states that "the Lord provided a great fish to swallow Jonah, and Jonah was inside the fish three days and three nights." Because such a statement initially strikes readers as implausible and might cause them to doubt the veracity of Scripture, Calvin took pains to point out that there are known instances of fish swallowing humans. "It is certain," he insisted, "that there are some fishes which can swallow men whole and entire."[6] The authority for this assertion was his almost exact contemporary, Guillaume Rondelet, a professor of medicine at the University of Montpellier in southern France, a Huguenot, and author of *De Piscibus Marinis*, published in 1554.[7] Rondelet was one of the great natural historians of the sixteenth century. Along with Pierre Belon (1517-1564) and Ippolito Salviani (1514-1572), Rondelet was one of the leading authorities on fishes of his time and, like them, considered as one of the founding fathers of the science of ichthyology. One of his achievements was the recognition that generally dark, sharp-edged triangular objects commonly found in unconsolidated sediment and popularly known as *glossopetrae* (literally, tongue stones) were really shark teeth. Rondelet's discovery was made a full century before Steno, who normally gets credit for the claim that *glossopetrae* were once shark teeth, made the same discovery.

Of Jonah's great fish, Calvin reported that Rondelet, "who has written a book on the fishes of the sea, concludes that in all probability it must have been the *Lamia*." Rondelet himself had seen that fish and claimed that "it has a belly so capacious, and a mouth so wide, that it can easily swallow up a man." Moreover, Calvin noted that "a man in armour has sometimes been found in the inside of the *Lamia*. Therefore, as I have said, either a whale, or a *Lamia*, or a fish unknown to us, may be able to swallow up a man whole and entire." In all likelihood, the *Lamia* of Rondelet was a large shark, most probably the great white shark, which does inhabit the Mediterranean Sea. Although accepting Rondelet's information about the stomach capacity of some fishes, Calvin had his doubts about the survivability of someone who had been swallowed. He went on to say that

> he who is thus devoured cannot live in the inside of a fish. Hence Jonah, that he might mark it out as a miracle, says that the fish was prepared by the Lord; for he was received into the inside of the fish as though it were into an hospital; and though he had no rest there, yet he was as safe as to his body, as though he were walking on land. Since then the Lord, contrary to the order of nature, preserved there his Prophet, it is no wonder that he says that the fish was prepared by the Lord.[8]

We do not know the extent of Calvin's acquaintance with Rondelet or with his book on fishes. Did he know Rondelet personally? Did he own a copy of Rondelet's book? Had he read it? Had an acquaintance simply called his attention to the relevant passage in Rondelet's book? The reference to Rondelet and his writing does indicate that Calvin had some awareness of contemporary scientific developments and literature.

Calvin's youthful commentary on the book *De Clementia* by Roman writer Seneca contained a couple of references to *muraenae*, a term translated as lampreys. Chapter 18 in Book I of Seneca's work contains a reference to one Vedius Pollio, an individual who was said, with ample justification, to be cordially hated by everyone because he would fatten his lampreys on human blood and then throw those who incurred his displeasure into his fishpond to be devoured by the lampreys. Seneca was understandably repelled by such behavior, whether Vedius Pollio threw slaves as food to lampreys that he eventually intended to eat, or merely fed the lampreys on such food. Calvin noted in his comments that Pliny the Elder corroborated Seneca's account of Vedius Pollio throwing slaves into ponds of lampreys. Pliny charged that creatures other than lampreys failed to produce the spectacle of a man being rapidly torn to shreds. Then Calvin mentioned that Marcus Terentius Varro (116-c. 27 B. C.) described the lamprey as a fish that was a very costly prime delicacy. He recognized that a lamprey is not too different from an eel. He also referred to one Roman woman who so highly prized her lamprey that she put earrings on it![9] It thus appears that Calvin knew, at least from the writings of classical authors, that lampreys are edible, eel-like fish that like to feast on blood. He did not mention their ability to attach themselves by their sucker-like mouths to extract blood from their hosts.

Although whales are classified as mammals by contemporary zoologists because they are warm-blooded, bear live young, and suckle their young, Calvin regarded them as fish. In his commentary on Genesis 1:21, the verse that describes the creation of sea creatures and birds on the fifth day of creation, he remarked that God "created whales (*balaenas*) and other fishes," thus classifying the whale among the fishes.[10] He seems, too, to have held the opinion that the biblical *leviathan* was a whale, or at least that whales might be considered as one among several large creatures designated by that name. He recognized that *leviathan* had been interpreted in a variety of ways, but he suggested that generally "it simply denotes a large serpent, or whales and sea-fishes, which approach to the character of monsters on account of their huge size."[11] Calvin also touched on the matter in his third sermon on Job 40 and first sermon on Job 41. In the former, he proclaimed that "as touching the word leviathan, through the whole scripture it signifies a whale."[12] In the latter sermon, he conceded that the description of *leviathan* did not exactly match that of a whale but suggested that similarities didn't have to match in every detail. More to the point was Calvin's description of the whale. He wrote that

> it might seem to us that the whale might be choked in the midst of the waters; and yet notwithstanding he is so great and huge a beast, as he cuts the sea asunder, makes it to boil like a pot with his snorting and sneezing and (as it is termed here) overturns ships, and is like to swallow up all that comes in his way.[13]

Calvin was clearly aware that whales spray water out of their blowholes.

Amphibians and Reptiles

Calvin made few informative comments about toads or frogs. Even his discussion concerning the plague of frogs in Egypt contains little out of the ordinary about the nature of these creatures. Although he did not use the term "reptile," Calvin made several allusions to "serpents" or "dragons." It may be presumed that in many of these instances he was thinking primarily about the snake, an animal that plays a prominent role in the biblical text. One need think only of the Garden of Eden temptation scene, or of the apostle Paul being bitten by a viper on the island of Malta, or of Moses and the Egyptian magicians converting their rods into snakes. I have found no clear references to turtles, lizards, or crocodiles. Although many commentators have suggested that *leviathan* in

Job 41 refers to the Nile crocodile, Calvin linked the term to the whale as we have just seen.

The Garden of Eden immediately comes to mind when we think of biblical references to snakes. Where Genesis 3 speaks of the serpent as "subtle," Calvin reckoned that the text was not indicating some flaw in the animal but was actually attributing "praise to nature, because God had endued this beast with such singular skill, as rendered it acute and quick-sighted beyond all others." For his own deceitful purposes, Satan then perverted this divinely imparted gift possessed by the serpent. Calvin regarded the serpent of the temptation literally: "I understand the name of the serpent, not allegorically, as some foolishly do, but in it genuine sense."[14]

God's judgment on the serpent recorded in Genesis 3:14 (you will crawl on your belly and you will eat dust all the days of your life) has led many a Christian to speculate that the snake was quite a different animal prior to the fall and that it may have walked on legs and climbed trees before being consigned to a degraded existence on the ground. Martin Luther was very much of that opinion. Luther wrote that the snake was not hated in the manner that it is now because "through the curse, something is added to the nature of the serpent. Although before the curse it was a very pretty little beast, it is now more frightful and more hated than all the other animals." He concluded that "before sin the serpent was a most beautiful little animal and most pleasing to man, as little mules, sheep, and puppies are today." Not only that, but "it walked upright. And so it is due to the curse and not to its nature that it now creeps on the ground." The serpent used to share in common with other animals like sheep and cows the glory that it ate herbs and fruits and produced things that were useful to people such as butter, milk, and meat. Because of sin, however, the snake "has been cast out from that company" and "is not permitted to eat even the lowliest herbs." In fact, so bad is the situation for the snake that it "dares not eat apples, pears, and nuts, on which even the mice feed; but it consumes raw earth."[15]

Calvin was far more reserved in his interpretation of the contrast between the pre-lapsarian and post-lapsarian natural history of the snake. Without mentioning Luther, he clearly disagreed with the German reformer's understanding of what happened to the snake. He maintained that there would be "no absurdity in supposing, that the serpent was again consigned to that former condition, to which he was already naturally subject." Apparently Calvin thought that snakes were originally created to crawl upon the ground. He said nothing about the snake walking upright or undergoing any kind of transformation. What happened is that the snake was "recalled from his insolent motions to his accustomed mode of going, in such a way as to be, at the same time, condemned to perpetual infamy. To eat dust is the sign of a vile and sordid nature."[16]

What is intriguing is that Calvin did not lump snakes with the toads, flies, and other "vermin" that he believed were created after the fall. This opinion is surprising, of course, because of the revulsion that most people feel toward snakes and because of the fact that many snakes are very poisonous and pose a threat to human life. Curiously, for Calvin, the snake was neither created anew

after the fall nor was it a transformed or deformed version of an original creature. The snake was fundamentally the same animal before and after the fall,
consigned to remain in its condition of crawling on the ground as a result of its
insolence in attempting to rise above its God-assigned lowly state.

Calvin's most intriguing references to snakes or serpents occur in comments on Jeremiah 14:6 and Lamentations 4:3. The former passage is translated
in the New International Version as "wild donkeys stand on the barren heights
and pant like jackals." The Hebrew word *tannim* is translated as "jackals." Calvin, however, translated *tannim* into the Latin word *serpentes*, in effect saying
that the wild asses snuffed up wind like "dragons." Whether he correctly translated the Hebrew term *tannim* here is beside the point. Correct or not, his translation and commentary shed light on his conception of the behavior of snakes or
of reptiles more generally. Of this text Calvin said, "great is the heat of serpents.
On account of inward burning they are constrained to draw in wind to allay the
heat within," that is, to cool themselves off.[17] It is not clear why he would say
this. Perhaps he had some inkling of the cold-blooded nature of snakes and for
their need not to spend too much time in the full sun lest they become over-
heated. Perhaps he was thinking of the fact that some snakes hiss. Or might he
have thought that the biblical description was a reference to the inflating of
throat sacs by lizards? Interestingly, Calvin's expression, "snuffing up of wind,"
makes much more sense in reference to mammals like jackals, animals that pant
in order to get rid of excess heat. Panting can readily be seen as a drawing in of
wind.

The Lamentations passage is translated in the New International Version as
"even jackals offer their breasts to nurse their young." As with the Jeremiah text,
Calvin used the Latin term *serpentes*, and the English translator of his commentary translated the verse as "even the sea-monsters draw out the breast, they give
suck to their young ones."[18] In Lamentations, however, we find the Hebrew term
tannin used. The same word is used in Genesis 1:21 with reference to the great
sea creatures. In Exodus 7:9, the term has a snake in view, and in Ezekiel 29:3
the reference may be to a crocodile. Calvin said that although these *serpentes* are
void of all humanity, they nourish their brood and give them the breast. They
draw out the breast when they give suck to their whelps. Although the word that
he translated as *serpentes* can mean snake, it is doubtful that Calvin thought that
snakes suckle their young. He may simply have envisioned *serpentes* as a catch-
all term for great sea creatures like whales that, as mammals, do indeed suckle
their young. The virtual identification of the terms *leviathan* and *tannin* in Psalm
74:13-14 strongly suggests that Calvin, who maintained that *leviathan* was a
whale, probably was thinking of whales when he used the word *serpentes* for
tannin in Lamentations 4:3. Where dealing with Psalm 74, Calvin maintained
that the terminology about breaking the head of *leviathan* or the dragons or sea
monsters was metaphorical language regarding Pharaoh and his army being destroyed in the sea. He said that Pharaoh was properly termed *leviathan*, "on account of the advantages of the sea possessed by his country, and because, in
reigning over that land with great splendor, he might be compared to a whale

moving up and down at its ease in the midst of the waters of the mighty ocean."[19] In summary, it would appear that Calvin regarded the *serpentes* that gave suck to their whelps not as reptiles generally or snakes specifically but rather as whales. If he was envisioning whales as those creatures that "give suck to their whelps," the nursing behavior of whales was undoubtedly known in his day. In fact, it was known already in Aristotle's time that dolphins, porpoises, and whales give milk to their young.[20]

Part of the reason for the confusion is that Calvin and many of his successors translated two different albeit very similar Hebrew words by the same Latin word, *serpentes*, then translated into French or English as "serpents," or "dragons." The word in Jeremiah 14:6, *tannim*, should, according to the best contemporary philological scholarship, be rendered as "jackals," a far cry from dragons! The word in Lamentations 4:3, *tannin*, is appropriately translated as dragons or sea-monsters.

One additional reference to snakes is worthy of mention. In Book I of *De Clementia*, Seneca likened cruel tyrants to snakes. The tiny snakes, he said, are generally ignored, but the inordinately wicked people, like exceptionally large snakes, become the object of organized hunts, namely wars. Said Seneca: "where one has exceeded the usual size and has grown into a monster, when it has poisoned springs by drinking from them, and with its breath scorches and destroys, then, wherever it advances, it is attacked with engines of war." As Calvin summed it up, Seneca's point was that "the more widely the tyrant's madness rages about, the more persons he has to fear." One need think only of Adolf Hitler, Idi Amin, or Saddam Hussein in recent decades.[21]

What is striking about Calvin's brief comments on the snake passage in Seneca is that he referred to a huge snake "sent to Rome by Regulus, of monstrous size, and quite exceeding credibility, were it not for the fact that so many writers unanimously affirm it."[22] Also of interest is that Calvin said nothing to deny that snakes could poison a spring by drinking from it or that a snake could scorch and destroy with its breath. As we will see later, Calvin apparently accepted the existence of creatures that could scorch vegetation by their breath.

Birds

The Scriptures are filled with dozens of references to a wide variety of common birds that inhabit portions of the Middle East.[23] In commenting on texts that refer to birds, Calvin often said little about the behavior and nature of the bird in question beyond what his readers already knew. For example, in Isaiah 10:14, the proud king of Assyria says that "as one reaches into a nest, so my hand reaches for the wealth of the nations; as men gathered abandoned eggs, so I gathered all the countries; not one flapped a wing, or opened its mouth to chirp." Calvin simply said:

> as if one were to seek a nest and find one deserted by the birds, and consequently to take the eggs without difficulty; for if the parent birds were sitting on

the eggs, having an instinctive desire to protect their nest, they would either fly at the robber, and attack him with their bill, or by loud and unpleasant noises endeavor to drive him away.[24]

We learn nothing unusual about Calvin's ideas on birds from this selection.

Another relatively uninformative passage relates to Jeremiah 8:7 where the prophet castigates Jerusalem for not considering the judgment of God even though the birds are wise enough to know their appointed times. Calvin wrote that storks, swallows, and cranes know the time when they should migrate from one country to another. At certain times they leave cold countries to seek out a warmer climate and escape the severity of winter. At other times they know when to return.[25] This passage lets us know that Calvin was cognizant of the migratory behavior of birds. Such knowledge does not seem out of the ordinary to us because we are familiar with bird migration.

Luther's comments, however, suggest that the nature and extent of avian migration may not have been fully appreciated in the sixteenth century. Where discussing the idea of spontaneous generation in his *Lectures on Genesis*, Luther said that he had no knowledge as to whether birds are spontaneously generated. Perhaps he simply meant that he had no personal, firsthand observation of spontaneous generation of birds because he went on to say that "it is not likely that they go to regions lying more toward the south, inasmuch as from experience it has been learned that the swallows lie dead in the waters throughout the winter and return to life at springtime."[26] From this statement, it seems that Luther did accept spontaneous generation of birds or at least some sort of resuscitation and was probably basing that belief on the observations of others. He suggested that birds were preserved in trees or in waters during the winters. Their "return" was seen as a proof of our resurrection. Luther appeared to be skeptical about bird migration.

Fortunately, Calvin did provide a remarkable amount of detail about birds in his analysis of several other texts, and his remarks provide a window on sixteenth-century conceptions. In one place or another, he wrote about sparrows, doves, goshawks, swans, peacocks, storks, bitterns, ravens, eagles, ostriches, and other birds. We begin with his ideas about eagles, very large birds of prey that make an indelible impression on the observer. There are a large number of species of eagles throughout the world. About half a dozen species live in Europe, most of them confined to eastern Europe. The golden eagle, *Aquila chrysaetos*, is the only eagle that resides in the Swiss and French Alps and is one of the two eagles, along with the bald eagle, that are familiar to North American birders. Very probably Calvin had seen golden eagles soaring in the vicinity of Lake Leman outside Geneva. The only other eagle that Calvin might have seen is the booted eagle, *Hieraetus pennatus*, known to occur throughout central and southwestern France. The biblical writers were acquainted with the golden eagle but also with species of eagles and other raptors distinct from those of central Europe. Whereas Calvin may have envisioned the golden eagle as he wrote about the text, the biblical writers may have had a different species in mind.

The Hebrew term used in Job 39 and frequently throughout the Old Testament for eagle is *nesher*. Although several species of eagle, including the golden eagle, are either resident in, or migrants through, the Holy Land, the one term *nesher* likely encompasses them all.[27] The golden eagle, a bird known for speed and power dives in attacking prey, summers around Mount Hermon and winters over all of Palestine.[28] Some authorities have suggested that, at least in some texts such as Micah 1:16, which refers to the bird's baldness, the biblical writer may have had a vulture, probably the griffon vulture (*Gyps fulvus*), in mind.[29] Some English translations do use "vulture." Quite possibly, the New Testament passage in Matthew 24:28, "there will the eagles be gathered together," is a reference to vultures congregating around a carcass.

Calvin wrote about eagles in at least three places. In commenting on Isaiah 40:31, "they will soar on wings like eagles," he observed that "the eagle is very long lived in comparison with other birds." He said that Aristotle and Pliny claimed that the eagle never dies of old age but dies of hunger when the upper part of its beak becomes so large that it cannot take food into its mouth. At that point the eagle subsists solely on what it can drink.[30] In his commentary on Habakkuk 1:8, he wrote that eagles are rapid in their flight and that the eyes of eagles are remarkably keen and strong. He then alluded to a claim that eagles "cast away their young, if they find that they cannot look steadily at the sun." Fledgling eaglets that could not gaze steadily at the Sun were considered to be spurious by the parent birds and thus ejected from the nest.[31]

Calvin repeated this claim in his third sermon on Job 39: "Some say that the eagles do cast away their young ones as bastard eagles if their sight be not strong enough to look full upon the shining sun." He further suggested that one kind of eagle casts the young ones out of the nest so that they will have to fend for themselves. It is also said, he preached, that these eagles "bring up none but the black ones," although he noted that not all who wrote about such matters agreed on that point.[32] Although providing these tantalizing bits of presumed natural history, Calvin backed off in order to return to the thrust of his sermon, saying that he did not "want to get into the curious points of the philosophers." What mattered most to Calvin was that in Job 39 God was pointing out the nature of eagles as it is known and that nature entails the fact that eagles have the property of sucking blood as soon as they emerge from their eggs. He considered it strange that a bird should feed itself that way. The birds, of course, did not make their own bodies or give themselves this inclination, so he assumed that the "cruelty" that is put into them must have been given them by God. As far as he was concerned, God had given all the birds their various inclinations and established the diversity between the various kinds of birds as signs of his providence so that we might worship his majesty.

Calvin did not link the "cruelty" of eagles as manifested in their inclination to feast on blood to the fall or to the sinfulness of humans. If he regarded such behavior on the part of eagles as abnormal or as evidence of disorder in the world, he gave no such indication in this sermon. The omission is striking in light of the fact that Calvin seemed to regard several features of the animal world as occasioned by the fall, and wherever possible he eagerly remarked that nature was full of pointers to God's displeasure with fallen men and with re- minders of our fallenness. The failure to make a connection between "feasting on blood" and the fallenness of the world at this juncture at least raises the ques- tion whether Calvin had fully thought through the matter of the extent of the fall. From his sermon on Job, we are left with the impression that he may have as- sumed that "bloodthirsty" eagles as we know them are simply a normal part of the creation of God.

Another question concerns the source of Calvin's information about eagles. The powerful, rapid flight and keen eyesight are and were common knowledge. Calvin had undoubtedly observed eagles in the Swiss mountains, but where did he learn about the beaks of old eagles and their presumed habit of throwing young impostors out of the nest? The former bit of information he claimed to have obtained from Aristotle and Pliny. In Book VIII of *History of Animals*, Aristotle had written that the beaks of eagles become increasingly curved as they age so that they die of starvation.[33] In Book X of *Natural History*, Pliny wrote that eagles die of hunger when their upper mandibles grow and become so hooked that they can no longer open their mouths.[34] And what of rejecting a young eagle that cannot stare at the Sun? One may legitimately doubt that Cal- vin had ever witnessed the alleged event but had derived the idea from classical writers. Pliny had written that sea-eagles beat their young until they gaze straight at the sun. A parent that notices one of the young birds blinking with watery eyes ejects it from the nest as illegitimate. In contrast, the eaglet that can stare straight at the light will continue to be raised.[35]

There is also reason to believe that some of Calvin's beliefs about eagles may have been derived from the bestiaries of the Middle Ages. Because of Cal- vin's possible dependence on bestiaries, a brief digression on the nature of the bestiary at this juncture is in order. This literary genre descended from an anonymous collection of tales about the characteristics of animals that was enti- tled *Physiologus* (The Naturalist), a work that originated around Alexandria in Egypt during the second century A. D.[36] Many of the stories in *Physiologus*, drawn from eastern Mediterranean folklore, had already been recorded by clas- sical writers like Aristotle, Pliny, and Seneca, and were, according to Florence McCulloch, widely known in the ancient world.[37] The entry for each animal in this compilation included information about observed physical and behavioral characteristics, popular lore, fable, and myth to which were added Christian moral lessons. According to McCulloch, scholars in that period preferred alle- gorical exegesis of the Scriptures and examined creatures to see what the might reveal of God's hidden power and wisdom.[38]

Physiologus was translated from Greek into Latin. Excerpts made their way into the writings of both Greek and Latin church fathers. Eventually *Physiologus* was translated into several vernacular languages. The medieval bestiaries that may have been familiar to Calvin descended from Latin versions of *Physiologus* that had been amplified by embellishments of the original entries and by incor- poration of lore about additional animals. These accretions were drawn from

Near Eastern, classical, and early Christian sources such as Ambrose's *Hexameron* or Isidore of Seville's *Etymologies*. Bestiaries might include as many as 100 different entries. No distinctions were made among fishes, birds, reptiles, and mammals. David Lindberg has characterized these bestiaries as an odd mixture of facts, fancy, and parables.[39] Very elaborate and colorful illustrations of the animals employing a profusion of bright metallic green, blue, red, and gold were added to later editions of *Physiologus* and became a routine feature of medieval bestiaries. Most of the medieval bestiaries were compiled in the twelfth and thirteenth centuries. Beryl Rowland has stated that the function of the bestiary was much like that of a sermon—to imprint indelibly on the mind Christian doctrine and ethics by means of illustrations and gripping stories.[40] Medieval bestiaries also became popular sources for sermon writers. It made sense that Calvin, as a preacher, might also make good use of this source of sermonic illustrations. Because bestiaries existed in several languages, including at least four versions in French, it is reasonable to assume that Calvin was exposed to some of the contents of *Physiologus* or of French bestiaries during his early education.

A couple of the bestiaries pick up on Pliny's claim that the eagle's upper beak grows so large with age that its eating is hindered. An *Aviarium* (book of birds) repeated Isidore's assertion that the eagle gets its name from the sharpness of its eyesight and then goes on to tell the story about the eagle being able to gaze directly at the Sun and holding up its young by the claws to see if they can look at the Sun. One beautifully illustrated thirteenth-century bestiary has this to say about the eagle:

> It is also said of the eagle that it tests its young by putting them into the sun's rays while it holds them in its claws in mid-air. In this way the young eagle which looks fearlessly at the sun without harming its eyesight proves that it is the true offspring of its race. If it looks away, however, it is at once dropped, because it is a creature unworthy of so great a father: just as it was unworthy of being carried up, so it is unworthy of being reared. The eagle carries out the sentence without any bitterness in its nature, but as an impartial judge. He does not turn from his own young, but refuses to accept a stranger.[41]

But there are other birds to consider. As already noted, Calvin referred to the migratory habit of storks in discussing Jeremiah 8:7. Because Job 39:13 says that the pinions and feathers of the ostrich are not comparable to those of the stork, he also took the occasion in his second sermon on that chapter to talk about the stork, another bird with which he was undoubtedly familiar. Both the white stork (*Ciconia ciconia*) and the black stork (*Ciconia nigra*) nest throughout portions of Europe after migrating from Africa. The white stork is the common stork of the Holy Land, but the black stork is also present.[42] Both species were more common and widespread in the past. The Hebrew term for stork is *chasidah*, literally meaning "kindness," perhaps an allusion to the stork's legendary parental instincts. In his sermon, Calvin suggested that the author of Job spoke about storks in order "to bring us to the reasonableness that is in them; for there is more kindness to be found in them, than there is oftentimes in men. For when the young storks are grown great, they reknowledge their dams and feed them in their old age, to requite that which they did to them in their youth."[43] The alleged kindly behavior of the younger generation of storks toward their aging parents then provided Calvin a springboard from which to launch a scathing indictment of ungrateful children. Although storks are known to be very solicitous parents, the kindness of stork offspring toward their parents in their old age has not been substantiated. Where, then, did Calvin get this idea? Here again we detect the influence of classical writers and the bestiaries. Pliny said that storks "nourish their parents' old age," and Aristotle wrote that "it is commonly reported of the storks that they are fed in return by their young."[44] Likewise, the *Aviarium*, following Isidore of Seville, made similar remarks.[45] A thirteenth-century English bestiary recorded that "the same length of time that they spend bringing up their young is spent in return by their offspring in caring for the parents."[46]

In Job 39, the stork was mentioned by way of contrast with the ostrich. Because that bird is described at some length in verses 13 through 18, Calvin devoted several sentences to these great birds in his second sermon on Job 39. Although now native only to Africa, the ostrich (*Struthio camelus*) formerly had a much wider range, extending into the Middle East and other parts of Asia during Calvin's day and even more so during biblical times.[47] The ostrich would have been familiar to educated Europeans from the medieval bestiaries and from Pliny's *Natural History*. Some kings who exchanged exotic animals as gifts may have known the ostrich firsthand. French royalty and nobility, who maintained menageries in Paris and elsewhere, may have been acquainted with ostriches. Just when zoological collections became available for viewing by the general public is not clear, however, so we do not know if Calvin ever saw an ostrich. He certainly had heard and read enough about them to be amazed by this peculiar bird. He may have seen illustrations of ostriches, albeit rather inaccurate ones, in some of the bestiaries. In his sermon, Calvin repeatedly described the ostrich as a "birdbeast," a nimble creature that is "half bird of the air and half beast of the earth."[48] Interestingly, the twelfth-century French bestiary compiled by Philippe de Thaon contains 23 entries on beasts and several more on birds, but the ostrich was listed as a beast.[49] Were Calvin's conceptions of the ostrich partly shaped by ideas drawn from the bestiaries?

The ostrich, Calvin said, has a weighty body and cannot fly, but it is so fast that a man cannot overtake it by running. It is faster than horses or any other beasts. Not only is the ostrich an extremely fast runner, but this birdbeast can also gather up stones by the way and throw them backward at those who might be following. Thus, the foolishness of the ostrich was said to be matched by its "advisedness" in gathering and casting stones at pursuers. The foolishness of the ostrich, said Calvin, could be seen in the fact that the birds "hide their heads and think that all their body is hidden despite the fact that their huge carcass can still be seen."[50] Moreover, because ostriches live in hot countries they do not sit on their eggs but hide them in the sand and let the Sun warm them. Following the biblical text, Calvin was under the impression that ostriches are very poor parents. He repeated this perception in his comments on Lamentations 4:3 by saying that ostriches are "very stupid because as soon as they lay an egg, they forget the egg and leave it."[51] Despite the supposed foolishness of ostriches, he perceived in their behavior evidence of a wonderful work of God in guiding them.

Calvin repeated some widely held misconceptions about this remarkable bird. Despite the popular myth that persists to this day, ostriches do not hide their heads in the sand. This alleged behavior may have come to be accepted as fact in part because the young birds, in order to escape danger, attempt to disguise themselves by sitting flush on the ground and spreading out their wings to maximum extent. Pliny's comment, one that Calvin may have read, about the "stupidity" of the ostrich "in thinking that it is concealed when it has hidden its neck among bushes, in spite of the great height of the rest of its body," may also have contributed to the misconception.[52]

Calvin's comments about ostriches picking up stones to throw at pursuers is quite strange. He did not seem at all baffled by the incongruity of a speedy ostrich wasting time to cast stones at pursuers. This peculiar belief may derive in part from the fact that ostriches, like the gallinaceous birds such as turkeys, pheasants, quail, and grouse, swallow stones of various sizes to grind up their food for better digestion. Given that the ostrich is a very large bird, it swallows pebbles that are capable of grinding the large amounts of vegetation that it has eaten. Thus, ostriches do pick up pebbles, but in view of their incredible speed there is little likelihood that they pick up stones to throw at anyone. Calvin sounds as if he thought the ostrich might have picked up and hurled stones at pursuers with its beak, but possibly he had in mind the statement of Pliny that the "cloven talons" of the ostrich foot were "useful for grasping stones which when in flight it flings with its feet against its pursuers."[53] Now the observational basis for Calvin's expression becomes somewhat clearer, because a fast-running ostrich streaking across desert floor would very likely unintentionally kick up rocks and pebbles that might accidentally be propelled backward. The fact that Calvin referred to the casting of stones as "advisedness," however, suggests that he thought this action was intentional and deliberate. Even Pliny's statement hints at intentional action by the ostrich, and in all likelihood, Calvin was influenced by Pliny on this point.

We must also consider the matter of the poor parenting skills of the ostrich. Calvin, of course, was unaware of documented evidence that ostriches are protective and solicitous parents. Ostriches lay their eggs on the ground in a slightly hollowed out depression out in the open. Several females may lay their eggs in the one nest, but the dominant female and her mate end up caring for the entire lot although her own eggs get preferential treatment. The secondary females leave the scene after laying their eggs, knowing instinctively that their eggs will be cared for. The dominant female faithfully tends the eggs, rolling them over from time to time with her beak to prevent them from boiling in the Sun, and sitting on them a great deal or shading them with her wings. The male stands guard as she does so and also feeds in the neighborhood. When the female is hungry she will go off to forage while the male cares for the nest. The parents are also extremely protective of the large, ungainly chicks after the eggs are hatched. Only on rare occasions do both parents leave the nest temporarily to satisfy their hunger. It is then that predators like hyenas or curious baboons might seek to raid the nest. In some cases, the ostrich may desert its eggs to serve as a decoy in the hopes that a potential predator will be tempted to follow the adult bird and leave the eggs alone. The alleged foolishness of the ostrich seems to be apparent foolishness only. Although some of the actions of ostrich parents might be perceived as foolish, the overall parenting skills of ostriches seem to stand in contrast to the portrayals of Job 39 and Lamentations 4, thus raising interesting questions about the proper understanding of these texts. We will revisit this puzzle in the final chapter.

Of course, the biblical texts alone were probably sufficient to convince Calvin that the ostrich is a foolish parent, but his idea may have been reinforced by the bestiaries. Some versions of the bestiary, including the thirteenth-century book of beasts, say this regarding the ostrich: "When, in about the month of June, it sees those stars [i.e., the Pleiades], it digs in the earth, lays its eggs, and covers them in sand. When it gets up from that place, it at once forgets them and never returns to its eggs."[54] Not quite so.

As with the blood-eating eagles, Calvin made no reference whatever to the foolish character of the ostrich in its egg-laying and the subsequent danger to which the eggs were exposed as being a result of the curse that God pronounced at the time of the fall. He wrote as if this situation were an original creation of God. God did not endow the ostrich with wisdom, says the Lord in Job 39:18. The implication of such a view is that the original creation did contain some violence and death. Either Calvin did not recognize this implication, was comfortable with the implication, or did not think through the issue in detail.

Calvin briefly mentioned other birds in his sermons on Job and throughout the commentaries. Doves, he said, are fearful, but goshawks are hardy. Swans are large birds, but unlike eagles, they are not birds of prey. Understandably, he was very impressed by the spectacular plumage of the peacock, a bird imported from Asia that he might have seen on the grounds of the nobility and royalty of France. In his second sermon on Job 39, he asked his parishioners to use their imaginations to "look upon a peacock's feather," suggesting that even they had seen peacocks before. He then asserted that the peacock feather is characterized by such wonderful workmanship that we would not know what to say about it "but only to glorify God." Even the unbelievers, he said, are compelled to glorify God in response to viewing the peacock feather. And if that is the effect of a single feather, how much more should the entire world lead us to glorify God. "If one feather of a peacock ravish," Calvin preached, and hold us as it were in a gaze at it, what shall all the workmanship which appears in the whole world do?"[55]

In his first sermon on Job 39 Calvin also observed that when ravens are hungry, the mothers fly off to seek their prey, and sometimes they find none. "In the meanwhile their young ones are half starved, and nobody provides for them.

Now is God feign to put to his helping hand, whether it be by giving them worms to jab at, or by some other secret means. Thus you see how the young ravens do cry unto God."[56]

Zephaniah 2:14 (New International Version) describes the desolation that God will bring on Nineveh and Assyria: "flocks and herds will lie down there, creatures of every kind. The desert owl and the screech owl will roost on her columns." The King James Version translated the verse as saying that "the cormorant and the bittern shall lodge there." The Hebrew term *kippohd* was translated "bittern" in the King James Version and as "owl" in the New International Version. Another Hebrew word *kippohz* is used but once in the entire Old Testament and appears in Isaiah 34:15. This term was translated as "great owl" in the King James Version. Clearly, the two Hebrew words are very similar to each other, perhaps contributing to the conflicting translations (bittern vs. owl) in the two versions noted above. The claim has also been made that the meaning of the word *kippohd* is uncertain. The Revised Standard Version has even translated the word as "hedgehog." Some scholars point out that a reference to the bittern, a common but secretive, stocky heron of the marshes of the Tigris River, would make sense in the context of an allusion to Nineveh, a city on the Tigris.[57] Calvin understood the word *kippohd* as a reference to the bittern and commented that "the bitterns, or the storks, or the cuckoos, and similar wild birds would be there. As to their various kinds, I make no laborious research."[58]

Mammals

Although the biblical text teems with allusions to mammals, e.g., lions, horses, cattle, sheep, goats, swine, foxes, dogs, camels, rabbits, conies, hyraxes, bear, and much else, Calvin said nothing out of the ordinary about most of them. He did, however, leave us with some fascinating comments about elephants, wolves, deer, and even unicorns! We begin with the elephants. Calvin included a reference to these great beasts in his commentary on Seneca's *De Clementia*, quoting a passage from Pliny the Elder to the effect that when an elephant notices a human footprint, it trembles in fear of an ambush, sniffs for the scent, breathes forth fury, and rather than trampling the footprint, digs it up and passes it on with a message to the next elephant and so on down to the end of the line of elephants.[59] Calvin claimed that this testimony from Pliny confirmed a statement by Seneca to the effect that elephants and lions pass by what they have stricken down. He expressed no misgivings about the validity of Pliny's assertion.

The second sermon on Job 40 contains the most intriguing claims about elephants that Calvin uttered. In that sermon, he was confronted with the need to guess the identity of *behemoth*. Job 40 suggests that *behemoth* is a large aquatic vegetarian animal, perhaps the hippopotamus, an animal now restricted to the rivers of Africa, but whose range in the past was considerably greater than it is today. How much Calvin knew about the hippopotamus is open to question. In any case, he did not identify *behemoth* with a hippopotamus. Nor can *behemoth* be an ox, because the text says that *behemoth* eats hay like an ox. Thus, in Calvin's judgment, the author of Job drew a distinction between *behemoth* and oxen. He did not think *behemoth* was a horse either. He opted for the elephant on the grounds of the "hugeness" of its body. He saw the elephant as an enormous, imposing, frightening animal that cannot help but arrest our attention. We ought to be afraid of elephants, he opined, just by looking at them because they are so big. The elephant is a "terrible huge beast that is enough to scare us out of our wits." Elephants are so unusual that they seem to be "made by art and not by nature." God created elephants not only to show us his wonderful order but also so that we would feel humbled by comparison to the elephant's massive bulk and thus be induced to worship God's majesty.

Calvin said that an elephant is so strong that it can strike down a "great sort of men" with one stroke of its foot. He marveled that elephants don't devour us all. They could execute such cruelty as to root out all mankind from the world, but God has tempered these great beasts so that they feed on grasses in the mountains, hide themselves under the shadow of trees, and don't break out into the kind of rage of which their size suggests that they are capable. God tames them and gives us room to dwell on the Earth. Given their great strength, one might think that elephants could rule over us, but instead they allow themselves to be ruled by men like little colts in a stable. However, God has left elephants destitute of many things. For example, elephants cannot bow their legs. They must stand up continually because if an elephant falls down on the ground it cannot get up again on its own power.[60]

Curiously, Calvin never mentioned the trunks, tusks, or large, floppy ears of elephants. Whether he ever saw an elephant we do not know. His failure to mention such striking features as the trunk and tusks suggests that he had not, for surely these characters make an indelible impression as much as the great mass of the animal. He may have seen illustrations of elephants in bestiaries. He almost certainly read about them in Pliny's *Natural History* where he would have encountered the author's description of the ways in which elephants were used by the Romans. He also undoubtedly knew of the use of elephants in warfare by Hannibal's army. The assertion about the inability of a fallen elephant to arise, however, indicates that Calvin had some familiarity with the folk tales repeated in the bestiaries. Neither Aristotle nor Pliny, to my knowledge, referred to the tale about fallen elephants. On the other hand, several versions of bestiaries do include this story. The thirteenth-century English bestiary, for example, claimed that the elephant's

> nature is such that, if he falls down, he cannot stand up again. Yet he will fall if he leans against a tree in order to sleep. For he has no joints in his knees, and the hunter cuts a little way into the tree, so that as soon as the elephant leans against it, he falls with the tree. When he falls, he trumpets loudly, and at once a huge elephant comes, but is unable to lift him. Then they both trumpet together, and twelve elephants come and are unable to lift him. They all trumpet,

and at once a little elephant appears and puts his trunk under the large elephant, and lifts him up.[61]

The fallen elephant was said to represent fallen man. The twelve elephants represent the law and the prophets, and the small elephant represents the Lord Jesus Christ who humbled himself to raise up the human race.[62] Here the difficulties of fallen elephants are linked to their allegedly unbendable, stiff legs, undoubtedly what Calvin had in mind when he mentioned their inability to bow their legs. Although Aristotle rejected the idea that elephants sleep standing against trees and maintained that the animal's hind legs can bend, the classical geographer Strabo wrote that the elephant's leg has a continuous, unbending bone. At what point belief in the rigid hind leg became connected to the story about elephants being unable to get up is not known for certain. As earlier noted, the bestiaries were intended to entertain and provide instruction in doctrinal and moral matters. Yet Calvin did not follow through in this sermon with any theological or moral lessons drawn from the bestiary in regard to fallen elephants. He simply threw out the statement, presumably common "knowledge" to his congregation, and left it at that. One gets the impression that Calvin assumed the factual correctness of the story about fallen elephants.

Calvin wrote that the wolf is a rapacious animal. When the wolf ranges about all day seeking in vain what it might devour, then in the evening hunger kindles its rage. There is, therefore, nothing more dreadful than hungry wolves. Unless they find some prey during the evening, they become all the more furious.[63] In another passage, Calvin said that the judges of Israel were like evening wolves in that wolves become furious in the evening when they have been roaming about all day and have found nothing to satisfy their hunger. "As their want sharpens the savageness of wolves," Calvin wrote, "so the Prophet says that the judges were hungry like evening wolves, whose hunger renders them furious."[64]

In the first four verses of Job 39, God poses a series of questions about the birthing habits of animals such as mountain goats, deer, and bear. In preaching about these verses in his first sermon on Job 39, Calvin briefly talked about deer. Unlike human mothers, he said, the brute beasts don't know what they are bearing when they are great with young. They only feel a cumbersome burden, and they may even be so grieved by the situation as to rush their bellies against something to "make their young one slink." The struggling of the young ones within them may even cast them into despair. Nevertheless, despite the fact that their "fruit" is heavy and troublesome, God preserves both the pregnant mother and its offspring almost as if it were a miracle. The red deer, for example, "cannot endure their own fatness" during pregnancy. If the does grow too fat, they will fast because they cannot bear with anything that hinders them. Still the doe carries its young with great pain. Calvin preached that the red deer are said to experience exceedingly great pain and grief during birth. The does position themselves as if they would "cleave asunder and strain themselves exceeding sore." The straining of the deer during birthing is much greater than that of women. The pain is so great that those who know about the secrets of nature say that the does use a certain herb as a medicine to help themselves deliver. Otherwise the birth process would come to a near standstill if they didn't take something to hasten their deliveries. Calvin marveled that the doe had no physician and had not learned in school the "skill to seek out an herb, and to know that it is expedient for their deliveries" and "for the voiding of their young ones out of their bodies." He also reported that does go a full eight months from the time that males and females go to rut until the time of delivery.[65]

There is little question that Calvin's views on deer were shaped by Pliny's comments. Pliny stated that the pregnancy of deer lasts eight months. He further wrote that "the females before giving birth use a certain plant called hartwort as a purge, so having an easier delivery." He made no reference, as Calvin had, to the pain and discomfort of deer pregnancy *per se* or to deer beating their bellies to relieve the discomfort. The only reference in Pliny to fat deer was to the males who, after gorging themselves at the conclusion of rutting season, "when they feel they are too fat, they look for lairs to hide in, showing that they are conscious of inconvenient weight."[66] Aristotle, too, mentioned the fatness of the bucks and noted that the gestation period of the mother is eight months.[67] Had Calvin simply relied on his memory of what he had once read about deer and transposed the reference about fatness from the males to the pregnant females? These claims about deer made by Aristotle, Pliny, and Calvin are generally lacking in the bestiaries.

Mythical Creatures, Animal Morality, and Hybrids

In accord with the perceptions of his era, Calvin also accepted the existence of the unicorn. Because the unicorn is a small beast, he said in his second sermon on Job 39, it has "nor more but a certain nimbleness in him, keeps always his sturdiness, insomuch that all the men in the world cannot by their cunning and strength bring him to subjection." Oxen and horses may be tamed, but not the unicorn. Because the unicorn cannot be tamed, we cannot use this animal "to our commodity." Even though the unicorn is "strong and light," it will not "till the earth at our pleasure, or draw the plough." Calvin considered our inability to bring the unicorn into subjection as an evidence of our fallen nature. "We should have reigned peaceably over all beasts," he preached, "if we had not been unthankful to our God, in breaking the allegiance which we owe unto him. That then is the cause why we be bereft of the lordship and sovereignty which was given us over all beasts." He envisioned our struggles to tame lions and unicorns as a means by which God subdued our pride. But, he continued, God can just as easily make a mockery of our pride by very small creatures: "God needs not to arm the lions or unicorns but can give us battle by lice and fleas if he thinks good and so make a scorn of all our pride."[68] Calvin probably drew his conception of the unicorn from medieval bestiaries where the fabulous creature is frequently mentioned in terms of characteristics borrowed from a variety of real creatures. The difficulty in capturing the unicorn was typically stressed in the bestiaries. The thirteenth-century English book of beasts says that the unicorn "is also called rhinoceros in Greek" but then goes on to describe an entirely different creature from what we know as the rhinoceros. The unicorn, it says, "is a little beast, not unlike a young goat, and extraordinarily swift. It has a horn in the middle of its brow, and no hunter can catch it."[69] The illustration that accompanies the description in the bestiary shows a deer-like animal with a single very long horn suggesting that the idea of the unicorn may have originated with sightings of various sorts of very swift antelope species on the plains of eastern Africa and then later conflated with the rhinoceros.

Calvin also seems to have accepted the existence of other mythological creatures. He referred to fauns and satyrs, creatures that were believed to look like hairy humans with beards and broad tails. Isaiah 13:21 promised a punishment of Babylon that would result in such devastation that the city would be desolated and inhabited by desert creatures, including jackals, owls, and wild goats. Calvin translated this text in terms of wild beasts of the desert, doleful creatures, owls, and satyrs (*Satyri*). He wrote that "the devil performs strange tricks by means of fauns and satyrs, and on that account their names are given to him."[70] This is not the only place where Calvin talked about such "creatures." The passage in Isaiah 34 that describes the desolating punishment of Edom also includes references to various wild animals having free reign. Verse 14 refers to creatures whose identity is not certain. Calvin noted that "it is not fully agreed what is the exact meaning of the Hebrew words" and pointed out that various commentators had referred to fauns, screech owls, goblins, and satyrs. Although acknowledging that "we cannot absolutely determine whether the Prophet means witches, or goblins, or satyrs and fauns," Calvin also maintained that "it is universally agreed that these words denote animals which have the shape of men." Presumably he assumed that some creature along these lines was intended. He referred again to the role of the devil in regard to these beings: "we see also what various delusions are practiced by Satan, what phantoms and hideous monsters are seen, and what sounds and noises are heard."[71] It appears that Calvin was under the impression that the powers of darkness might invent strange creatures to deceive and terrify people who found themselves in extremely desolate, isolated places.

We saw earlier that Calvin uncritically accepted Seneca's reference to creatures that could scorch vegetation with their breath. In fact, he made his own reference to such fire-breathing creatures in discussing Isaiah 5:10. This text refers to a vineyard that would produce a pitifully small amount of wine in the context of judgment pronounced on God's vineyard. Calvin noted here that God had cursed the soil as a punishment for the extortions of men. "These men," he asserted, "destroy the fruits of the earth by their extortions." In that respect, those guilty of extortion resembled "certain animals that by their breath, scorch the branches, and wither the corn."[72] He did not name the animal, but he may have had in mind the basilisk, another mythical creature of deadly characteristics. The thirteenth-century bestiary claimed that the basilisk has a fiery breath. In some bestiaries, it was alleged that no bird can fly away unharmed from the sight of a basilisk because the bird will be consumed by fire from the mouth of the beast.[73] There is no hint that Calvin considered this animal to be purely imaginary. One additional reference to the basilisk occurs in the commentary on Jeremiah 8:17, but there he made no mention of a scorching breath.

Despite his occasional portrayals of furious, savage animals, whether a real animal like the wolf or an imaginary beast like the animal that can wither corn with its breath, Calvin's acceptance of the doctrine of the depravity of the human race was so firm that he also virtually envisioned animals, despite the ferocity of many of them, as living on a higher moral plane than human beings. He clearly relished likening human beings either to some of the less desirable animals or to some of the less desirable traits of animals. As is well known, Calvin's theological opponents particularly were frequent targets of zoological epithets. In the tract *Contre le Sect Phantastique et Furieuse des Libertins* he compared the Libertines to a variety of wild beasts. And how often he spoke of his opponents as "barking dogs!" Calvin was always looking for creative, vivid, memorable ways to describe the utter depravity of human beings. And yet, he considered humans as even worse than the animals with which he so often compared them.

Isaiah 9:19 refers to God's wrath against Israel as a scorching of the land. The people of Israel are portrayed as the fuel for the fire. During this judgment, "no one," says the text, "will spare his brother." Calvin used this verse as an opportunity to rail against human cruelty. "The beasts themselves," he wrote, "are restrained by similarity of nature from cruelty against their own kind; for a wolf does not devour a wolf, and a bear does not devour a bear."[74] Calvin undoubtedly picked up this notion from the classical authors. In *De Clementia* Seneca had written that lions, bears, and serpents are "devoid of reason and condemned by us on the charge of bestial cruelty, yet spare their kind, and even among wild beasts likeness of habits and kind forms a safeguard; but among men tyrants do not withhold their fury even from their kin."[75] In his brief commentary on this passage, Calvin noted that Pliny the Elder had made similar observations. According to Pliny, "all other living creatures pass their time worthily among their own species . . . the fierceness of lions is not directed against lions; the serpent's bite attacks not serpents; even the monsters of the sea and the fishes are only cruel against different species; whereas to man, I vow, most of his evils come from his fellow man."[76] Calvin provided similar observations from Juvenal, Quintilian, Horace, and Augustine. Of course, he never observed Tasmanian devil mothers eating their excess babies, male crocodiles consuming their own offspring, male sea horses devouring some of their unfortunate progeny, or hippopotami and elephant seals fighting over females or turf. Many animal taxa are not quite so lacking in cruelty to their own kind as Calvin and the classical authors may have suspected.

Calvin also disapproved of the hybridization of animals. Genesis 36:24, a portion of a listing of the descendants of Esau, mentions Anah as one of the sons of Zibeon. In the New International Version, Anah is said to have discovered hot springs in the desert while grazing his father's donkeys. There is, however, some uncertainty over the meaning of the Hebrew term *yehmeem* that is translated as "hot springs," in part because that word occurs only once in the Old Testament. Both Calvin and the King James Version translated the Hebrew word as "mules." Thus, Anah found "mules" in the desert, but not "hot springs." Whether Calvin's rendering is correct or not, he expressed his opinion about mules in commenting on the text. Mules, he said, are the "adulterous offspring" of the horse and the ass. He even claimed that Moses said that Anah was the author of this "connection." He did not think that Moses' statement was made to praise Anah's industry,

> for the Lord has not in vain distinguished the different kinds of animals from the beginning. But since the vanity of the flesh often solicits the children of this world, so that they apply their minds to superfluous matters, Moses marks this unnatural pursuit in Anah, who did not think it sufficient to have a great number of animals; but he must add to them a degenerate race produced by unnatural intercourse. There is more moderation among brute animals in following the law of nature, than in men, who invent vicious admixture.[77]

Calvin was, no doubt, unaware that on rare occasions different species of animals interbreed without any human intervention. At present, for example, there is considerable concern that the koloa (Hawaiian duck), found primarily on the island of Kauai, may eventually lose its identity through interbreeding with the mallard. Several different species of gulls, too, frequently interbreed.

Invertebrates

Calvin had relatively little to say of significance about invertebrates. There are, of course, biblical passages that refer to plagues of flies and locusts and prophetic texts that allude to infestations of insect pests. Calvin commented on many of these texts but said little beyond what the text itself states. His most extensive comments about insects are found in two places. The first of these is in the commentary on Seneca's *De Clementia*. After commending the quality of clemency in a king, Seneca remarked that nature had conceived the idea of kingship and provided a kind of example of how a king should behave. He described the role of a king bee (a drone) in the beehive. Unlike the smaller worker bees, the king had no stinger because nature did not wish the king to be cruel. Seneca thought that great kings should find a pattern here for their own behavior. He maintained that it would be shameful not to learn a lesson from the ways of these little creatures. In commenting on Seneca's passage, Calvin adduced quotations from Pliny the Elder, Virgil, and Varro about the habits of bees in protecting and defending their king and of their utter confusion when the king is lost or hurt. He quoted Columella on the physical characteristics of king bees and other authors about the stinging capabilities of bees. He noted that it was a matter of controversy whether the king has a stinger or not. According to Pliny, those who dispute the existence of the king's stinger were agreed on the point that the king did not use his stinger. Aristotle thought the king had a stinger but that it was unsuited for combat. Calvin did not know whether the king bee had a stinger and was content to interpret Seneca as saying that the king bee does not have "a sting effective to do harm, lest he should be cruel or desirous of vengeance."[78]

A second major reference to invertebrates is in the commentary on Isaiah 7:18-19, a passage stating that "the LORD will whistle for flies from the distant streams of Egypt and for bees from the land of Assyria." Calvin wrote that there is a connection between "the climate of those kingdoms of which he speaks" and the various insects. "Egypt abounds in flies," he said, "because the country is hot and marshy; and when the air is both hot and moist, there must be produced a great abundance of flies." By way of contrast, Assyria "abounded in bees; and when he says that he will bring them by a hiss, he alludes to the natural habits of bees and flies." Calvin went on to observe that "bees commonly seek nests for themselves in caverns, or valleys and bushes, and such like places."[79]

Plants

Calvin also had little to say that conveys a sense of the scientific conceptions of plant life in his day. Of some interest are a few brief remarks about mildew in connection with Haggai 2:15-19, a passage in which Yahweh is said to have sent mildew and hail as warnings upon the people of God. Calvin wrote that "Irkun [the Hebrew term *yehrahkohn*] is mildew, or a moist wind, from which mildew proceeds; for we know that corn, when it has much wet, contracts mildew when the sun emits its heat." He then suggested that when "famine happens only from the cold or from the heat, it may be ascribed to chance or to the stars." He recognized that there are "ordinary" famines that the majority of people might be tempted to explain strictly in terms of natural processes, including the influence of the stars. He went on, however, to argue that famine, whether its cause is a natural scourge such as heat, hail, or mildew, should lead us to acknowledge God's wrath and to recognize that the Lord intends through that famine to correct our neglect.[80] Elsewhere, Calvin intimated that the stars might indeed have some effect on the behavior of plants. In *A Warning against Judiciary Astrology* he commented that "the stars are signs which show us the season to plant or to sow."[81] The fact that he conceded the influence of heavenly bodies on animal and human life indicates that he was not averse to accepting some degree of their influence on plants as well. Nevertheless, it may be that he simply recognized the close connection between the seasons of the year and the positions of the stars without implying that the positions of the stars *per se* exerted a physical influence on plant growth.

Trees are mentioned in the commentary on Isaiah 6:13, a verse that refers to the *terebinth* and oak trees. Calvin said that the biblical "casting of leaves" referred to the throwing down of leaves which takes place when trees are stripped of their leaves as of their garment; for trees, in that state of nakedness, appear to be dry and withered; though there remains in them a hidden vigor, through which they are at length quickened by the returning mildness of the season.

He viewed this phenomenon as a "spiritual grace of God in the very order of nature" that served to confirm us in faith. For him, the behavior of trees served to illustrate the restoration of the church.

In the same vein, he compared the sowing of the corn to the resurrection.[82] Similar thoughts were expressed in regard to herbs of the meadow. The occasion for these thoughts was provided by Isaiah 26:19, "but your dead men will live, their bodies will rise. You who dwell in dust, wake up and shout for joy. Your dew is like the dew of the morning; the earth will give birth to her dead." Both the King James Version and Calvin understood the text as referring to "the dew of the herbs." Evidently, the Hebrew can bear either meaning: "the dew of the morning" or "the dew of the herbs." The herbs, Calvin noted, dry out in winter and are completely dead as far as all outward appearance is concerned. Still, the concealed roots imbibe dew at the return of spring, put forth their vigor, and grow green again.[83] He applied the metaphor of plant growth to the nation of Israel regaining its former vigor after being plentifully watered with the dew of the grace of God, even though the nation appeared to be completely withered and decayed.

Calvin provided just a tiny glimmer of scientific thinking in his treatment of Isaiah 18:4: "For so the Lord said to me, I will take my rest, and I will consider my dwelling-place like a clear heat upon herbs, and like a cloud of dew in the heat of harvest." He interpreted the text as "heat that dries up the rain" (*calor siccans pluviam*) and said that such rains were "exceedingly adapted to ripen the fruits." The heat that followed these rains, he said, penetrated the fruits with its force and drove the moisture more inward so that the maturity of the fruit was hastened.[84] He envisioned the heat as driving moisture on the surface of a fruit through the skin into the fruit itself. Although mosses, lichens, and epiphytes can absorb moisture directly from the air, fruit-bearing plants absorb soil moisture through the roots. Increased heat is much more likely to evaporate any moisture on the skin of fruit.

Calvin's treatment of thorns and thistles also deserves notice. Genesis 3:18 states that the ground would "produce thorns and thistles for you." Calvin observed simply that God had declared "that the earth would degenerate from its fertility, and bring forth briers and noxious plants. Therefore, we may know, that whatsoever unwholesome things may be produced, are not natural fruits of the earth, but are corruptions which originate from sin."[85] In this case, he seemed to suggest that thorns are new things introduced into the world as a result of sin, but he did not suggest that the plants on which thorns occur were totally new kinds of plants that had not existed before. He may have conceived of them as deformed versions of originally created plants. In some way, thorns and thistles are corruptions of the original order of nature. But then, in interpreting passages in Isaiah 5 and Hosea 9, Calvin intimated that he understood that thorns and thistles, described in terms of a biblical context of judgment and punishment, arose naturally where formerly inhabited land became uninhabited and, as a result, uncultivated, which is exactly how it is today.[86] A back yard, a garden, or a field that is completely left to itself will, in time, revert to a patch of weeds that will generally choke out some of the desirable flowers and vegetables. That patch of weeds is very likely to include a good many thistles or thickets of brambles. It may be that Calvin understood Genesis 3 in somewhat the same fashion, namely, that fallen humans would fail to cultivate the land in a sufficiently thorough manner as to prevent the appearance of thorny plants. When all is said and done, perhaps it is safe to suggest that Calvin had not really thought through in detail exactly how the organic world changed in response to the fall, just that it did.

The Origin of Animals

In light of the controversial nature of the question of the origin of various organisms in Christian circles, Calvin's observations would be of considerable interest. Unfortunately, he made relatively few comments along this line. In writing about Genesis 1:20, for example, he said that it didn't seem to be consonant with reason that Moses declares birds to have proceeded from the waters. He understood why this biblical statement served as the occasion of calumny on the part of scoffers. In response, however, he asked

> why should it not be lawful for him, who created the world out of nothing, to bring forth the birds out of water? What greater absurdity has the origin of birds from the water than that of the light from darkness. Nevertheless, if we must use physical reasoning in the contest, we know that the water has greater affinity with the air than the earth has.[87]

Calvin did not simply appeal to the raw supernatural power of God to account for the origin of birds. At the very least, his conception entailed God's use of pre-existent material in the creation of birds, and he briefly introduced scientific argument regarding the nature of water and air as suitable media for the origination of birds. He invoked the idea that water has a greater affinity with the element, air, than it does with the element, earth, presumably on account of its fluidity and wetness. In Calvin's mind, it was not foolish to envision the birds, creatures of the air, being fashioned from the element that is most closely related to the air, namely water.

Calvin held that some of the animals that are present in the world today had not been created during the initial week of creation and were not a part of the original good creation. For him, some creatures appeared specifically as a result of Adam's rebellion. His primary assertion in this regard occurs in his discussion of Genesis 2:2, the very passage that refers to the completion of the work of creation prior to the entry of sin. The comments are as follows:

Many things which are now seen in the world are rather corruptions of it than any part of its proper furniture. We must come to this conclusion respecting the existence of fleas, caterpillars, and other noxious insects. In all these, I say, there is some deformity of the world, which ought by no means to be regarded as in the order of nature, since it proceeds rather from the sin of man than from the hand of God. Truly these things were created by God, but by God as an avenger.[88]

Did Calvin regard fleas, caterpillars, and the like as deformities of previously existing animals or did he regard them as *de novo*, *ex nihilo* creations that did not exist in any form before the fall? Because he did not belabor the point it is not entirely certain just what he intended. In any case, he was much more cautious on the point than Luther was. For example, in his *Lectures on Genesis*, Luther's discussion of the work of the fifth day of creation included reflections on "harmful worms or vermin, such as toads, flies, butterflies, among which there is an amazing fertility." He ventured the opinion that generally "the more harmful one is, the greater its fertility is." After promising a more extended discussion of the issue in his lectures on Genesis 3, Luther offered the general view that "at this time those troublesome and harmful creatures were not yet in existence but were brought into being later on out of the cursed earth as a punishment for sin, to afflict us and to compel us to call upon God."[89] Luther observed that the Earth "does not bring forth the good things it would have produced if man had not fallen." And besides all that, the Earth "produces many harmful plants, which it would not have produced, such as darnel, wild oats, weeds, nettles, thorns, thistles. Add to these the poisons, the injurious vermin, and whatever else there is of this kind. All these were brought in through sin."[90]

Although God had brought the "vermin" out of the cursed ground after the fall, Luther also believed that the creator still used spontaneous generation as a method of making some creatures right up to the present. Luther used mice as an example. He agreed that mice gave birth to baby mice, but he also believed that mice could be generated from decayed material by the warmth of the Sun under the guidance of God. "God had to say by his divine power, 'Let a mouse come out of the decay,'" according to Luther. Hence the mouse is a divine creature. He even likened mice to a land bird and envisioned birds as products of a kind of spontaneous generation at the end of wintertime.[91] Fishes, too, he regarded as spontaneously generated in some instances. For example, he mentioned that fishes are "brought into existence directly out of the water. Ponds and lakes generate fish, since we see that carps have been brought forth in ponds in which there were none before."[92] This process, he thought, was much the way it was in the beginning when God spoke the word and the seas teemed with living creatures. Calvin was considerably more cautious than Luther in committing himself to mechanisms of divine creation or to the concept of spontaneous generation.

Effects of the Fall on Animals

For Calvin, the curse upon nature extended beyond the inorganic realm and the lower aspects of the organic world to include the animals, particularly in their relation to human beings to whom they were originally subject. He inferred from the judgment passage of Isaiah 34, which speaks of weeds, brambles, and wild animals taking over the citadels of the kingdom, that "the animals would have continued to be subject and obedient to man, had not his own rebellion deprived him of that power and authority; but when he revolted from God, the animals at the same time began to refuse subjection and to attack him."[93] Of course, Calvin derived his understanding of the distorted relationship between animals and human beings from the Genesis passage that describes the original dominion of humans over the animal realm and the subsequent disruption of that dominion. Conceiving of the original relationship as one of placidity and gentleness toward people, he thought that "the gentleness towards man would have remained also in wild beasts, if Adam, by his defection from God, had not lost the authority he had before received." Unfortunately, ever since Adam rebelled, humanity has "experienced the ferocity of brute animals against himself." Calvin, however, did not teach that the disruption of the relationship extended to the entire animal realm, but only to higher animals, for "Moses speaks only of those animals which approach the nearest to man, for the fishes live as in another world."[94] But then, neither did he teach that the relationship of animals to humans was completely disrupted. Despite their fallen condition and despite the divinely pronounced curse, humans retained some remnant of their original authority and dominion, as indicated by Calvin's observations regarding the renovation of the Earth after the great flood. Even though "the beasts were endued with new ferocity" after the fall, he maintained that there were still "some remains of that dominion over them, which God had conferred on him in the beginning." And he envisioned that God now restrained the wild beasts from being even more ferocious.[95] One very striking passage in which Calvin asserted the notion that the animals have risen up against us comes from the commentary on Hosea. In Hosea 2:18, the prophet proclaims that the Lord would make a covenant between the people of God and the beasts of the field, the birds of the air, and the creatures that move along the ground such that all may lie down in safety. The passage led Calvin to reflect on the tenuous relationship between humans and animals that pertains at present. He observed that now the

wild beasts rise up so rebelliously against us; for otherwise they would have willingly and gently obeyed us. Now since there is this horrible disorder, that brute beasts, which ought to own men as their masters, rage against them, the Lord recalls us here to the first order of nature.

When men repent of their rebellion against God and are restored to a state of favor with him, then the disorder indicated by the disrupted relationship between animals and their human masters will be removed and "the regular order of nature would prevail."[96] The notion of God's restraining the beasts comes clearly to the fore in some of the sermons on the latter chapters of Job where, for example, Calvin was simply astounded that humans are not all swallowed up and trampled under foot by those monstrous beasts, the elephants.

But Calvin did not restrict the effects of the fall on animals to changes in their behavior toward human beings such that humans had lost some of their authority over them. He also saw animals as being direct recipients of God's punishment because of their close linkage to people. Jeremiah 7:20, for example, mentions that God would pour out his wrath on the house of God and its environs and that wrath would be extended not only to humans but also to the beasts, the trees of the field, and the fruit of the ground. The question arises as to why God would punish the innocent, amoral animals. Calvin dealt with the problem by claiming that inasmuch "as the whole world was created for man and for his benefit, it is nothing strange that God's vengeance should extend to innocent animals and to things not endued with reason." The reason is that God inflicts punishment on brute animals and on the fruits of the Earth to show "by extending the symptoms of his wrath to all the elements, how much displeased he is with men." The whole world, he said, bears in some measure the punishment that Adam deserved. He suspected that it was little cause for wonder that God, in order to terrify men, would "daily set before their eyes the various forms of his vengeance as manifested toward animals as well as trees and the fruits of the earth."[97] Similar comments appear in regard to the passage in Jeremiah 21 in which the Lord threatened Zedekiah with the destruction of Jerusalem by the siege of Nebuchadnezzar. Here God promised to "strike down those who live in this city—both men and animals—and they will die of a terrible plague." "It was no wonder," Calvin insisted, "that God's vengeance extended to horses, and oxen, and asses; for we know that all these were created for the use of man." As a result, the point of God's pouring out wrath on animals was "to fill men with greater terrors; for they thus saw oxen and asses, though innocent, involved in the same punishment with themselves."[98]

Calvin also envisioned the relationships among various animals as disturbed in the post-lapsarian world. The messianic passages of Isaiah that speak of the coming kingdom in metaphorical terms of a harmonious relationship between humanity and animals readily lend themselves to the interpretation that such harmonious relationships existed in the Garden of Eden, and to some extent Calvin adhered to the view that a passage like Isaiah 11 teaches that conditions in the future kingdom represent an exact restoration of conditions in the original creation. In this context he saw restored harmony not only between man and animals but also among the various animals. Writing of the text of Isaiah 11 that describes a world in which "the wolf will live with the lamb, the leopard will lie down with the goat, the calf and the lion and the yearling together, and a little child will lead them," Calvin suggested that the passage amounted to a promise of a "blessed restoration of the world." He then claimed that Isaiah was describing "the order which was at the beginning, before man's apostasy produced the unhappy and melancholy change under which we groan." Then he asked the question as to "whence comes the cruelty of brutes, which prompts the stronger to seize and rend and devour with dreadful violence the weaker animals?" There could not have been, in Calvin's view, any discord among the creatures of God if they had remained in their original condition. He concluded that when animals exercised cruelty toward one another such that the weak needed to be protected from the strong, that was an evidence of a disorder in the world that had sprung from the sinfulness of man. Moreover, the fact that straw would be the food of the lion as well as the ox was an indication that "if the stain of sin had not polluted the world, no animal would have been addicted to prey on blood," a claim he did not bring up in his comments on eagles in the third sermon on Job 39. The fruits of the Earth would have provided sufficient food for all, according to the method that God had appointed, Calvin affirmed in reference to Genesis 1:30. From this passage alone it is clear that Calvin regarded the original animal creation as vegetarian. Interestingly, even though he interpreted the passage literally in regard to the original and future condition of animal life, he took the main thrust of the passage metaphorically as referring to the benevolent dispositions of the people of Christ. The redeemed would behave like sheep rather than like lions, he said.

> By these modes of expression he means nothing else than that those who formerly were like savage beasts will be mild and gentle; for he compares violent and ravenous men to wolves and bears which live on prey and plunder, and declares that they will be tame and gentle, so that they will be satisfied with ordinary food, and will abstain from doing any injury or harm.[99]

Calvin briefly touched on the question of death in the animal realm in relation to the fall. In his discussion of the grant of vegetation to men and animals for food described in Genesis 1:29, he noted that some maintained on the basis of this text that it was unlawful for men to eat flesh even until after the deluge, at which time God finally granted the use of flesh. He did not feel that this argument was sufficiently compelling on the grounds that the first men offered sacrifices and did so rightly in that they did not "offer unto God anything except what he has granted to our use." He also noted that men were clothed in skins in which case it was lawful for men to kill animals for their skins. In the end, Calvin adopted an agnostic position, suggesting that we should "assert nothing in this matter."

Although most of his discussion could apply simply to the lawfulness of eating animal flesh and killing animals after the fall, we still need to recognize that Calvin did not find the argument compelling that the eating of flesh was prohibited to pre-fall man by the grant of plants for food mentioned in the Genesis text. The way that Calvin argued the point at least leaves open the possibility that he might have looked favorably, if not on natural animal death before the fall, at least on the death of animals at the hands of humans to whom the use of animals had been given in the mandate to subdue the Earth.[100]

Was Calvin an Evolutionist?

Our discussion of Calvin's ideas about the origin of animals and plants would be incomplete without some attention to the matter of biological evolution. Although Calvin lived long before Lamarck and Darwin and knew nothing of fossils or of the concept of natural selection, the suggestion has nevertheless been made that his thinking about the creation of animals bore an evolutionary character. In other words, it has been alleged that Calvin's conception of origins might have been compatible with the idea of evolutionary development of organisms. Theories of development had been worked up by the Greeks, including Aristotle, and met with relatively little resistance in Christian thinking in the Middle Ages. Was Calvin sympathetic to such theories of development? We now turn to the specific claim that Calvin was an "evolutionist."

The claim in question was made by the Reformed theologian, Benjamin B. Warfield (1851-1921), a professor of didactic and polemic theology at Princeton Theological Seminary who was surprisingly sympathetic to the concept of biological evolution when cast in an appropriately theistic form.[101] Warfield was favorably disposed toward biological evolution in part because of his experience with cattle breeding as a young man on the farm of his father, a noted expert and writer on the subject. Warfield's positive attitude toward biological evolution may have colored his interpretation of Calvin as expressed in a lengthy article on Calvin's doctrine of creation written in 1915 toward the end of his distinguished career.[102] His article deals to a considerable extent with Calvin's views on the creation of angels and the spirit world, but for our purposes we will consider only Warfield's comments regarding Calvin's doctrine of creation of the material world. Warfield based his treatment mainly on material in the *Institutes*.

Warfield argued that Calvin drew a sharp distinction between creation in the strict sense and the perfecting and subsequent government of the world. Creation is an act in which God created the heavens and the earth. Subsequent to that, the gradual molding of the world is a "formation." There is the primal act of creation, and then there are subsequent acts of molding. Warfield thought Calvin restricted the term "creation" in its strict conception to the primal act of creation out of nothing. "God has acted in the specific mode properly called creation only at the initial step of the process," as Warfield interpreted Calvin's view.[103]

Warfield suggested that Calvin's distinction was not the same as is commonly made by Reformed theologians when they used such terms as "first" and "second creation" or "immediate' and "mediate creation." Such distinctions, he claimed, would posit "a sequence of truly creative acts of God throughout the six days" and would entail the idea of subsequent creations from pre-existing material. "It is," he asserted, "precisely this sequence of truly creative acts which Calvin disallows." In this regard, he appealed to Calvin's exegesis of Genesis 1:21, the verse that refers to God's creation of the great sea creatures. He pointed out that Calvin traced the "creation" of these creatures back to the beginning.[104] Calvin stated the following:

God, then, is said to have 'created' the sea monsters and other fishes because the beginning of their 'creation' is not to be reckoned from the moment in which they received their form, but they are comprehended in the universal matter (corpus, corpore) which was made out of nothing.[105]

Warfield, therefore, envisioned Calvin as repudiating mediate creation. Calvin wanted "to preserve to the great word 'create' the precise significance of 'to make out of nothing' and he will not admit that it can be applied to any production in which preexistent material is employed."[106] This desire of Calvin to set aside the notion of mediate creation was then "mediated by the height of his doctrine of providence."[107]

Particularly striking is Warfield's assertion that Calvin's insistent thinking that the works of the six days were not creations includes "only the lower creation, inclusive, no doubt, of the human body." The soul is different, however, and is to be regarded "throughout the whole course of human propagation" as an immediate creation out of nothing. But what is really arresting is Warfield's assertion that "it should scarcely be passed without remark that Calvin's doctrine of creation is, if we have understood it aright, for all except the souls of men, an evolutionary one." The original "indigested mass" was truly created, truly made out of nothing at God's fiat, but then "all that has come into being since—except the souls of men alone—has arisen as a modification of this original world-stuff by means of the interaction of its intrinsic forces." Warfield was as thoroughgoing a theist as was Calvin, so he reassured the reader that these intrinsic forces are not acting apart from God. After all, "Calvin is a high theist, that is supernaturalist, in his ontology of the universe and in his conception of the whole movement of the universe." All the modifications of the world-stuff took place under God's governing hand and ultimately in his will.[108] Nevertheless, these modifications "find their account proximately in second causes, and this is not only evolutionism but pure evolutionism."[109]

Lest we fail to get Warfield's point, he restated it. Calvin, he pointed out, always envisioned second causes as acting in complete concurrence with God's purpose and government. And in the present instance, Calvin

ascribed to second causes as their proximate account the entire series of modifications by which the primal indigested mass called heaven and earth has passed into form of the ordered world which we see, including the original of all forms of life, vegetable and animal alike, inclusive doubtless of the bodily form of man. And this, we say, is a very pure evolutionary scheme.

In Warfield's judgment, however, Calvin had no theory of evolution, even though his conception of world formation was evolutionary. Calvin's interest was to preserve the creative act to immediate production out of nothing. Everything not so produced is evolved. But because Calvin, a child of his times, saw the "evolutionary unfolding process being compressed into a period of six ordinary days, his doctrine of evolution is entirely unfruitful." Now if the doctrine of evolution were to be useful "as an explanation of the mode of production of the ordered world" the six days would need to be lengthened into six periods. If Calvin had done that, Warfield suggested, he "would have been a precursor of the modern evolutionary theorists." But given the times and Calvin's assumption of six ordinary days, he "forms only a point of departure" for the modern evolutionary theorists in that "he teaches as they teach that by the instrumentality of second causes—or as a modern would put it, of intrinsic forces—the original world-stuff was modified into the varied forms which constitute the ordered world."[110]

The question is whether Warfield correctly assessed Calvin's view of creation. The definitive counter interpretation of Calvin's doctrine of creation came from the pen of John Murray (1898-1975), a professor of systematic theology at Westminster Theological Seminary.[111] After laying out in some detail the distinction between immediate and mediate creation in the writings of several Reformed theologians subsequent to Calvin, Murray examined Calvin's teaching about creation, concluding that, although Calvin did not use the expression "mediate creation," he, nevertheless, held to a view that others might have designated by that terminology.

From an examination of Calvin's discussion of Genesis 1:1-2 and Genesis 1:21, the verses on which Warfield based his argument, Murray conceded that Warfield's contention that Calvin taught "pure evolutionism" seemed to be confirmed. For example, regarding Calvin's designation of the originally created heaven and earth as a "confused mass" that served as the "seed" of the whole world, Murray granted that "one is distinctly liable to derive from such a statement as this the impression that the confused mass had inherent in it the potencies or germs which were capable of producing the innumerable variety of things, animate and inanimate."[112] He went on to show, however, that such a conclusion was unwarranted. Murray pointed out that Calvin *did* employ the term "creation" in reference to "an act of God which was subsequent to the creation of the shapeless mass of Genesis 1:1, 2." He further claimed that Calvin did not regard the subsequent ordering of creation over the six days as occurring in response to the outworking of "intrinsic forces." Upon examining Calvin's commentary on Genesis 1:11, Murray showed that Calvin used the term "create" in reference to the production of herbs and trees on the third day and again of the Sun on the fourth day. These were clearly not creations *ex nihilo* but rather formations *ex materia*. In other words, Calvin did not exclusively reserve the term "create" to the initial *ex nihilo* fiat, as Warfield claimed. Beyond that, Murray showed that Calvin taught that new virtue had to be added by God to the originally created earth before it could bring forth plants because it lacked a "germinating principle." Murray contended that Calvin's description "is in no way consonant with the notion that the earth was endowed with certain intrinsic forces which were developed by a process of 'pure evolution.'"[113] Calvin also said that the Earth was not fit to produce anything.

Had Warfield looked more thoroughly at Calvin's Genesis commentary, he would have seen, as Murray made clear, that, although Calvin appeared to define creation as a making of essence out of nothing, he also used the word "create" with great freedom in reference to the successive acts of God in perfecting the heavens and the earth. Nor did Calvin, according to Murray, regard the "unformed mass as containing within itself the living germs and potencies or the intrinsic forces by the development or evolution of which the various forms of life were subsequently produced."[114]

In my judgment, Murray more accurately portrayed Calvin's handling of the concept of creation than did Warfield. We are left with the fact that Warfield, rightly or wrongly, favored a form of providentially directed biological evolution, but we are not warranted in looking to Calvin as some sort of proto-evolutionist.

In summary, Calvin's knowledge of the biological realm was very heavily dependent on the writings of classical authors, particularly Pliny the Elder, Aristotle, and Seneca, but he showed intimations of an acquaintance with the popular tales about animals that were enshrined in various versions of medieval bestiaries. He showed surprisingly little inclination to doubt the deliverances of either the classical writers or the bestiaries. Nowhere did he display the slightest hint of acquaintance with any of the discoveries of animals in the New World, something we might have expected him to allude to in his discussion of the animals on the ark. Calvin was in no danger of being *avant garde* with regard to natural history!

NOTES

1.   On the animals of the Bible, see Roy Pinney, *The Animals of the Bible: The Identity and Natural History of All the Animals Mentioned in the Bible* (Philadelphia: Chilton Books, 1964); George S. Cansdale, *All the Animals of the Bible Lands* (Grand Rapids, Mich.: Zondervan, 1970); and Donald Ray Schwartz, *Noah's Ark: An Annotated Encyclopedia of Every Animal Species in the Hebrew Bible* (Northvale, N.J.: Jason Aronson, 2000).

2.   Aristotle, *Historia Animalium*, 3 vol., trans. A. L. Peck and D. M. Balme, (Cambridge, Mass.: Harvard University Press, 1965, 1970, 1991).

3.   Pliny the Elder, *Natural History*, vol. 3, trans. H. Rackham (Cambridge, Mass.: Harvard University Press, 1940).

4.   Commentary on Leviticus 11. Deuteronomy 14:3-20 incorporates a condensed listing of clean and unclean animals, but Calvin did not discuss this passage either.

5.   Commentary on Genesis 1:21. Calvin wrote here: "God then, it is said, created *whales* (balaenas) and other fishes, not that the beginning of their creation is to be reckoned from the moment in which they received their form; but because they are comprehended in the universal matter which was made out of nothing. So that, with respect to species, form only was then added to them; but creation is nevertheless a term truly used respecting both the whole and the parts." In the same passage Calvin also suggested that the word commonly rendered whales (*tanninim*) might also be properly translated as "tunny fish."

6.   Commentary on Jonah 1:17.

7.   For an overview of Rondelet's life and work, see Jane M. Oppenheimer, "Guillaume Rondelet," *Bulletin of the History of Medicine* 4, (1936): 817-34.

8.   Commentary on Jonah 1:17.

9.   Ford Lewis Battles and Andre Malan Hugo, *Calvin's Commentary on Seneca's De Clementia* (Leiden: E. J. Brill, 1969), 269-75. All future references to this work in the notes will be listed as "Commentary on Seneca." The quotation is from Pliny the Elder, Natural History IX.39.

10.   Commentary on Genesis 1:21.

11.   Commentary on Isaiah 27:1.

12.   Third Sermon on Job 40.

13.   First Sermon on Job 41.

14.   Commentary on Genesis 3:1.

15.   Pelikan, *Luther's Works*, vol. 1, 186-87.

16.   Commentary on Genesis 3:14.

17.   Commentary on Jeremiah 14:6.

18.   Commentary on Lamentations 4:3.

19.   Commentary on Psalm 74:13-14.

20.   Aristotle, *Historia Animalium*, III.20.

21.   Commentary on Seneca, 315.

22.   Commentary on Seneca, 321.

23.   On birds of the Bible, see Virginia C. Holmgren, *Bird Walk through the Bible* (New York: Seabury Press, 1972).

24.   Commentary on Isaiah 10:14.

25.   Commentary on Jeremiah 8:7.

26.   Pelikan, *Luther's Works*, vol. 1, 52.

27. On eagles, see Cansdale, *All the Animals of the Bible Lands*, 142-46 and Pinney, *The Animals of the Bible*, 147-48.

28. On the golden eagle, see Holmgren, *Bird Walk*, 94-98 and Schwartz, *Noah's Ark*, 196-99.

29. On the griffon vulture and other vultures, see Cansdale, *All the Animals of the Bible Lands*, 146; Holmgren, *Bird Walk*, 171-73; Pinney, *The Animals of the Bible*, 148-50; and Schwartz, *Noah's Ark*, 250-53.

30. Commentary on Isaiah 40:31.

31. Commentary on Habakkuk 1:8.

32. Third Sermon on Job 39.

33. Aristotle, *Historia Animalium*, VIII.32.

34. Pliny the Elder, *Natural History*, X.4.

35. Ibid., X.3.

36. Willene B. Clark and Meradith T. McMunn, eds., *Beasts and Birds of the Middle Ages: The Bestiary and Its Legacy* (Philadelphia: University of Pennsylvania Press, 1989). See also Michael J. Curley, trans., *Physiologus* (Austin, Tex.: University of Texas Press, 1979).

37. Florence McCulloch, *Mediaeval Latin and Greek Bestiaries* (Chapel Hill, N.C.: University of North Carolina Press, 1962).

38. Ibid., 17.

39. Lindberg, *The Beginnings of Western Science*, 351-53.

40. Beryl Rowland, "The Art of Memory and the Bestiary," in Clark and McMunn, *Beasts and Birds of the Middle Ages*, 12.

41. Richard Barber, trans., *Bestiary: Being an English Version of the Bodleian Library, Oxford M. S. Bodley 764 with All the Original Miniatures Reproduced in Facsimile* (Woodbridge, Suffolk: The Boydell Press, 1993), 119.

42. On storks, see Cansdale, *All the Animals of the Bible Lands*, 157-58; Holmgren, *Bird Walk*, 63; Pinney, *The Animals of the Bible*, 142-44; and Schwartz, *Noah's Ark*, 211-13.

43. Second Sermon on Job 39.

44. Pliny the Elder, *Natural History*, X.32. and Aristotle, *Historia Animalium*, VIII.13.

45. McCulloch, *Mediaeval Latin and Greek Bestiaries*, 174.

46. Barber, *Bestiary*, 132.

47. On ostriches, see Cansdale, *All the Animals of the Bible Lands*, 190-93; Holmgren, *Bird Walk*, 120-29; Pinney, *The Animals of the Bible*, 136-38; and Schwartz, *Noah's Ark*, 261-66.

48. Second Sermon on Job 39.

49. McCulloch, *Mediaeval Latin and Greek Bestiaries*, 47.

50. Second Sermon on Job 39.

51. Commentary on Lamentations 4:3.

52. Pliny the Elder, *Natural History*, X.1.

53. Ibid.

54. Barber, *Bestiary*, 137.

55. Second Sermon on Job 39

56. First Sermon on Job 39.

57. See discussions by Cansdale, *All the Animals of the Bible Lands*, 147-49, 175, and Pinney, *The Animals of the Bible*, 141-42 and 165-67.

58. Commentary on Zephaniah 2:14.

59. Commentary on Seneca, 119. The passage is from Pliny the Elder, *Natural History*, VIII.5.

60. Second Sermon on Job 40.

61. Barber, *Bestiary*, 41.
62. Ibid., 42.
63. Commentary on Habakkuk 1:8.
64. Commentary on Zephaniah 3:3.
65. First Sermon on Job 39.
66. Pliny, *Natural History*, VIII.50.
67. Aristotle, *Historia Animalium*, VIII.5 and VI.29.
68. Second Sermon on Job 39.
69. Barber, *Bestiary*, 36.
70. Commentary on Isaiah 13:21.
71. Commentary on Isaiah 34:14.
72. Commentary on Isaiah 5:10.
73. Barber, *Bestiary*, 184.
74. Commentary on Isaiah 9:19.
75. Commentary on Seneca, 323-25.
76. Commentary on Seneca, 327. Pliny the Elder, *Natural History*, VII.1.
77. Commentary on Genesis 36:24.
78. Commentary on Seneca, 277-85.
79. Commentary on Isaiah 7:18-19.
80. Commentary on Haggai 2:15-19.
81. Calvin, "A Warning against Judiciary Astrology," 179.
82. Commentary on Isaiah 6:13.
83. Commentary on Isaiah 26:19.
84. Commentary on Isaiah 18:4.
85. Commentary on Genesis 3:18.
86. Commentary on Isaiah 5:6 and Hosea 9:6.
87. Commentary on Genesis 1:20.
88. Commentary on Genesis 2:2.
89. Pelikan, *Luther's Works*, vol. 1, 54.
90. Ibid., 204.
91. Ibid., 52.
92. Ibid., 54.
93. Commentary on Isaiah 34:16.
94. Commentary on Genesis 2:19.
95. Commentary on Genesis 9:2.
96. Commentary on Hosea 2:18.
97. Commentary on Jeremiah 7:20.
98. Commentary on Jeremiah 21:6-7.
99. Commentary on Isaiah 11:6.
100. Commentary on Genesis 1:29.
101. For the writings of Warfield that pertain to evolution and other scientific issues, see Benjamin B. Warfield, *Evolution, Science, and Scripture: Selected Writings*, ed. Mark A. Noll and David N. Livingstone, (Grand Rapids, Mich.: Baker Books, 2000).
102. Benjamin B. Warfield, "Calvin's Doctrine of Creation," *Princeton Theological Review* 13, (1915): 190-255.
103. Warfield, "Calvin's Doctrine of Creation," 204.
104. Ibid., 204-5.
105. Commentary on Genesis 1:21.
106. Warfield, "Calvin's Doctrine of Creation," 206.
107. Ibid., 207.

108. Ibid., 207-8.
109. Ibid., 208.
110. Ibid., 209-10.
111. John Murray, "Calvin's Doctrine of Creation," *Westminster Theological Journal* 17, (1954): 21-43.
112. Murray, "Calvin's Doctrine of Creation," 32.
113. Ibid., 38.
114. Ibid., 40.

CHAPTER 6

CALVIN ON THE HUMAN BODY, MEDICINE, AND ORIGINS

John Calvin had a well-developed *theological* anthropology. His primary interest in human beings was centered on the relationship that they bear to their Creator, Sustainer, and Redeemer. Given the intensity with which he imbibed the Bible's teaching about the depravity of humanity and of the individual person, Calvin was a perceptive observer of human behavior. He was acutely attuned to both the blatant and subtle ways in which sin manifested itself in human thought, attitudes, speech, and action. His writings certainly offer a wealth of insight into human psychology. In contrast, his attention to matters of human anatomy, physiology, and medicine was incidental. Occasionally he did offer glimpses into his thinking about human beings as inhabitants of the natural world, as creatures who are subject to influences of the heavens, as creatures who possess biological characteristics, and as creatures who are afflicted by disease and pain.

Man as Animal

Unlike those Christians who cringe at the thought of describing a human being as an animal, Calvin had not the slightest hesitation in referring to man as an animal. Human beings were considered unique animals, to be sure, radically different from all other animals, not simply animals, but animals nonetheless. He repeatedly drew a distinction between humankind and the other animals, indicating that he regarded humans as "animals." Human beings, he said, "excel other animals."[1] They differ from other animals in the manner of their creation. "Concerning other animals," he said, "it had before been said, Let the earth produce every living creature." Although the body of Adam was formed of clay, that body was destitute of sense so that we would not exult in our flesh. Thus, God designed "to distinguish man by some mark of excellence from the brute animals." For Calvin, that distinguishing mark pertained to the timing of the act of origination. On the one hand, he said, the brute animals "arose out of the earth in a moment; but the peculiar dignity of man is shown in this, that he was gradually formed." God did not command Adam to spring alive out of the Earth immediately but, by a "special privilege," formed him gradually so that he might outshine all the creatures that the Earth produced. The Creator, therefore, exercised special care in bringing man into existence. That is his distinguishing mark of excellence compared to the "other animals."[2]

In what other ways does the human animal differ from the other animals? In addition to method of production, Calvin suggested that humans differ from them in regard to posture. When commenting on the Isaianic passage that calls upon us to "lift your eyes and look to the heavens," he observed that "while God formed other animals to look downwards for pasture, he made man alone erect, and bade him look at what may be regarded as his own habitation." Following the prophet Isaiah, he complained about "the wickedness of men who do not acknowledge what is openly placed before their eyes concerning God, but, like cattle, fix their snout in the earth; for, whenever we raise our eyes upwards, with any degree of attention it is impossible for our senses not to be struck with the majesty of God."[3]

Calvin, of course, also appealed to the non-material capacities of human beings as distinguishing marks in comparison to other animals. In discussing the apostle John's assertion that Jesus the Logos was "the true light that gives light to every man," he pointed out that "men have this unique quality above the other animals, that they are endowed with reason and intelligence and that they bear the distinction between right and wrong engraven in their conscience."[4] Of the passage in I Corinthians 1:20 that deals with the foolishness of the wisdom of the world in comparison to the wisdom of God, Calvin asked "what is more noble than the reason of man by which he stands out far above all other animals?"[5] He thought of humans as rational, intelligent, and moral animals.

Although Calvin noted other characteristics of humans without contrasting them with those of the "other animals," he sometimes used these characteristics as adjectives modifying the word "animal." For example, he claimed that "man was formed to be a social animal"[6] and that "man is a social animal."[7] Writing about the prophecy in Isaiah 3:6 that "a man will seize one of his brothers at his father's home, and say, 'you have a cloak, you be our leader: take charge of this heap of ruins!'" he observed that "in every age the whole world has been convulsed by the desire of obtaining kingly power; and there is not a village so inconsiderable as not to contain men who willingly undertake to become rulers: and all this proves that man is an animal desirous of honor."[8] Despite the many astounding characteristics of the human animal, Calvin took note of the fact that man, like the other animals, is subject to the rule of death. "When any one is asked as to his condition," he asserted, "he must necessarily confess that he is a creature, and that he is also, as the ancients have said, an ephemeral animal, that his life is like a shadow."[9] Given that men were constrained to make such a confession about themselves, he wondered how it were possible that people would dare to make gods for themselves. After all, men and women are rational, intellectual, moral, social animals, unique in their mode of creation by God, created to stand upright and observe the God-given world around them so that they might give God glory for it. Despite their exalted status, however, men and women are also humble creatures of the dust that will one day depart this life.

Heavenly Influences on Humans

Let us review some of what we saw in Chapter 2 pertaining to the effect of the heavens on the human body. We saw that Calvin complained in his little book, *A Warning against Judiciary Astrology*, that the "judicial" astrologers carried the legitimate principles of astrology too far by misapplying knowledge of the heavens. He granted that the astrologers "take a true principle--namely, that terrestrial bodies and in general all subcelestial creatures are subject to the order of the heavens and draw from them whatever qualities they possess."[10] Given that human beings are indeed "subcelestial creatures," Calvin envisioned them as being subject, in some manner, "to the order of the heavens." Humans draw from the heavens "whatever qualities they possess." Precisely what qualities are these that are drawn from the "order of the heavens?" "Natural" astrology had shown that "bodies here below receive some influence from the moon" such as the amount of marrow in the bones varying as the Moon waxes and wanes.[11] Clearly Calvin assumed that at least some aspects of human anatomy are subject to the influences of the Moon. He further recognized that doctors could legitimately learn much from astrology. Physicians were guided by astrological knowledge in determining "the appropriate time to order blood-lettings, infusions, pills, or other medical necessities." There is, he said, "some correspondence between the stars and planets and the dispositions of human bodies." Such matters he viewed as falling under the purview of a legitimate "natural" astrology.[12]

We noted that Calvin believed that the complexion of human beings is influenced by the order of the heavens. By complexion, he was not referring solely to skin quality. He probably had in mind the general appearance of a person, that is, body shape, height, facial characteristics, and so on. He granted that "for the complexions of men and especially their affections, which participate in the qualities of their bodies, these do depend in part upon the stars. At least there is some correspondence between them."[13] He acknowledged that "the stars do indeed have some concurrence in forming our complexion and especially influence those things which have to do with the body," but he denied that the stars are the chief cause of such things.[14] The influence of the heavens might be considered as a partial determinant, but not the sole determinant, of our bodily characteristics. In some instances, he thought that the influence of the heavens was vastly overrated. In discussing twins, he wondered why a set of twins might manifest different features if the influence of the heavens was so powerful. He especially wondered why there should be a set of twins consisting of a brother and a sister. These phenomena suggested to him that the "seed of the father and the mother have an influence one hundred times more powerful than all the stars put together" in determining the appearance of children.[15] Calvin was, therefore, concerned to "limit the power of the stars to those things which have to do with the world and which belong to the body and to the first inclination of nature."[16] He faulted judicial astrology for not being "content with determining the character and complexion of men" and then wanting to extend its capabilities even further to the business of foretelling "what will happen to people throughout their lives." "At the most" he insisted, "the stars are able to imprint people with certain qualities; they cannot make this or that happen to them besides."[17] And likewise "although the stars are signs which show us the season to plant or to sow, to heal or to give medicine, to cut wood, etc., this does not mean that they are signs which tell us whether or not we should wear new clothes."[18] Calvin said that he confessed the natural signs but detested the sorcery that the devil had invented in connection with the stars.

Anatomy, Physiology, and Nutrition

Throughout his commentaries and sermons Calvin occasionally referred to bone, blood, nerves, sweat, and childbirth. As we have seen, he posited a connection between the influence of the heavens and the amount of marrow in the bones. He also envisioned the bones as being connected by nerves. "We know that the strength of the arm depends on the structure of the nerves," he said. "Except the bones were bound together by the nerves, a dissolution would immediately follow."[19] In regard to the flow of blood and water from the spear-pierced side of the crucified Jesus, he stated that "it is natural for congealed blood to lose its red colour and become like water. It is also well known that water is contained in the membranes next the heart."[20]

The question of Job 37:17, "You who swelter in your clothes when the land lies hushed under the south wind, can you join him in spreading out the skies, hard as a mirror of cast bronze?" induced Calvin to make some observations about sweat in the third sermon on Job 37. He asserted that although we see that our clothes become soaked on a hot summer day, we are unable to explain why the sweat issues from our bodies. "How is the sweat engendered?" he asked. He suggested that it is because the body is "loosened." This loosening opens up the body sufficiently that it cannot retain its moisture. In calm weather, he said, the pores are shut up "and the moisture shrinks inward to nourish a man's life." Heat causes the opposite. In fact, heat engenders feebleness which "makes the humors to melt."[21] Calvin did not explain why heat drives moisture inward in fruits but brings it outward to the skin of humans. Why should heat "loosen" the human body, but not "loosen" a piece of fruit? We don't know if he was even aware of an inconsistency here.

Some very graphic comments about childbirth were offered in Calvin's first sermon on Job 39. He asked if it was not a remarkable miracle "that the child should be nourished in uncleanness and infection in his mother's womb even among all the excrements; and yet notwithstanding receiving sustenance and grow so big as to find means to come into the world?" He also mentioned that the little babies in the womb had a vent to take a breath at within their mother's womb, namely, by means of the navel. Did Calvin think that a fetus actually breathes through the umbilical cord, or was he merely recognizing that it receives its entire life support in that manner? We do not know. In any case, the child was said to be sustained in the midst of all manner of corruption. "He lies there among all manner of excrements and all kinds of wretchednesses," Calvin preached,

> insomuch that if it be considered how he is borne there by the space of eight months, and how he is maintained, and man may see God's mighty hand, yes and that so passingly as we must needs be amazed to think upon it, and acknowledge that it is God which governs all things and which had the ordering of us all.[22]

The pastor urged his congregation to be "ravished" at these "excellent miracles of God." He thought that birth among the brute beasts was an even greater miracle than human childbirth, because the animals do not even understand what is inside them and might not be as protective of the fetus as a human mother. And as great as the pain and stress of human mothers during childbirth might be, Calvin believed that the birthing process was even more difficult to endure for some of the wild beasts. We noted in the previous chapter, for example, his perception of the pains endured by pregnant does.

Calvin commented on nutrition in reference to Daniel 1:14, a passage reporting that Daniel and his three friends determined not to eat the Babylonian King Nebuchadnezzar's luxurious food but only "pulse." He observed that "if any one asks the medical profession whether pulse and other leguminous plants are wholesome, they will tell us they are very injurious since they know them to be so."[23] The term that Calvin and the King James Version translated as "pulse" literally means "seeds." Some contemporary writers interpret the word as a general term for legumes such as lentils, peas, and beans. On the other hand, some commentators suggest that the word refers generally to vegetables and has the sense of "things that are grown." Many recent Bible translations including the Revised Standard Version, New American Standard Bible, and New International Version translate the word as "vegetables."[24] Calvin regarded "pulse" as derived from a leguminous plant, but it is not clear if he identified it with beans, peas, lentils, some other specific legume, or a combination of these. Regardless of his exact understanding of what pulse is, leguminous vegetables and vegetables generally are now regarded as nutritious, highly beneficial components of the diet. Calvin's negative assertion about legumes provides just one more illustration of the shifting opinions within the medical profession about the benefits and risks of particular diets!

Why would Daniel and his friends deliberately choose to subsist on a diet of presumably injurious food? Calvin stressed that there is no necessary virtue in bread or any other kind of food to nourish us. It is not the bread in and of itself that imparts strength to us when we eat. He did not mean to imply that various foods do not have certain nutritional values. One can assume that he agreed with the sixteenth-century medical profession about the poor nutritional value of pulse, and by implication, the beneficial nutritional value of other foods. His point, however, was that nourishment and sustenance are ultimately conveyed to us by "the secret blessing of God." In general, God has, as it were, chosen to breathe virtue into bread. The nutritional value is emplaced in the bread at God's behest. In other instances, such as the situation in which Daniel and his friends survived on pulse, God may impart nourishment in spite of the available food. "The properties of various viands," Calvin concluded, "do not support us by their own inherent qualities, but by God's blessing, as he sees fit."[25]

Death and Disease

Calvin was quite clear that death was the penalty for sin, and yet he also maintained that, had Adam not sinned, he would not have remained in his originally created condition. There would ultimately have been some kind of transition or transformation to a heavenly state. Thus we read in his comments on Genesis 2:16 that

> man's earthly life truly would have been temporal; yet he would have passed into heaven without death, and without injury. Death, therefore, is now a terror to us, first, because there is a kind of annihilation, as it respects the body; then, because the soul feels the curse of God.[26]

Much the same thought appears in the commentary on Genesis 3:19, namely, that "truly the first man would have passed to a better life, had he remained upright; but there would have been no separation of the soul from the body, no corruption, no kind of destruction, and, in short, no violent change."[27]

But more than death affected humans personally as a result of the fall. Disease and pain, likewise, he attributed to the curse. "Nor is there any other primary cause of diseases" than sin.[28] And, elsewhere, he expanded on that claim by stating that "to our sins it ought to be imputed, that we are liable to diseases, pains, old age, and other inconveniences."[29]

Perhaps much of what Calvin was driving at can be summed up by his reflections on Genesis 2:8. Here he confessed that

> if the earth had not been cursed on account of the sin of man, the whole as it had been blessed from the beginning would have remained the fairest scene

both of fruitfulness and of delight; that it would have been not dissimilar to Paradise when compared with that scene of deformity which we now behold.[30]

Medical practice in Calvin's era was still very much under the influence of the medical theory and practice of Greece and Rome.[31] Although ancient Mesopotamia and Egypt had their healers and their medical remedies, Greek medicine tended to follow its own course. Early Greek medical practice had strong religious overtones, but beginning with Hippocrates (c. 460-377 B.C.), medicine became a field that broke away from supernatural explanations of illnesses and from reliance on supernatural cures. A prolific writer, Hippocrates wanted to place medicine on a sound rational and observational basis, to gain respect for medical practitioners, and to establish professional standards of conduct for physicians. He was very patient-oriented, stressed the importance of diet and exercise, was suspicious of drastic healing measures, and often looked to the body to restore itself naturally.

By the fifth century B. C., the external anatomy of human beings was rather well known. On the other hand, knowledge of internal human anatomy and physiology was greatly limited by the fact that dissection of cadavers was prohibited by the Greek respect for the dignity of the human body. The body, therefore, was something of a "black box" whose inner workings and parts could only be inferred from behavior, manifestations of disease, and comparison with animals. Examination of wounds did provide some idea of the insides, and dissections of various animals yielded putative analogies to the structure and function of the human body. Even surgery was not regarded as the task of physicians but was left to individuals who were accomplished in treating war wounds.

Hippocrates believed that health and illness were a matter of balance among four humors (χυμοι) within the human body. These four bodily humors, or fluids, were yellow bile, black bile, phlegm, and blood. Hippocrates maintained that illness occurred when a humor flowed in abnormal amounts or when it became concentrated in one part of the body. Thus, a flow of humors to the feet caused gout, too much flow of phlegm produced colds, and a flow of phlegm from the head to the lungs resulted in coughing. The humors could readily be linked to the four elements, the four human temperaments, the four seasons, and the four primary qualities: hot, cold, dry, and wet. Phlegm seemed to predominate in the winter, hence so many colds. Blood was thought to become more vigorous in spring, an appropriate time for relieving the body of excess blood. Summer brought on an excess of yellow bile, when fevers became more commonplace, and autumn was considered a more likely time for diarrhea and vomiting, thanks to excess black bile. In Hippocratic thought, the body discharged the excess of harmful fluid in an effort to restore equilibrium among the humors. Because the body also naturally discharged blood, the beneficial, life-giving fluid, during nosebleeds and menstruation, it made sense that blood might be extracted as a therapeutic measure. Blood-letting, therefore, remained a standard medical procedure for centuries to come until it finally passed from the scene in the nineteenth century. Given that Calvin himself was subject to a wide spectrum of illnesses throughout his lifetime, it is probable that he personally experienced the therapy of blood-letting.[32]

Hippocractic medicine was developed further by Galen of Pergamon, a flamboyant self-promoter, skilled physician and experimentalist, and incredibly productive writer who became a physician to gladiators and ultimately to Roman emperors. So strong was Galen's impact that he shaped the course of western medicine at least until the Renaissance when some of his errors were finally detected. Thanks to his experience in patching up the wounds of many gladiators, Galen developed surgical skills as well as considerable insight into human anatomy. To this work he added the knowledge gleaned from many public dissections of apes, pigs, sheep, goats, and other animals. Because dissection of corpses was still prohibited, Galen's work with animals did lead him into some errors. He had the misconception, for example, that the human liver, somewhat like that of pigs and apes, had appendages extending from the main mass that grasped the stomach in finger-like fashion. He further maintained that the veins originated in the liver and that blood from the liver carried nutrition to various parts of the body. In contrast, he thought that arteries originated in the heart. Galen was also a vigorous advocate of blood-letting as a measure for cooling the body and preventing illness. He developed detailed ideas about the best times to employ the procedure based on the time of year, weather, and the age and constitution of a patient. He further laid great stress on the character of the pulse as a diagnostic tool.

During the early Christian era, Oribasius (325-397), Aëtius of Amida (527-565), Paul of Aegina (c. 625-c. 690), and other medical authors simplified, refined, and systematized the writings of Galen. This process was later carried forward by Islamic scholars. In the meantime, improvements in medical practice took place, such as increased skill in the removal of cancerous tumors. Galenism increasingly came under challenge during the Renaissance. In the sixteenth century, for example, Calvin's contemporary Andreas Vesalius (1514-1564) undertook dissections of human corpses and demonstrated that the internal organs were not always as Galen had maintained. Among other things, he showed that the heart is a muscle.

Given that John Calvin experienced poor health and a host of maladies throughout much of his adult life, it is appropriate to ask what knowledge he had of the medical field and perhaps even what medical procedures he and his family might have experienced. Calvin had quite a bit to say about disease, a phenomenon that he attributed to the presence of sin. Although he did not maintain that there is a direct correlation between commission of a specific sin and a consequent disease in every case, he did take the view that disease in general is a punishment sent as the result of sin upon a fallen race. His view can be summed up by his assertion that "to our sins, therefore, it ought to be imputed, that we are liable to disease, pains, old age, and other inconveniences."[33]

The specific diseases that Calvin discussed were cancer, gangrene, lunacy, epilepsy, and blood disease. In his second letter to Timothy, the apostle Paul warned against people like Hymenaeus and Philetus who indulged in godless chatter and quarreling about words. The teaching of such individuals, said Paul, would "spread like gangrene." This passage provided Calvin with an opportunity to discuss gangrene and cancer at length. The discussion is one of the very few places in all of his writings in which he specifically mentioned the names of individuals who had made contributions to natural knowledge.

One such individual was Benoit Tixier (d. 1560) who Latinized his name to Benedict Textor. Textor had been a physician in Macon, north of Lyons, prior to establishing his medical practice in Geneva in 1543. Shortly after his arrival he became Calvin's personal physician. Textor was the author of an early work on plants drawn from Dioscorides. In 1551, he published *De la Maniere de Preserver de la Pestilence*, a treatise on the plague, and around the same time he also authored *De Cancri Natura et Curatione*, a book dealing with the nature and cure of cancers.[34] So highly did Calvin regard Textor's diligence, faithfulness, and competence that he dedicated his commentary on II Thessalonians to the medical doctor, and, in the dedication, Calvin praised him for faithfully treating his wife's illnesses and seeing her through the disease that ultimately took her life. He also expressed gratitude for the medical ministrations to himself and was particularly indebted to Textor for his great concern for the church should anything happen to Calvin. We also get the impression that Textor refused to charge Calvin anything for his medical services. After Textor's death, Philibert Sarasin succeeded him as Calvin's personal physician.

Calvin obtained much of his information about cancer and gangrene in his discussion of II Timothy 2:17 from Textor, a recognized expert in the field. Textor informed Calvin that II Timothy 2:17 had been poorly translated by the Renaissance humanist Desiderius Erasmus (1466-1536). Presumably Erasmus had made one disease out of two diseases that are quite different from one another. Instead of "gangrene," he had used the word "cancer." Calvin then launched into a detailed dissertation on the ways in which previous authorities on medicine had defined cancer and gangrene. According to Calvin, Galen distinguished gangrene from cancer "in many passages throughout his writings, and especially where he lays down definitions in his small work *On Unnatural Swellings*." Calvin may have read Galen's little book upon the advice of Textor. He may simply have taken Textor's word on the matter. Or he may have obtained his information about cancer and gangrene from the *Epitome Medicae Libri Septen*, a seven-volume medical encyclopedia compiled by Paul of Aegina, a seventh-century physician who was educated in Alexandria and practiced medicine in the same city where he had a substantial influence on subsequent Islamic medicine. Much of his medical encyclopedia consisted of extracts from earlier writers such as Galen.[35] Calvin referred specifically to the sixth book of Paul of Aegina (sometimes called Paul Aegineta), undoubtedly a reference to the sixth volume of *Epitome*, which is devoted primarily to surgery. In that volume, Paul of Aegina, following Galen, defined a "cancer" as "an irregular swelling, with fearful rims, of hideous appearance, bluish red in colour and unaccompanied by pain." According to Calvin, Paul of Aegina enumerated two kinds of cancers. He said that "some cancers are concealed and have no ulcers while others, where there is a preponderance of the black bile from which they originate, do ulcerate."[36]

In regard to "gangrene," Calvin referred to Galen's work on unnatural swellings and second book addressed to Glauco; to the fourth book of Paul of Aegina's *Epitome*, a volume devoted to skin diseases including cancers; and to the fourteenth book of Aëtius of Amida, a physician who lived primarily in Constantinople. Like Paul of Aegina, he also published compilations of extracts from earlier medical writers. Calvin wrote that all three of these authors had written to the effect that gangrene proceeds from great "phlegmons" or "inflammations" that may "attack any member, deprive the affected part of heat and vital energy so that it begins to die." If the part is dead, Calvin said, the Greek writers called the disease σφακελος, the Latins called it *sideratio*, and the common people called it "St. Anthony's fire." Calvin further mentioned Aulus Cornelius Celsus (c. 25 B. C. -c. A. D. 50), a Roman physician and author of *De Medicina*, who drew a distinction between "cancer" and "gangrene" by regarding "cancer" as the genus and "gangrene" as the species. Calvin considered this mode of distinction as mistaken on the grounds that it was "clearly refuted in many passages by physicians of proved authority." He thought it possible that Celsus might have been led astray by the similarity between the Latin words *cancer* and *gangraena*. But, he asserted, there can be no mistake of that kind if one attends to the Greek where "καρκινος corresponds to the Latin *cancer* and both a crab and the disease." In contrast, he said, "grammarians think that γαγγραινα is derived .απoτouγραινειν which means 'to eat.'" Calvin concluded that students of Scripture should "abide by the term gangrene, which is the word Paul uses and which agrees with what he says about eating or consuming."[37] He concluded his discussion by claiming that

> all medical authorities agree that the nature of the disease is such that unless counteracted as quickly as possible it will spread to adjoining parts and penetrate right into the bones, and not cease to consume until it has destroyed the man. Since therefore gangrene is quickly followed by mortification (νεκροσις or sideratio) which soon infects the rest of the members till it ends in the complete destruction of the body, Paul aptly compares false doctrines with this deadly contagion. For if once they are allowed in, they spread till they completely destroy the Church.[38]

It is reasonable to assume that Calvin was directed by Benedict Textor to the several relevant passages in these ancient medical authorities. In all probability, Calvin did not read Galen and the other medical writers during his early education, but it does make sense that a medical specialist would be familiar with the works of Galen, Aëtius of Amida, and Paul of Aegina and would be in possession of personal copies, particularly since the writings of both Aëtius of Amida and Paul of Aegina had been translated into Latin during the sixteenth century.

Lunacy and epilepsy were noted by Calvin in discussions of a pair of passages from the gospels. Matthew 4:23 states that Jesus went throughout Galilee "preaching the good news of the kingdom, and healing every disease and sickness among the people." Calvin commented that "*lunatics* is the term given to those in whom the force of the disease increases or declines according to the phases of the moon." As an example of such a disease, he referred to "those who suffer from epilepsy and the like."[39] Disease of this sort, he maintained, could not be healed by natural means. As a result, Christ proved his divinity when he miraculously healed such diseases. Mark 9:17 and Matthew 17:14-18 mention the episode of a man who brought his son to Jesus for healing. Since childhood, the son had been possessed by a spirit that robbed him of speech, seized him, threw him to the ground, and caused him to foam at the mouth, gnash his teeth, and become rigid. Calvin wrote that

> they are called *lunatics* who during the waning of the moon, suffer from epilepsy or are tormented with dizziness. I do not accept what Chrysostom imagines, that this name was devised as a trick of Satan to defame the good creation. For sure experience teaches us that those illnesses increase or decrease according to the course of the moon.[40]

Clearly, Calvin regarded epilepsy as a form of lunacy that afflicted some of the biblical characters and as a disease that was subject to heavenly influences, in this case the phases of the moon.

Calvin commented very briefly on blood diseases. Regarding Paul's stay at the estate of Publius, the chief official of the island of Malta on which Paul had been shipwrecked, the book of Acts records that the father of Publius was in bed suffering from fever and dysentery and was subsequently healed by Paul. Calvin marveled that although "the cure of dysentery is difficult and slow, especially when fever goes along with it, the old man at death's door was not restored to health so suddenly, by the laying on of hands alone and prayers, without the power of God."[41]

A prophetic reference in Isaiah 4 to "the cleansing of bloodstains from Jerusalem by a spirit of judgment and a spirit of fire" drew the remark that "it is necessary that God should earnestly warn us, and, like a physician, apply physic, and the lancet, and sometimes proceed to burning."[42] The assertion in Zephaniah 3:11 that God would "remove from this city those who rejoice in their pride" led Calvin to visualize a medical procedure. "When disease is removed from the human body," he wrote,

> the body itself is necessarily weakened; and it is sometimes necessary to amputate a member, that the whole body may be preserved. In this case there is a grievous diminution; but as there is no other way of preserving the body, the remedy ought to be patiently sustained.[43]

These remarks provide confirmation that surgical procedures, practiced since classical times, were still followed in the sixteenth century.

Anthropological Issues

In the ancient, early Christian, and medieval periods, human artifacts and skeletal remains of pre-historic humans were unknown. In Mesopotamian, Egyptian, and Greek civilization knowledge about the origin and antiquity of the human race was shrouded in mystery and clothed in the language of myth. In some way, the human race was believed to be derived from the action of the gods. In contrast, the Jews and Christians relied on Scriptural revelation as their source of information about humanity. Calvin's contemporaries in Europe, inextricably enmeshed as they were in western Christian culture, took it for granted on the authority of the Bible, literally interpreted, that the entire human race originated from a single pair, Adam and Eve, only a few thousands of years ago in the Garden of Eden in the Mesopotamian valley. Virtually everyone understood, too, that the early human race, entrenched in wickedness of staggering proportions, was wiped out by a global deluge approximately 1656 years after the creation of Adam and Eve with the exception of righteous Noah and his family. The human race as we know it began anew after the flood with all people descending from the three sons of Noah: Ham, Shem, and Japheth. Perhaps Calvin believed much the same.

In light of this historical setting, what were Calvin's ideas about the origin of humans, the unity and antiquity of the human race, and the early history of humanity? For starters, Calvin taught the origin of humans by a creative act of God. As we observed earlier, he said that humanity is distinguished from the other animals by virtue of the gradual manner of his creation. Lest one think, because of his emphasis on gradual creation that he entertained an evolutionary origin for humans from animals, it must be observed that an origin by gradual evolution from animal ancestry, whether under the guidance of God or not, was not an issue in Calvin's day. Even B. B. Warfield recognized as much while suggesting that Calvin's approach could be characterized as evolutionary. It is not surprising, then, that Calvin offered neither explicit agreement with, nor refutation of an evolutionary view. The concept of biological evolution was not a significant part of the thought universe of the sixteenth century.

In reference to the apostle Paul's assertion in the book of Acts that God had made all nations on the Earth from one man, Calvin took for granted that the human race is a physical and biological unity, that "all were created of one blood." Although affirming a monogenetic origin of humanity, he was particularly concerned to stress the lack of *religious* unity displayed by the human race. He virtually subordinated the importance of biological unity to religious unity. Consanguinity and the same point of origin, he said, should have been a bond of mutual consent among all people. It is religion that is the strongest unifying force among all men. Calvin concluded that those who disagreed so much in matters of religion and the worship of God had revolted from nature. The natural thing, he said, would be for all men, wherever they were born and in whatever place they inhabited, to seek with one consent the Maker and Father of them all. Calvin asserted that Paul

> wanted to teach that the order of nature was violated when as religion was torn to pieces among them, and that the dispersion, which is to be seen among themselves, is evidence of the overthrow of godliness, because they have broken loose from God, the common Father, from whom all blood-relationship is derived.[44]

A good many theologians throughout church history have regarded Adam and Eve as exclusive vegetarians prior to their fall on the basis of Genesis 1:29-30, the text in which God is said to have given seed-bearing plants and fruit-bearing trees to humans and to the other animals for food. Calvin exercised some caution on this point. He began by observing that some writers inferred that humans were actually content with herbs and fruits until the great flood. Not only that, these writers inferred that it was unlawful for humans to eat flesh. Calvin conceded that this view had some basis of support in that God did seem to confine the food of humans within certain limits and then expressly granted the use of flesh after the deluge. "These reasons, however, are not sufficiently strong," he countered,

> for it may be adduced on the opposite side, that the first men offered sacrifices from their flocks. This, moreover, is the law of sacrificing rightly, not to offer unto God anything except what he has granted to our use. Lastly, men were clothed in skins; therefore it was lawful for them to kill animals.

For these reasons, Calvin thought that it was the better part of wisdom not to be dogmatic about the issue of the original human diet and about the killing of animals. Perhaps, he thought, it was better "to assert nothing concerning this matter." He believed that it was enough to accept that herbs and fruits were given as the common food of early men.[45]

A question that has long perplexed Christian readers of the Bible concerns where Adam's son Cain found his wife after he had killed his brother Abel and had been driven from the presence of the Lord and his family to roam as a vagabond in the land of Nod. In Genesis 4:17, Cain's wife appears from nowhere. The text does not say where she came from or when they were married. Was she a sister or a niece of Cain? Was she a so-called pre-Adamite, a member of a group of human beings who lived in the vicinity of the family of Adam and Eve? The text is silent, and we are left with speculation. The discovery in the last couple of centuries of numerous human skeletal remains that are undoubtedly more than ten thousand years old has led many Christian scholars to entertain the pre-Adamite hypothesis very seriously.[46] Because such fossil remains were completely unknown in Calvin's day, he would not likely have entertained the idea of pre-Adamite or syn-Adamite peoples in any serious way. He probably also had theological reasons for not considering pre-Adamitism. Calvin concluded that Cain had already married one of his sisters prior to killing Abel. Had she married Cain after the murder, he thought, Moses would probably have said something about the marriage. Calvin supposed this to be the case because

> it would be a fact worthy to be recorded, that any one of his sisters could be found, who would not shrink with horror from committing herself into the hand of one whom she knew to be defiled with a brother's blood; and while a free choice was still given her, should rather choose spontaneously to follow an exile and a fugitive, than to remain in her father's family.

One could well ask if it would not also be remarkable for someone who had already married Cain to freely follow a murderer of her brother into exile rather than stay behind with her family. But Calvin did not raise that possibility. Perhaps he assumed that a wife would have absolutely no choice in the matter of following Cain once she was married to him. One might argue that it makes a lot of sense for Cain to have married a wife after he had fled to the land of refuge where any prospective wife would more likely be unaware of his sordid past. But Calvin did not pursue this view because he clearly assumed that Cain married "any one of his sisters," one of Adam's daughters.[47]

Calvin did not ponder the significance of Cain's paranoid and guilt-ridden concern about someone finding him and killing him, a concern that also makes some sense if there were non-Adamite peoples in the vicinity of the land of Nod. He opined that Cain justly reasoned that he would be "exposed to injury and violence from all men." Cain, moreover, considered himself "deprived of God's protection, but also supposes all creatures to be divinely armed to take vengeance of his impious murder." Because man is a social animal who desires mutual intercourse, "this is certainly to be regarded as a portentous fact, that the meeting with any man was formidable to the murderer."[48] Nowhere did Calvin discuss whom Cain had in mind when he spoke of "all men," "all creatures," or "any man." Almost certainly he thought of them as Cain's brothers and nephews, but he did not explicitly say so, and he did not ask why Cain did not speak of "his brothers" killing him. Calvin acknowledged that "many persons, as well males as females, are omitted in this narrative."[49] It was Moses' design, he said, to follow just one line of his progeny until he came to Lamech.

Another biblical statement that has led many Bible students to wonder about the existence of pre-Adamites is that "Cain was then building a city, and he named it after his son Enoch." Does not city-building indicate at the very least a permanent settlement with a substantial number of people? Were all of those people merely Cain's offspring? Calvin's answer indicates his awareness that some individuals had hinted at the possibility of pre-Adamites, but he neglected to mention who these individuals might be. In regard to the city-building, he wrote:

> When captious men sneeringly inquire, whence Cain had brought his architects and workmen to build his city, and whence he sent for citizens to inhabit it? I, in return, ask of them, what authority they have for believing that the city was constructed of squared stones, and with great skill, and at much expense, and

that the building of it was a work of long continuance? For nothing further can be gathered from the words of Moses, than that Cain surrounded himself and his posterity with walls formed of the rudest materials: and as it respects the inhabitants, that in that commencement of the fecundity of mankind, his offspring would have grown to so great a number when it had reached his children of the fourth generation, that it might easily form the body of one city.[50]

Calvin obviously held the view that Cain had married a sister and, after fleeing from Adam and Eve, produced a sufficient number of offspring to establish a permanent settlement that Genesis refers to as a "city."

Another passage from early Genesis that has perplexed Christians for a long time includes references to the intermarriage of the sons of God and the daughters of men and to the Nephilim. It is commonly held that these "heroes of old" and "men of renown" were giants, a unique brand of human being. Calvin evidently discounted such notions about the Nephilim, observing that "Moses does not indeed say, that they were of extraordinary stature, but only that they were robust." The Nephilim, he maintained, were distinguished from other humans not so much "by the size of their bodies, as by their robberies, and their lust for dominion."[51]

Although Calvin did not dwell on the matter to the degree that Luther did, he seemed to regard very early humanity as in some way more vigorous than are we. God had adorned Adam with "excellent gifts," he said, not least of these was longevity.[52] In his discussion of Cain, Calvin had referred to the "fecundity of mankind" being such that Cain's offspring could have grown to a sufficiently great number in four generations as to populate a small city.[53] Although he did not explicitly state that he regarded the ages of the patriarchs mentioned in Genesis 5 as literally true, he clearly assumed that these specimens of early men did in fact live for hundreds of years.

A strictly literal view of these patriarchal ages leads to the conclusion that they had overlapping life spans. On this view, Lamech and Methusaleh, for example, both lived almost to the onset of the flood, and Adam lived well into the time of Lamech. Calvin seems to have accepted that notion, writing that "in the number of years here recorded we must especially consider the long period which the patriarchs lived together." He believed that the voice of Adam daily resounded through six successive ages when the family of Seth had grown into a great people to "renew the memory of the creation, the fall, and the punishment of man; to testify of the hope of salvation which remained after chastisement, and to recite the judgment of God." Although Adam's descendants would continue to rehearse from generation to generation these great events, Calvin believed that "far more efficacious would be the instruction from the mouth of him, who had been himself the eye-witness of all these things."[54]

So, Calvin believed that Adam lived to see several generations of his descendants. By the same token, he thought that Shem lived well into the time of Abraham. In discussing the episode of Genesis 14 in which several kings engaged in battle in the valley of Siddim and in which Abraham needed to rescue his nephew Lot, Calvin claimed that the recording of the names of so many "kings" during the lifetime of Shem would not appear absurd if only people would "reflect that this great propagation of the human race, was a remarkable miracle of God."[55] Human longevity and vigor exceeded that of the present even as late as the age of Abraham and Sarah, in Calvin's opinion. "There is no doubt that there was then greater vivacity in the human race than there is now," he suggested in his comments on Abraham's observation of the exceptional beauty of his wife Sarah, then 65 years old.[56]

As in so many other matters, however, Calvin exercised considerably more restraint than Luther. Consider, for example, the following passage from Luther's *Lectures on Genesis* about Adam prior to his fall:

> Both his inner and his outer sensations were all of the purest kind. His intellect was the clearest, his memory was the best, and his will was the most straightforward—all in the most beautiful tranquility of mind, without any fear of death and without any anxiety. To these inner qualities came also those most beautiful and superb qualities of body and of all the limbs, qualities in which he surpassed all the remaining living creatures. I am fully convinced that before Adam's sin his eyes were so sharp and clear that they surpassed those of the lynx and eagle. He was stronger than the lions and the bears, whose strength is very great; and he handled them the way we handle puppies. Both the loveliness and the quality of the fruits he used as food were also far superior to what they are now.[57]

If Calvin entertained such opinions about Adam, he wisely refrained from giving written expression to them.

NOTES

1. Commentary on Isaiah 40:6.
2. Commentary on Genesis 2:7.
3. Commentary on Isaiah 40:26.
4. Commentary on John 1:9.
5. Commentary on I Corinthians 1:20.
6. Commentary on Genesis 2:18.
7. Commentary on Genesis 4:14.
8. Commentary on Isaiah 3:6.
9. Commentary on Jeremiah 16:20.
10. Calvin, "A Warning against Judiciary Astrology," 166.
11. Ibid., 166-67.
12. Ibid., 167.
13. Ibid., 168.
14. Ibid., 169-70.
15. Ibid., 169.
16. Ibid., 170.
17. Ibid., 171.
18. Ibid., 179.
19. Commentary on Hosea 7:15.
20. Commentary on John 19:34.
21. Third Sermon on Job 37.
22. First Sermon on Job 39.
23. Commentary on Daniel 1:14.
24. On pulse, see, for example, Edward. J. Young, *The Prophecy of Daniel* (Grand Rapids, Mich.: William B. Eerdmans, 1949), 46, and Charles F. Pfeiffer, Howard F. Vos, and John Rea, eds., *Wycliffe Encyclopedia*, vol. 2 (Chicago: Moody Press, 1975), 1369.
25. Commentary on Daniel 1:14.
26. Commentary on Genesis 2:16.
27. Commentary on Genesis 3:19.
28. Ibid.
29. Commentary on Isaiah 65:20.
30. Commentary on Genesis 2:8.
31. Much of the following overview of ancient medicine is derived from Roy Porter, *The Greatest Benefit to Mankind: a Medical History of Humanity* (New York: W. W. Norton, 1997) and Lawrence I. Conrad, Michael Neve, Vivian Nutton, Roy Porter, and Andrew Wear, *The Western Medical Tradition: 800 BC to AD 1800* (Cambridge: Cambridge University Press, 1995).
32. Some indication of Calvin's physical woes can be found in his letters. On March 2, 1559, for example, he wrote to Peter Martyr that "the debility of my stomach is especially a cause of suffering to me, and it is increased by a catarrh which brings along with it its accompaniment a cough. For as vapours arising from indigestion trouble my brain [not the only time Calvin referred to vapors affecting his brain], the evil reacts in its turn upon my lungs. To all this has been added for the last eight days a pain occasioned by hemorrhoids from which it is not possible to force the blood." In subsequent letters he complained of violent headaches, a violent pain in the side, colic, inflammation of blood and lungs, and convulsions of nerves. Especially revealing was a letter that he wrote on February 8, 1564, to the physicians of Montpellier regarding medical consultation. Noting

that when he had consulted three distinguished physicians in Paris twenty years earlier, he had not been plagued by ailments that were now assailing him in full force: arthritic pains, colic, expectoration of blood, ague, severe pains in his calves, an ulcer in the hemorrhoid veins that caused excruciating suffering, intestinal worms, profuse discharges of blood after passing several kidney stones that caused exquisite pain, and gout in his feet. In addition, he complained that imperfectly digested food turned into phlegm and that he had difficulty breathing. He lamented that the sedentary way of life to which the gout in his feet condemned him precluded all hope for a cure. A little more than three months later Calvin was dead. For the letters see volumes 4 through 7 of Henry Beveridge and Jules Bonnet, *Selected Works of John Calvin: Tracts and Letters* (Grand Rapids, Mich.: Baker Book House, 1983).

33. Commentary on Isaiah 65:20.
34. Textor's little book on cancer was translated into English as early as 1587.
35. On Paul of Aegina and Galen see Porter, *The Greatest Benefit to Mankind*.
36. Commentary on II Timothy 2:17.
37. Ibid.
38. Ibid .
39. Commentary on Matthew 4:23.
40. Commentary on Mark 9:17 and Matthew 17:17.
41. Commentary on Acts 28:7.
42. Commentary on Isaiah 4:4.
43. Commentary on Zephaniah 3:11.
44. Commentary on Acts 17:26.
45. Commentary on Genesis 1:28.
46. On pre-Adamitism see David N. Livingstone, *Preadamite Theory and the Marriage of Science and Religion* (Philadelphia: American Philosophical Society, 1992).
47. Commentary on Genesis 4:17.
48. Commentary on Genesis 4:14.
49. Commentary on Genesis 4:17.
50. Ibid.
51. Commentary on Genesis 6:4.
52. Commentary on Lamentations 1:7.
53. Commentary on Genesis 4:17.
54. Commentary on Genesis 5:4
55. Commentary on Genesis 14:1.
56. Commentary on Genesis 12:11.
57. Pelikan, *Luther's Works*, vol. 1, 62.

CHAPTER 7

CALVIN, THE NATURAL WORLD, AND SCRIPTURE

After the rise of modern science, Christian thinkers have expended count-less hours attempting to determine the precise bearing of biblical texts on mat-ters of scientific interest. Such attempts have focused not only on general rela-tionships between the teaching of Scripture and the scientific enterprise, broadly conceived, but also on the factual content of specific scientific theories and on the validity of scientific theories. For example, one might ask the question, "Does an infallible biblical text require belief that the outer portion of the Earth rests upon some sort of subterranean body of water?" Certain texts seem to sug-gest that the Earth does rest on such a body of water. Psalm 24:2, for example, says that God founded the Earth upon the seas and established it upon the wa-ters. Psalm 136:6 says that God "spread out the earth upon the waters." The flood story includes the statement of Genesis 7:11 that "all the springs of the great deep burst forth." Other verses convey a similar idea. Influenced by such texts, many Christians throughout the earlier phases of church history believed that the Bible includes a literal physical description of the structure of the Earth and that beneath the Earth, there is, or was, at least until the time of the deluge, a large body of subterranean water.

With the development of modern techniques for investigating the interior of the Earth, however, geologists have concluded that such a body of water never existed in the past nor does it exist now. If there is no mass of subterranean wa-ter, then how should we understand the texts quoted above? A wide variety of approaches to this question has emerged. Some Christians argue that such texts are speaking poetically and, therefore, should not be understood as a literal physical description. Others claim that such texts employ ancient Near Eastern conceptions of the structure of the Earth. Still others might say that such texts are simply referring to springs and groundwater. And still others will insist that the Bible does in fact teach the existence of a subterranean ocean and, therefore, there must be one despite the assertions of geologists to the contrary. In reply, some will maintain that it is a perversion of the biblical text to have it making scientific assertions. They claim that it is neither the purpose nor intent of biblical authors to make scientific claims. God has left that business up to us, they say. On the other hand, others maintain that God has conveyed some scientifically accurate information in the Bible and that we must accept what he has told us. Clearly, there may be many approaches to texts that bear on scientific matters.

A very different contemporary example of the attitude which posits that the Bible contains scientifically accurate data concerns the field of radioactivity. Scientific knowledge of the rates of radioactive decay of certain isotopes such as ^{238}U (uranium 238), ^{40}K (potassium 40), ^{87}Rb (rubidium 87), and ^{147}Sm (samarium 147) and of the distribution of these isotopes in a wide range of minerals and rocks indicates that planet Earth is an extremely old object, several billions of years in age. Many Christians are persuaded that the Bible rules out this scientific conclusion on the grounds that Scripture does give valid scientific information. In this case, these believers will point to a six-day creation and the biblical genealogies as proof of a *very* young Earth. To resolve the problem of the apparent conflict, some have suggested that rates of radioactive decay have been speeded up spectacularly, and perhaps miraculously, during the creation period and the Noachian deluge. At least one writer has written that the Bible "suggests," "hints at," or "favors" such a speed-up in decay rates. D. Russell Humphreys, for example, wrote that Deuteronomy 32:22 offers "support for the idea of accelerated nuclear decay." This verse says: "For a fire has been kindled by my wrath, one that burns to the realm of death below. It will devour the earth with its harvests and set afire the foundations of the mountains." Humphreys preferred not to adopt a metaphorical view of the verse because from other verses he had "learned interesting new scientific facts by looking for a straightforward meaning first." He thought that biblical talk about fire being kindled in the foundations of the mountains had to refer to nuclear decay. "Taken straightforwardly," he claimed, "the verse is a graphic and accurate picture of the effects of nuclear decay." Humphreys also proposed that Psalm 18 and Habakkuk 3 contain language that refers to the deluge, an occasion when God kindled "nuclear fires." In the New Testament, II Peter 3 was said to relate to nuclear decay.[1] Others claim that this approach to the Bible represents a misguided and disastrous mishandling of the sacred text.

A question that substantial segments of the contemporary church need to resolve, therefore, is whether the Bible includes the germ of valid scientific theories or contains infallible data that must be incorporated into such theories. In light of contemporary discussions about how we ought properly to regard the Bible when it comes to scientific issues, we can learn some helpful lessons by considering how Calvin read the Bible in addressing the scientific issues of his own day. Because he framed his views about the proper handling of the Bible *vis à vis* science prior to the advent of the modern scientific revolution, he is not susceptible to serious accusations of "compromising" on the authority of Scripture because of eagerness to accept the conclusions of "godless scientists" about the age of the Earth, the big bang, or biological evolution. So how did Calvin handle the Bible in relation to the scientific issues of his day?

Calvin on Science and Scripture

Calvin believed that Scripture taught that the Earth is only a few thousand years old and that the globe was covered by the flood of Noah. The Christian church had traditionally assumed a very young Earth and a global deluge, and Calvin's contemporaries believed the traditional views. Should he have been any different? Calvin also adopted a geocentric cosmological theory that has long since been completely repudiated by the scientific community. The reason that he accepted the theories of geocentrism, four elements, and natural places was because they were the best theories available in light of then current evidence. Moreover, they seemed to Calvin and many of his predecessors and contemporaries to be reasonably consistent with the biblical text. In his day, of course, there was no recognition by natural philosophers of the geological evidence that is available to us today that compels acceptance of an extremely ancient Earth. Nor was there recognition of the lack of physical evidence in support of a global deluge. Given the status of scientific endeavor in the sixteenth century, it is hardly surprising that he would adopt the views aforementioned. Given the absence of the mountains of physical evidence that support an old Earth and call into question a global deluge, Calvin did not have to deal with this powerful extra-biblical impetus to thorough re-examination of traditional views. In his day there was no compelling reason to doubt that the Bible contained at least some scientific information.

Despite the fact that Calvin adopted a particular scientific theory or idea such as a young Earth, a global flood, or a geocentric universe because he thought it was called for by, or consistent with, the biblical evidence, he was extremely reticent, as we have pointed out before, to draw detailed, specific scientific inferences from the biblical text. I have already contrasted his caution on this score with Luther's boldness. Luther pointed to fossils as relics of the flood; Calvin kept mum about fossils and, in fact, shied away from drawing scientific implications of the deluge apart from mention of some animals on the ark and the general location of the ark's landing site. Luther envisioned the rainbow as something new in creation that appeared only after the flood; Calvin did not wish to take that route. Luther advocated spontaneous generation of birds and fish; Calvin was non-committal about spontaneous generation. Luther thought the serpent in the Garden of Eden had originally walked on all fours; Calvin exercised great caution and maintained that the serpent was the same animal before the fall as after. In short, Calvin was often quite reluctant to indulge in scientific speculation beyond what was stated in the text. For example, he might hold that there was a great deluge that killed all life, but he did not then begin to draw conclusions about erosion of the land, sedimentation, burial of dead animals, volcanic eruptions, or earthquakes associated with the flood. In other words, he did not "read into" the text scientific conclusions that were not explicitly mentioned by the text. As a result, we can conclude that Calvin would probably have disapproved of the method adopted by Humphreys by which subtle hints of a change in nuclear decay rates are detected in the Bible. Humphreys stands more in line with Luther than with Calvin in regard to finding scientific data in Scripture.

Next let's ask how Calvin dealt with perceived weaknesses in the scientific theories that he accepted. Specifically, how did he handle those weaknesses in light of biblical doctrines? There were, in fact, situations in which he viewed the natural explanations of some of the aspects of scientific theory available to him as unconvincing. On the contrary, he thought that the biblical doctrines of providence and miracle provided more satisfying explanations. I will recall here two examples that we reviewed earlier. In one case, Calvin did not think that the available explanations of how the Earth could maintain its stability at the center of the universe surrounded by huge whirling spheres did the job. His solution was not to reject either the geocentric idea in its totality or the notion of whirling spheres. Rather, he introduced an *ad hoc* exercise of God's ongoing miraculous providential power to stabilize Earth. In short, he did not try to come up with a different natural cause. Without saying so, he felt that current scientific theorizing had effectively reached the limits of its explanatory power. When *scientific* explanation failed completely, then it became needful for Calvin to bring in God's *miraculous* power.

For our second case, remember that Calvin could not see how the dry land could be protected from the ocean in terms of the theory of natural places. That theory maintained that the natural place of water is above that of the element, earth. By all rights the waters of the ocean should drown the landmasses. But obviously they do not, and Calvin could think of no compelling scientific explanation as to why the ocean should be kept at bay. Explanation in terms of natural, secondary causes had again reached its limit. The solution laid in the *miraculous* exercise of God's providential power in heaping back the sea. What we find is that there were times when Calvin employed what is referred to today as the "God-of-the-gaps" strategy. In essence, if all scientific, natural explanations fail to explain a given phenomenon, if we cannot think of any new explanations of the phenomenon to put to the test, and if we cannot even conceive how anyone in the future can ever come up with a scientific explanation for that phenomenon, we fall back on a miraculous intervention of divine power to account for the phenomenon. That is the essence of the God-of-the-gaps procedure, a method that has been frequently introduced in discussions of how biblical interpretation interacts with scientific explanation.

But now we must consider how Calvin responded when he confronted situations in which science apparently conflicted with the biblical text. What we find is that he typically accepted the scientific data and adjusted his interpretation of the text accordingly. In so doing, he invoked a principle of accommodation. This is such an important principle in Calvin's overall thought, that we will now focus our attention on his use of this principle for the remainder of the chapter.

Calvin's Principle of Accommodation

As a recipient of thorough training in the classical writers such as Seneca and Cicero, Calvin learned to appreciate the skills and techniques of rhetoric early in life. Upon his conversion, however, his classical learning was "transmuted," and, as Ford Lewis Battles (1915-1979), a Calvin scholar who taught at Pittsburgh Theological Seminary and Calvin Theological Seminary, put it, "he exchanged for human rhetoric a divine rhetoric."[2] Especially as a pastor and biblical exegete, Calvin, perhaps following the model of John Chrysostom, became concerned to communicate the divine message of the Scripture in plain terms so that his hearers and readers would understand that message, but he also recognized that God himself engaged in a kind of pedagogical rhetoric in creation, incarnation, and Scripture. In Calvin's view, God accommodated himself to humanity by acting and speaking in ways that finite creatures can grasp. Battles summed it up as follows:

> As in human rhetoric there is a gulf between the highly educated and the comparatively unlearned, between the convinced and the unconvinced, a gulf which it is the task of rhetoric to bridge so that through simple, appropriate language the deeps of human thought yield up their treasure, or at least the views of the speaker are persuasively communicated—analogously in divine rhetoric the infinitely greater gulf between God and man, through divine condescension, in word and deed, is bridged. And the divinely appointed human authors and expositors of Scripture express and expound the divine rhetoric under the Spirit's guidance for the benefit of all.[3]

Because God, the transcendent, incomprehensible "rhetorician," condescends to his finite creatures in Scripture to communicate with them, the principle of accommodation becomes profoundly important for the appropriate interpretation of biblical texts. Our examination of the instances in which Calvin appealed to this principle will make it clear why this is so. In the commentaries, in sermons, and in the *Institutes*, Calvin repeatedly emphasized the fact that God accommodated himself to our limited capacity so that we might understand his message. He constantly stressed that God, the Holy Spirit, or the human authors of Scripture, particularly Moses, David, or the prophets, accommodated themselves in deed or in language to the hearers or readers of Scripture. Calvin spoke of that accommodation as a "condescension," a "descent," an "adaptation," a "stooping far below God's proper height," or an "approaching near to fallen creatures" who were variously described as an "unlearned multitude," "unlearned men," "rude and unlearned" or "humble and unlearned people," "infants," or "little children." Because we are but infants or unlearned creatures in comparison to the infinite Creator of heaven and earth, we are folk of limited capacity. Calvin, thus, spoke of God or the biblical writers as accommodating themselves to the "capacity of men," "the capacity of the age," "the common capacity of every most simple man," "the capacity of the people," "the capacity of the unlearned," "our feeble capacities," "the mutable and diversified capacities of man," "our capacity," "our small capacities," or "our limited capacity."

Although favoring the term "capacity," Calvin also used other expressions to describe the human condition that necessitated God's accommodating to us. Thus, God was said to accommodate himself variously to "our rudeness and homeliness," what was "common to the simplest and most uneducated persons," "the puerile age of the church" when it was "unable to receive any higher instruction," the "ignorance of the generality of men," "our weakness," "our standard," "mistaken, though generally received opinion," "the measure of man's understanding," "our sense," or else "their carnal view." This accommodating was also said to be "suited to the lowest apprehension" of humans, given with "respect to the common apprehension of men," or "expedient to each age." God, of course, lowered himself to us, as it were, with our limited capacity, precisely so that his message to us would be "intelligible," or "so that the least informed might understand." The message, pertaining to godliness, was given for our sake. And, in the last analysis, God's condescension, his accommodating himself to meet our need, Calvin viewed as a marvelous exhibition of his infinite love for us.

But the question arises as to the ways in which God accommodated himself or the biblical authors accommodated themselves to us. This question may be answered both positively and negatively. Negatively, we note that Calvin frequently wrote about the ways in which biblical authors did not pursue their teaching. Paul and Barnabas *did not* speak to the citizens of Lystra by means of "subtle entreaties as the philosophers do." When talking about the stars or geography, Moses *omitted* "higher subtleties," "abstained from acute disputations," and *did not* speak "scientifically," "acutely," or "philosophically," nor according to "the rules of philosophy." Jeremiah *did not* "philosophize, as the astrologers do." David *did not* "dispute philosophically" nor "discourse scientifically" when talking about the heavens. Such technical modes of reasoning that are well suited to those who are educated, schooled, or learned were, in Calvin's judgment, passed over by the biblical writers in many cases so that ordinary people could grasp what they were saying.

How, then, did God and the human authors speak? Positively, accommodation meant for Calvin that God "prattled in Scripture in a rough, popular style" and "lisps with us as with nurses." The Holy Spirit "spoke childishly rather than unintelligibly," made use of "popular language," and even spoke to us "grossly." God, of course, descended to us through the human authors like Paul and Barnabas who "plainly set forth what the most ignorant know." Moses wrote in a "common style," spoke in a "homely style" or a "popular manner," "popularly," and "in a popular style." Jeremiah spoke "popularly, according to common notions." David used "popular language," "phraseology well known," language in "familiar use," and adopted a "homely style."

In employing the principle of accommodation for rhetorical purposes, Calvin was not an innovator. The Latin verb *accommodare* (to accommodate) was also used by Latin rhetoricians such as Cicero, Livy, and Cato in their writings. According to Battles, Calvin, in his reading of the classics, "frequently came across *accommodare* in Cicero, Quintilian, and the minor rhetoricians."[4] It is the same Latin term that Calvin typically used in his applications of the idea of accommodating.

Neither was Calvin the first Christian theologian to employ the principle of accommodation. Among the church fathers, Clement of Alexandria (2nd century A.D.), Origen (185-254), Augustine, Theodore of Mopsuestia (c. 350-428), John Chrysostom (c. 347-407), Tertullian (c. 160-c. 240), Hilary of Poitiers (d. 368), and others all made use of the principle. Chrysostom, for example, in his fourth homily on Genesis called upon his hearers to notice, with respect to the creation of the firmament, "the extent of the considerateness of the language to accommodate human limitations." Thomas Aquinas wrote that "Moses, accommodating [*condescendens*] himself to uneducated people, followed the things which appear to the senses."[5] In many instances, writers used the idea of accommodation as an apologetic device in response to challenges to the Scriptures by opponents of Christianity. Some of the expressions of these church fathers regarding accommodation are similar to those employed by Calvin.

Although Calvin may have been influenced by both classical rhetoricians and the church fathers in his employment of the principle of accommodation, David F. Wright has maintained that the source of Calvin's principle of accommodation is not fully clear. In Wright's judgment, a convincing demonstration that Calvin had derived the principle from Origen, Chrysostom, or Augustine has not yet been made. He did, however, propose that a study of Chrysostom by Erasmus may have helped Calvin to focus his attention on divine accommodation as expounded by Chrysostom and on pedagogical accommodation as practiced by that Greek Father. Wright also pointed out the remarkable similarity in Erasmus' language to that of Calvin in regard to accommodation: "Almost everything he [Chrysostom] wrote he accommodated to popular ears, and to this end he lowered the character of his speaking to their capacity, as a teacher prattles with an infant pupil."[6]

Regardless of the primary influences behind Calvin's pervasive use of the idea of accommodation, Battles maintained that "unlike an Origen, or an Augustine, or a John Chrysostom, or a Hilary of Poitiers, Calvin makes this principle a consistent basis for his handling not only of Scripture but of every avenue of relationship between God and men."[7] Similarly, Clinton Ashley stated that "no other theologian in the history of the Christian church has applied the principle of accommodation as extensively and as effectively as Calvin."[8] Again, according to Battles, "for Calvin, accommodation has to do not only with Scripture and its interpretation, but with the whole of created reality to which, for the Christian, Scripture holds the clue."[9] Battles claimed that the principle of accommodation was everywhere assumed throughout the *Institutes* as a working principle.

Having said this, I would stress that Calvin definitely did invoke the principle in his handling of Scripture. As we will shortly see, he commonly employed the principle where there seems to be some clear contradiction or disparity between the statement of the text and what he knew about the world from other sources. The principle became a strategy for harmonization in Calvin's hands. As Battles put it, "the starkest inconsistencies in Scripture are harmonized through rhetorical analysis, within the frame of divine accommodation to human capacity," but Calvin's method, he claimed, did not serve merely as an apologetic device, a way of explaining away discrepancies or presumed mistakes. Rather the application of the principle of accommodation "unlocks for Calvin God's beneficent tutelage and pedagogy of his wayward children."[10] This principle above all else had a pastoral function, serving for the edification of believers.

The term "pedagogy" leads to Romans 1:14, a text in which the apostle Paul stated his obligation to bring the good news of salvation to both Greeks and non-Greeks, to the wise and the foolish. Calvin viewed Paul's evangelistic work as that of a teacher. He laid it down as a generality that "all teachers also have here a rule to follow, viz., to accommodate themselves in a modest, courteous way to the ignorant and unlearned." If teachers would only keep this rule of accommodating themselves to their students in mind, Calvin said, they would better be able "to patiently endure much stupidity of conduct and bear with innumerable instances of pride which might otherwise overcome them."[11] The effective teacher adjusts to the student's level, explains things in terms suited to the student, and often tolerates mistakes that are peripheral to the main point being taught. God, in effect, plays the role of a wise and effective teacher because he accommodates himself to our limited spiritual and intellectual capacities by revealing himself and by communicating to us in ways that we can comprehend. Moreover, God also tolerates many of our own deficient understandings about the world and does not always attempt to correct them in the interests of achieving the infinitely higher goal of leading us to Christ.

The Principle of Accommodation and the Nature of God

Let us now examine many of the specific passages in which Calvin appealed to the principle of accommodation. First we will look at a wide range of instances that have no immediate relevance to scientific questions just so that we can get a sense of the overall importance of this principle to Calvin. Then we will look at the application of the principle of accommodation to texts that do have scientific implications. The depth of conviction with which Calvin applied this principle may be gauged from his commentary on John 3:12, the verse in which Jesus asked how Nicodemus would be able to believe heavenly matters if he did not believe the Savior when he spoke to him about earthly matters. In writing about this episode, Calvin scolded individuals who thought that it was beneath God's dignity to condescend to human ignorance and who scoffed because God "prattles with us in Scripture in an awkward and common style." Such individuals, Calvin accused, were "very wicked." What they need to realize is that the very reason that God condescends to our human weakness is precisely because of the great love that he bears toward us.[12]

Because he was intensely aware of the incomprehensibility of the infinite, eternal, unchangeable, and omnipotent God who created and sustains the entire cosmos, Calvin repeatedly invoked the concept of accommodation in his reflections on the nature of God. He deeply appreciated the fact that mere creatures simply cannot grasp the immensity of God. If one is to form any understanding at all of his maker, God must somehow adapt his portrayal of himself to the capabilities and limitations of finite creaturely minds. Calvin's reflection on a Psalm text that referred to God's abandonment of the tabernacle at Shiloh led him to observe that God "fills both heaven and earth; but as we cannot attain to that infinite height to which he is exalted, in descending among us by the exercise of his power and grace, he approaches as near to us as is needful, and as our limited capacity will bear."[13] Ezekiel 9 mentions the vision of the glory of God moving to the threshold of the temple from between the cherubim. Calvin wrote that the prophet was taking the glory of God as a representation of God himself because

> God cannot be comprehended by us, unless as far as he accommodates himself to our standard. Because therefore God is incomprehensible in himself, nor did he appear to this Prophet as he really is (since not angels even bear the immense magnitude of his glory, much less a mortal man) but he knew how far it was expedient to discover himself, therefore the Prophet there takes his glory for himself; that is, the vision, which was a sign or symbol of the presence of God.[14]

In discussing Romans 1:19 which says that "what may be known about God is plain to them, because God has made it plain to them," Calvin again maintained that "we cannot fully comprehend God in His greatness, but that there are certain limits within which men ought to confine themselves, even as God accommodates to our limited capacity every declaration which He makes of Himself."[15] In the *Institutes*, he observed that one might easily refute the error of the Anthropomorphites "who imagined a corporeal God from the fact that Scripture often ascribes to him a mouth, ears, eyes, hands, and feet." Calvin asked "who even of slight intelligence does not understand that, as nurses commonly do with infants, God is wont in a measure to "lisp" in speaking to us?" These modes of expression about God having bodily parts, he said, "do not so much express clearly what God is like as accommodate the knowledge of him to our slight capacity. To do this he must descend far beneath his loftiness."[16] Because the personal beings that we encounter every day speak with mouths, see with eyes, hear with ears, and act with hands and feet, God refers to his own activity in images that are familiar to us without intending to teach us that he actually possesses physical eyes, ears, mouth, and so on.

A particularly arresting example of the manner in which God may represent himself to humans for their instruction may be found in Psalm 78:65 where God depicts himself as a drunken man: "Then the Lord awoke as from sleep, as a man wakes from the stupor of wine." The Lord bestirred himself to beat back his enemies and put them to shame. Of this verse, Calvin commented that

> the figure of a drunken man may seem somewhat harsh; but the propriety of using it will appear, when we consider that it is employed in accommodation to the stupidity of the people. Had they been of a pure and clear understanding, God would not have thus transformed himself, and assumed a character foreign to his own.[17]

In Jacob's dream at Bethel in which the angels ascended and descended upon the ladder to heaven, God revealed himself to the patriarch as Yahweh, the eternally self-existent one, but also as the God of Abraham and the God of Isaac. This identification as the God of Jacob's fathers impressed Calvin as another example of divine accommodation. Since God's "majesty is in itself incomprehensible" as intimated in the divine name Yahweh,

> he accommodates himself to the capacity of his servant, by immediately adding, that he is the God of Abraham and Isaac. For though it is necessary to maintain that the God whom we worship is the only God; yet because when our sense would aspire to the comprehension of his greatness, they fail at the first attempt; we must diligently cultivate that sobriety which teaches us not to desire to know more concerning him than he reveals unto us; and then he, accommodating himself to our weakness, according to his infinite goodness, will omit nothing which tends to promote our salvation.[18]

Jacob's subsequent act of worship in constructing the altar at Bethel when he fled from his brother Esau commended a faith that was confined within divinely prescribed bounds. It was not a rash act in which he behaved in a too familiar manner toward God. His faith was

> praiseworthy, seeing it does not desire to know more than God permits. And as when God descends to us, he, in a certain sense, abuses himself, and stammers with us, so he allows us to stammer with him. And this is to be truly wise, when we embrace God in the manner in which he accommodates himself to our capacity.

In short, Jacob did not try to penetrate farther into the being of God than was meet. Instead, he responded in a manner that comported with the way in which God revealed himself to Jacob. As Calvin said, Jacob "does not keenly dispute concerning the essence of God." He asked his readers to recall that God "descends to us in order to raise us up to himself. For he does not speak to us in this earthly manner, to keep us at a distance from heaven, but rather by this vehicle, to draw us up thither."[19] Calvin clearly believed that God must accommodate himself to our limited capacity in giving us a sense of his being because as creatures we are totally incapable of grasping the essence and glory of God as he is in himself.

Appeal to accommodation crops up in the first chapter of Ezekiel where the prophet reported his vision of the expanse or the firmament. Above the firmament, said Ezekiel, was something in the likeness of a throne looking like sapphire, and on the likeness of the throne was the likeness of an appearance of a man. Calvin remarked here that, in this passage, God "accommodates his discourse to the measure of our capacity." In his exposition, he refuted those who argued that God has a bodily form or that the vision referred to a material throne. He emphasized that a picture of the glory of God was in view in this text and that, by means of the "likenesses" and "appearances" in the vision, the reader was enabled by steps to "penetrate to so great a height." In effect, the glory of God is something that we cannot see directly but must be conveyed to us in terms of pictures or images that convey a sense of heavenly things.[20]

Finally, a reference to the stability of the throne of God in Psalm 93:2 was interpreted by Calvin as a symbol for righteousness and the power of government rather than as a literal throne, which, of course, would be difficult to envision as God is a spirit and does not have a body like man. By way of explanation, Calvin noted that it was "customary to transfer such images taken from men to God, in accommodation to our infirmity."[21]

Calvin also used the notion of accommodation in regard to the alleged changeability of God in Book 1 of the *Institutes* where he talked about divine providence. In that context he explained what was meant by the "repentance" of God. Recognizing that "God is not a man that he should repent," he attributed references to God's repentance to a divine accommodation in which he appears to repent or change his mind. "Because our weakness does not attain to his exalted state," Calvin wrote,

> the description of him that is given to us must be accommodated to our capacity so that we may understand it. Now the mode of accommodation is for him to represent himself to us not as he is in himself, but as he seems to us. Although he is beyond all disturbance of mind, yet he testifies that he is angry toward sinners. Therefore whenever we hear that God is angered, we ought not to imagine any emotion in him, but rather to consider that this expression has been taken from our own experience; because God, whenever he is exercising judgment, exhibits the appearance of one kindled and angered. So we ought not to understand anything else under the word "repentance" than change of action.[22]

The same issue was addressed in the commentary on Amos 7:3. Here the Lord is said to have repented of sending a plague of grasshoppers to devour the land in response to a petition from Amos. In this instance, Calvin wrote that as to the word repent, as applied to God, let us know, as it has been elsewhere stated, that God changes not his purpose so as to retract what he has once determined. He indeed knew what he would do before he showed the vision to his Prophet Amos, but he accommodates himself to the measure of men's understanding, when he mentions such changes.[23]

Calvin further employed the idea of accommodation in explaining the apparent change in attitude on God's part toward the repentant citizens of Nineveh. The book of Jonah tells us that "when God saw what they did and how they turned from their evil ways, he had compassion and did not bring upon them the destruction he had threatened." But Calvin argued that there is no internal change within the deity. Rather, "it is according to our perceptions that there is any change." He postulated a "two-fold view of God." On the one hand, there is that view of God "as he sets himself forth in his word," and, on the other hand, there is that view of God "as he is as to his hidden counsel." In regard to his secret counsel, God "is always like himself, and is subject to none of our feelings." In contrast, "with regard to the teaching of his word, it is accommodated to our capacities. God is now angry with us, and then, as though he were pacified he offers pardon and is propitious to us. Such is the repentance of God."[24]

The principle of accommodation was introduced, too, in regard to God's taking an oath. Amos 6:8 says that "the sovereign LORD has sworn by himself—the Lord God Almighty declares: 'I abhor the pride of Jacob and detest his fortresses. I will deliver up the city and everything in it.'" God's coming judgment on Israel is then described by Amos. Calvin granted that "the form of swearing, as it is, may seem apparently improper," but he evaded the problem by claiming the "God in this place puts on the character of man, as he often does in other places. He swears by his soul, that is, by his life, as though he were one of mankind." He further observed that "God borrows from men their mode of swearing: as though he said, 'If men be believed when swearing by their life, which yet is evanescent, of how much greater weight must that oath be, by which I pledge my own life?'" Calvin thought that we should get accustomed to God's use of such forms as swearing an oath, forms "in which God familiarly accommodates himself to our capacities."[25]

If we are to know anything of the being and nature of the living God, he must stoop to our level. As finite creatures we are constitutionally unable to comprehend God as he is in himself. Were we capable of doing so, we would be as God himself.

The Principle of Accommodation in God's Dealings with Men

In all of his dealings with us, God takes into account our weakness and need. Because God even created the world in a manner that was for our benefit, Calvin applied the notion of accommodation to the question of how long God took to create the world. In his comments on the meaning of "the first day" in Genesis 1:5, Calvin addressed that question. Some of the church fathers, in particular Augustine, had taught that God created the entire cosmos essentially complete in an instant and so did not understand the days of creation as referring to the passage of certain amounts of time. Calvin regarded this view as an error. "It is too violent a cavil to contend that Moses distributes the work which God perfected at once [i.e., in a moment] into six days, for the mere purpose of conveying instruction," he argued. Instead, he concluded "that God himself took the space of six days, for the purpose of accommodating his works to the capacity of man." And exactly how did Calvin envision God's using six days to create the world as an accommodation to our capacity? He asserted that "God applied the most suitable remedy when he distributed the creation of the world into successive portions, that he might fix our attention, and compel us, as if he had laid his hand upon us, to pause and to reflect."[26] In essence, God created the world over a stretch of time to stimulate us to pause and reflect on the glory of God and his works. Calvin made the same claim in his reflections on the compound miracle by means of which Peter was delivered from prison. He regarded the miracle as even more beneficial to faith because it consisted of several steps each of which was quite remarkable in its own right. In Calvin's judgment, Peter was liberated from prison more than ten times. He likened the miracle to the work of creation. "God," he asserted,

> could have hurried Peter out in a single moment, but one after the other He overcomes various difficulties, so that the glory of the miracle might be greater. Thus he created the world in six days, not because He needed that space of time, but that He might keep us in meditation of His works. For He accommodates His method of acting to our capacity, and the progress of our faith.[27]

In some way, the passage of time during creation enables us to see more strikingly the wonder of God's works. One wonders if Calvin, following this line of reasoning, might not have felt that our faith and opportunity to meditate on God's works would have been enhanced even more if he had believed that God had taken billions of years to produce the universe and the Earth. Many of my Christian geologist friends and I have marveled at the amazing artistry and inventiveness of the Creator in molding and shaping this Earth through an incomprehensibly long series of events of erosion, sedimentation, burial, igneous intrusion, metamorphism, deformation, and mountain uplift over vast stretches of time. For them and for me, the glory of God seems to break through in a far more dramatic and compelling fashion through this providentially directed, ingeniously conceived, unimaginably complex and lengthy dynamic history of the planet than through a few instantaneous miracles only a few thousands years ago.

Calvin also regarded the creation of angels as, in part, an accommodation to human need. In discussing angels in the chapter on the creation of the world in the *Institutes*, he observed that the angels were provided for our protection and care as attendants. God, indeed, is free to act without angels but generally employs the agency of angels in manifesting his power, for providing for the safety of his people, and for imparting gifts of his beneficence. When God uses the agency of angels, it is primarily "to comfort our weakness." God will use all means "to raise up our minds to good hope, or confirm them in security." Thus, even though it should suffice for the Christian that God "declares himself to be our protector," he nonetheless reinforces us by sending us the aid and comfort of angels. "When we see ourselves beset by so many perils, so many harmful things, so many kinds of enemies," Calvin wrote, "such is our softness and frailty—we would sometimes be filled with trepidation or yield to despair if the Lord did not make us realize the presence of his grace according to our capacity." Thus he supplies us with numberless angelic attendants.[28]

Having created the world, placed us in it, and provided the angels to watch over us, God then communicated with us. In so communicating, he accommodated himself to us by representing himself under the figures of a father who cares for his children, a physician who heals our diseases, and a teacher who instructs us. Although revealing himself in this way, God, nevertheless, did not always act in the same manner throughout human history, as Scripture makes clear. God adapted his message to the stage of development of the human race, according to Calvin, just as any effective teacher would do.

This sense of the idea of accommodation emerges clearly in a chapter in the *Institutes* on the difference between the Old and New Testaments. After discussing the variety of ways in which God governed and instructed his people and the fact that there were changes in rites and ceremonies, Calvin answered the objection that it is unreasonable to suppose that God would permit such a change in which he would come to disapprove of something that he had previously ordered and commanded. The grounds for such an objection were thought to lie in the consistency of God with himself, a point that Calvin often stressed in other contexts. How could a consistent, unchangeable God change his mode of instruction or action? In response, Calvin answered "that God ought not to be considered changeable merely because he accommodated diverse forms to different ages, as he knew would be expedient for each." He then listed examples from family life in which a parent might pursue one course of action, instruction, or management for a child at one time and a different course at a later stage of the child's development. Such a parent would not be charged with being fickle or of changeable opinions for so doing. Why then should God be so charged? "What was irregular," Calvin asked, "about the fact that God confined them to rudimentary teaching commensurate with their age, but has trained us through a firmer and, so to speak, more manly discipline?" In fact, God's constancy really was conspicuous in his delivering the same doctrine to all ages and in requiring the same worship of his name that he originally commanded. Thus, he concluded, "in the fact that he has changed the outward form and manner he does not show himself subject to change. Rather, he has accommodated himself to men's capacity, which is varied and changeable."[29] Elsewhere in the *Institutes*, he stressed that the Old Testament differed from the New Testament because the Messiah had not yet come and the Jews "had not yet come to know Christ intimately." Because of that lack of intimate acquaintance with the Messiah in the Old Testament era, the Jews "were like children whose weakness could not yet bear the full knowledge of heavenly things."[30]

The very forceful manner in which our need for salvation is presented in Scripture entailed pedagogical accommodation on God's part. Pointing out that the Holy Spirit says that God is our enemy until we are restored to favor through the death of Jesus Christ; that we are cursed until the sacrifice of Christ expiates our sin; and that we are separated from God until we are received into union with God by means of Christ's body, Calvin referred to "expressions of this sort" as being "accommodated to our capacity that we may better understand how miserable and ruinous our condition is apart from Christ." We would be far less attuned to our wretched condition without the mercy of God and less disposed to value the "benefit of liberation" if Scripture had not clearly stated "that the wrath and vengeance of God and eternal death rested upon us."[31]

Where Scripture exposes the folly and madness of the world "in searching for God when all the while each one clings to his own speculations," it generally does not do so by reproving the elegant and subtle teaching of the philosophers. Rather "having regard for men's rude and stupid wit" the Bible normally "speaks in the manner of the common folk." As a result, when the object of Scripture is "to distinguish the true God from the false, it particularly contrasts him with idols."[32] The common man is far more likely to understand the significance of an idol than the significance of a convoluted anti-theistic philosophical speculation.

Calvin further saw the establishment of the church as an example of divine accommodation. According to the reformer, "in our ignorance and sloth (to which I add fickleness of disposition) we need outward helps to beget and increase faith within us." Because of this reality, "God has also added these aids that he may provide for our weakness." And so that the preaching of the gospel might flourish, the Lord "deposited this treasure in the church." Moreover, because we have "not yet attained angelic rank," our God "in his wonderful providence accommodating himself to our capacity, has prescribed a way for us, though still far off, to draw near to him," namely, the church of Jesus Christ.[33]

Perhaps the manner in which God has related to his creatures entails the notion that God "accommodated Himself to us and to our weakness in such a way that He has neither forgotten nor left behind anything which might be good and profitable to us."[34]

Jesus and the Principle of Accommodation

The supreme revelation of God to his creatures in the person of Jesus Christ is the prime example of condescension on the part of the heavenly father. Philippians 2:5-11 is arguably the leading text in which that condescension is manifested. The notion of accommodation unavoidably pervades Calvin's discussion of the self-abasement of Christ in his commentary on this passage. Surprisingly, however, he did not once use the term "accommodation" in the analysis of the text. But he did specifically mention accommodation elsewhere in reference to the person of Jesus. One example occurs in his discussion of I Peter 1:21, the passage that speaks of our redemption by the precious blood of Christ by whom we believe in God. Calvin explained that there are two reasons why faith in God is not possible apart from the mediatorship of Christ. One reason is that "the greatness of the divine glory must be taken to the account, and at the same time the littleness of our capacity." Because we are very far from being able to ascend sufficiently high as to comprehend God, any and all knowledge of God without Christ is a vast abyss that swallows all our thoughts.

The second reason is that, on account of our sin and the state of enmity between God and man, we naturally dread and avoid access to God unless a "Mediator comes who can deliver us from fear." In essence, Calvin concluded, it is

> evident that we cannot believe in God except through Christ, in whom God in a manner makes himself little, that he might accommodate himself to our comprehension; and it is Christ alone who can tranquilize consciences, so that we may dare to come in confidence to God.[35]

Elsewhere he maintained that without the intercession of Christ as the mediator between God and men, any faith that we might place in God will gradually disappear, because "God's majesty is too lofty to be attained by mortal men, who are like grubs crawling upon the earth." Speaking of the church father Irenaeus (second century A. D.), who approvingly referred to the statement of an unnamed writer that the unmeasurable Father was himself subjected to measure in the Son, Calvin wrote that God "has accommodated himself to our little measure lest our minds be overwhelmed by the immensity of his glory."[36]

During his earthly ministry, Jesus accommodated his own teaching to the level of his hearers. In the John 6 passage that recounts the miraculous sign of the loaves and fishes, Jesus accused the crowd of seeking him out later, not on account of the sign he had performed, but because they had their stomachs filled. The crowd requested that Jesus perform a sign so that they might believe in him. After all, God, through Moses, had given the miraculous sign of manna from heaven to their forefathers in the desert. In response, Jesus said that he is the true bread of heaven, which, unlike manna, provides genuine life. In a discussion of this passage in the *Institutes*, Calvin again brought in accommodation. He wrote that "because the Lord was then talking to hearers who were trying only to fill their bellies with food, but were not concerned about the true food of the soul, he accommodated his language somewhat to their capacity; especially making the comparison of manna and their bodies in accordance with their understanding."[37] In essence, Jesus accommodated himself to the fixation of his listeners on eating, manna, and temporal bodily needs by employing the image of bread to draw attention to their need for eternal sustenance.

The announcement of the gospel, a manifestation of God's hidden wisdom, was likewise viewed as a gracious accommodation on God's part. "If God established everything to some purpose," Calvin argued, "it follows that we will lose nothing in hearing the Gospel, which He intended for us, for when He speaks to us He accommodates Himself to our capacity."[38]

The Principle of Accommodation and Textual Interpretation

A host of Calvin's uses of the principle of accommodation related to the proper interpretation of specific texts. In some cases, he invoked the principle of accommodation to account for perceived omissions in a text, that is, the failure of a given text to supply all the information that one might expect or wish it to supply. In his treatment in the *Institutes* of the creation of the world and all things in it, Calvin introduced his section on the creation of the angels by noting that Moses said nothing about angels in Genesis 1:

> to be sure, Moses, accommodating himself to the rudeness of the common folk, mentions in the history of the Creation no other works of God than those which show themselves to our own eyes. Yet afterward when he introduces angels as ministers of God, one may easily infer that he, to whom they devote their effort and functions, is their Creator.

Speaking in "after the manner of the common people," Moses "did not in laying down basic principles immediately reckon the angels among God's creatures," but our knowledge of them must be drawn from other portions of Scripture.[39]

In his commentary on the text in which the serpent appears in the Garden of Eden, Calvin again dealt with the failure of the text to mention something. In this case, the text makes no mention of Satan. Calvin perceived a problem in this omission. It appeared to him as scarcely consonant with reason "that the serpent only should be here brought forward, all mention of Satan being suppressed." He acknowledged that, from the Genesis 3 text considered by itself, "nothing more can be collected than that men were deceived by the serpent." The numerous testimonies elsewhere in the Bible, however, provided the grounds for the belief that "the serpent was only the mouth of the devil." But why did Moses keep back the name of Satan in Genesis 3? Calvin argued that the Holy Spirit then "purposely used obscure figures." He then reminded his readers that he had previously said

> that Moses, by a homely and uncultivated style, accommodates what he delivers to the capacity of the people; and for the best reason; for not only had he to instruct an untaught race of men, but the existing age of the Church was so puerile, that it was unable to receive any higher instruction. There is, therefore, nothing absurd in the supposition, that they, who, for the time, we know and confess to have been but as infants, were fed with milk.

He said that Moses was not to be blamed for insisting on "the rudiments suitable to children" inasmuch as he was "considering the office of schoolmaster as imposed upon him." Despite the noises of the impious to the contrary, Calvin saw nothing offensive in Moses' mode of speaking about Satan, "the prince of iniquity, under the person of his servant and instrument [i.e., the serpent], at the time when Christ, then Head of the Church, and the Sun of Righteousness, had not yet openly shone forth." Those who had an aversion to such simplicity of instruction on the part of God and his servant Moses "must of necessity condemn the whole economy of God in governing the Church." The reader should not be surprised, that, "while intent on the history he purposed to relate," Moses did not "discuss every topic which may be desired by any person whatever."[40]

Another usage of accommodation crops up in a passage in which Calvin dealt with one of the seeming factual contradictions in Scripture, namely, that pertaining to the worship action of the patriarch Jacob as he neared death. The text of Genesis 47:31 states that Jacob worshiped as he leaned upon his bed whereas Hebrews 11:21 has Jacob leaning on his staff. The writer of Hebrews adopted the Septuagint Greek translation of the Genesis text. In dealing with the discrepancy, Calvin suggested that the Septuagint translators made a mistake in their translation because the Hebrew vowel points in use in his own day were not in use when the Septuagint version was produced. Otherwise, he thought, the mistake would probably have been avoided. So why would the writer of Hebrews adopt a mistaken translation in using the word "staff?"

According to Calvin, the author of Hebrews did not hesitate to use for his own purpose what was "commonly received." The dispersed Jews to whom Hebrews was addressed were now using Greek, and so they would have been familiar with the Septuagint translation of the Old Testament. And here Calvin brought in accommodation. "We know," he said, "that the apostles were not too particular in the matter of adjusting themselves to the ignorant who still had need of milk." He saw no danger in such accommodation "provided always that the readers are brought back to the pure, original sense of Scripture."[41] The author of Hebrews was simply accommodating himself to the rendering of Genesis regarding Jacob's staff that was contained in the Septuagint, the form of the Old Testament familiar to the Jews of the *diaspora.*

Calvin also had an interesting take on Jeremiah 10:2, a verse in which the Lord warned the house of Israel not to be terrified by celestial signs. Do we not have here an inconsistency, he asked rhetorically, because God appointed the Sun, the Moon, stars, planets, and twelve constellations of the Zodiac to serve as signs? So why did the prophet forbid the Jews to fear such signs? After all, the signs were not "vain fictions" of men but creations of God. Thus, "if the stars presage to us either prosperity or adversity, it follows that they ought to be dreaded by us."

The solution to the apparent dilemma again lay in the application of accommodation. Calvin alleged that Jeremiah did not "use the word 'signs' in its proper meaning." Rather, the prophet was not referring to the true origin of signs "but accommodates himself to the notions which then prevailed." Calvin then took occasion to chastise those wicked and unprincipled people who profaned the word "signs" by the "foolish divinations" that they intermingled with genuine science.[42] In his judgment, Jeremiah accommodated himself to the erroneous understanding of the nature of signs fostered by judiciary astrology in his use of the word.

Calvin rejected literalistic interpretations of many texts, reasoning that employment of metaphors and familiar images represented an instance of divine accommodation. For example, in Isaiah 40:12 the Creator is pictured as using scales and balances to measure out the waters, the heavens, the dust of the Earth, and the mountains and hills. Clearly such a text should not be interpreted literally. God does not literally "measure" things. He does not use literal physical balances. In referring in the text to the measuring devices that are used by human beings, Calvin said, the Creator "accommodates himself to our ignorance; for thus does the Lord often prattle with us, and borrow comparisons from matters that are familiar to us, when he speaks of his majesty; that our ignorant and limited minds may better understand his greatness and excellence." In the same vein, of the following verse in which Isaiah asked who has counseled the spirit of the Lord, Calvin suggested that the term "spirit" is not a reference to the "essential Spirit of God," that is, the third person of the Trinity, but rather "denotes reason, judgment, or understanding; for he borrows a comparison from the nature of men, that he may more fully accommodate himself to them."[43]

Along these same lines, Calvin referred to the statement "let them be blotted out from the book of the living" in Psalm 69:28 as "an improper manner of speaking." One may infer that he was denying that there is a literal, physical "book of life" and that we must understand the "book" as an image or metaphor for something higher. Thus, he said that the reference to the book of life "is one well adapted to our limited capacity, the book of life being nothing else than the eternal purpose of God, by which he has predestinated his own people to salvation." He continued that "as God's eternal purpose of election is incomprehensible, it is said, in accommodation to the imperfection of the human understanding, that those whom God openly, and by manifest signs, enrols among this people, *are written*." David, moreover, desiring that the vengeance of God might be manifested, "properly speaks of the reprobation of his enemies in language accommodated to our understanding" when he refers to their being blotted out of the book.[44]

Like any good teacher or preacher, the divine author of Scripture employs word pictures or images to get across his point in terms that are familiar to the reader or hearer.

The Principle of Accommodation in Relation to the Natural World

Of particular significance for our present purposes is the fact that Calvin commonly appealed to the principle of accommodation in discussing the natural world. Reijer Hooykaas has pointed out not only that Calvin applied the principle in dealing with texts that pertain to nature but also that Calvin's "theory" exerted considerable influence on subsequent men of science and theologians with Calvinist sympathies such as Reformed minister-astronomer Philips van

Lansbergen (1561-1632) and John Wilkins (1614-1672) who frequently wrote about the Bible and nature.[45] Calvin's appeals to accommodation in relation to scientific issues fall into two categories. On the one hand, he noted that, where biblical writers discussed elements of the weather like rain, they made no effort to talk about the natural phenomena in scientific, philosophical, or technical terms. They simply referred to those characteristics of natural occurrences that even the most uneducated person could observe. In this way, the biblical author in question accommodated himself to his unlearned readers. On the other hand, Calvin dealt with other texts in which the biblical statements about some natural phenomenon do not seem to agree with knowledge about that phenomenon obtained via scientific investigation. Here he appealed again to accommodation and made several claims that may strike many contemporary Christians as rather provocative. We will closely examine examples from this latter category shortly.

There are several examples of the first category of Calvin's application of accommodation, particularly in relation to the Old Testament. In interpreting the statement in Stephen's sermon that "Moses was instructed in all the wisdom of the Egyptians," he noted that Moses did not use his learning as an excuse for looking down on the common people. He repeatedly made this point in discussing astronomical, geographical, and geometrical references contained in the early chapters of Genesis. Moses, he said, "could argue acutely with learned and sharper-witted men about the secrets of nature," but displayed excellent modesty by cutting out "the loftier subtleties of speech," coming down "to the ordinary capacity of everyone, even the humblest," and speaking to "uneducated people in ordinary language about things they understand from their own experience."[46] It was in handling the "secrets of nature," what we might call "natural science," that Moses was careful to speak and write in understandable language rather than with complicated concepts and technical jargon.

Calvin regarded the description of Noah's ark and its various rooms, including its dimensions, as an example in which Moses displayed his "excellent modesty." Although the great lawgiver of Israel was "educated in all the science of the Egyptians" and "was not ignorant of geometry," Calvin was unable to persuade himself that Moses had employed any geometrical subtlety in his description of the ark. Such a use would have been contrary to Moses' ordinary method. Here, too, Calvin said that Moses "everywhere spoke in a homely style, to suit the capacity of the people" and that he "purposely abstained from acute disputations, which might savour of the schools and of deeper learning."[47] Calvin further alleged that that is exactly how Moses had written about the heavenly bodies in Genesis 1, namely, in a popular manner rather than scientifically.

Calvin found the principle of accommodation in relation to the natural world at work in much of the wisdom literature. The book of Job includes a lengthy discourse (chapters 32-37) by Elihu, Job's young friend, in which Elihu referred to God's employment of atmospheric phenomena such as clouds, rain, thunder, and lightning. In his fifth sermon on Job 36, the chapter in which Elihu alluded to many of these atmospheric phenomena, Calvin expounded on the weather to his congregation. He acknowledged that the natural causes of rain and other atmospheric phenomena are not immediately apparent to ordinary people. It was true, he said, that the reasons for the works of nature that are observed in the air are neither common nor ordinary. "If one should ask a poor silly soul how rain is engendered," he asserted, "he could not resolve him of it, because we do not see how the water mounts up, nor how the water can be engendered in the air, and it might seem a thing against reason." As a result, the "plain countryman" is in no position to discuss things that are known by philosophy. The "country folk," for example, do not understand why the middle regions of the atmosphere are colder than at the Earth's surface in spite of being closer to the Sun. But, despite the fact that God has such works that are high and difficult to comprehend, it was the intent of the Holy Spirit in the book of Job "to teach us grossly according to our rudeness and homeliness." Consequently, in his discourse, "Elihu set down an example of the works of nature that we say are common. We do not need to go to school nor to be great clerks in order to have knowledge of the rain, of hail, of fair weather, and of the changes that we see in the air," because we all observe the phenomena of the air without fully comprehending their causes. The Spirit of God simply referred to phenomena with which we are acquainted through daily experience rather than talking abstrusely about the physical causes of those phenomena. Ironically, Calvin did not fully apply to himself the principle of accommodation to his own audience at this point, because he proceeded to preach a few sentences about the current philosophical explanations for the origins of rain and other atmospheric phenomena![48]

In Psalm 19, David wrote that God had established a tent or tabernacle for the Sun. He said that the Sun runs its course across the heavens. Calvin suggested that David had especially chosen the heavens, out of the entire fabric of the world, to exhibit an image of God to our view. In the heavens, that image of God is more distinctly to be seen, just as a person is seen better when set on an elevated stage. Thus, Calvin said, David showed us the Sun as placed in the highest rank, because in its wonderful brightness "the majesty of God displays itself more magnificently than in all the rest." He mentioned that the planets had their motions and their "appointed places within which they run their race" and that "the firmament, by its own revolution, draws with it all the fixed stars." Despite these various heavenly motions, he maintained that "it would have been lost time for David to have attempted to teach the secrets of astronomy to the rude and unlearned; and therefore he reckoned it sufficient to speak in a homely style." His object was to "reprove the whole world of ingratitude, if, in beholding the sun, they are not taught the fear and the knowledge of God." That was why David said that "a tent or pavilion has been erected for the sun, and also why he says, that he goes forth from one end of the heaven, and quickly passes to the other and opposite end." According to Calvin, David

> does not here discourse scientifically (as he might have done, had he spoken among philosophers) concerning the entire revolution which the sun performs, but, accommodating himself to the rudest and dullest, he confines himself to

the ordinary appearances presented to the eye, and, for this reason, he does not speak of the other half of the sun's course, which does not appear in our hemisphere.[49]

David accommodated to his readers by not talking about what happens to the Sun after it sets and before it rises again in the morning. One might, of course, question Calvin' assumption that David (or Moses) was sufficiently knowledgeable about the heavens to discuss "scientifically" the structure of the cosmos with the learned of his day. It is possible that David simply wrote his poetry in terms of the naive observations that would have been familiar to any Jewish shepherd boy. Be that as it may, Calvin detected the use of accommodation on the Psalmist's part.

Calvin also saw hints of accommodation in Psalm 148 where the psalmist called upon the waters above the heavens to give praise to God. He thought that it would be "adhering too strictly to the letter of the words employed, to conceive as if there were some sea up in the heavens, where the waters were permanently deposited." After all, he wrote, "Moses and the Prophets ordinarily speak in a popular style, suited to the lowest apprehension" and it would be absurd to try to reduce what they said to "the rules of philosophy." In the passage under consideration, the Psalmist "notes the marvelous fact that God holds the waters suspended in the air, because it seems contrary to nature that they should mount aloft, and also, that though fluid they should hang in vacant space." Calvin observed that the Psalmist had borrowed his form of expression from Moses who had said in Genesis 1 that the waters were divided from the waters.[50]

Calvin found the principle of accommodation operating in the prophetic writings, too. Of Jeremiah 31:35-36, a passage in which the weeping prophet talked about the daily course of the Sun and the Moon, he pointed out that Jeremiah "spoke popularly, and according to the common notions," as the prophets generally did. If, however, the prophets had "philosophized" as the "astrologers" do by talking about the monthly course of the Moon or of the annual course of the Sun, Calvin reasoned, then the common people would not have understood them, because these motions of the Sun and the Moon are much less obvious to ordinary folk than are the daily movements. The prophets were content to state things that could be comprehended by children. Even they can plainly see that the Sun, the Moon, and the stars orbit the Earth every day. Nor was there any need for Jeremiah to indulge in a subtle discussion about whether or not the center of the Earth can be discovered. It is not that such inquiries are wrong or useless, for, after all, "the philosophers do indeed bring some probable reasons as to the extent of the heavens, and the dimension of the earth is also conjectured by them." Jeremiah's purpose, however, was to declare, "according to the common and popular mode of speaking, that God's mercy would be perpetual and immeasurable towards the children of Abraham, like the immensity of the earth and the heavens, which exceeds the comprehension of the human mind."[51] Scientific discourses would only distract from the establishment of that main point.

The New Testament apostles, likewise, followed Moses' lead in regard to accommodation. In comments on a text that describes the apostle Paul as speaking to the people of Lystra about the goodness of God in sending rains, fruitful seasons, and food, Calvin observed that the apostles did not offer "a closely reasoned discourse in the philosophical manner about the secrets of nature." Paul did not begin to explore theories of the origin of rain, for example. Because the apostles were speaking to an unlearned multitude, it behooved them to set before that multitude in very plain terms that which the most ignorant among them already knew.[52]

There are, therefore, a sufficient number of examples to support the claim that Calvin thought that the authors of Scripture, when discussing aspects of the natural world, always spoke in the daily language of ordinary people. They did not discuss the natural world scientifically, technically, or philosophically, in Calvin's judgment.

Accommodation and Astronomy

Calvin invoked the principle of accommodation in his discussions of specific phenomena of nature, particularly with respect to geography and astronomy. In regard to the phenomena of astronomy, there seemed to him to be some disjunction between the biblical affirmations and the scientific knowledge of his day. Application of the principle of accommodation to deal with these presumed disjunctions showed up in Calvin's commentary on the first chapter of Genesis. After bringing in the idea of accommodation in regard to creation of the universe in six days (Genesis 1:5), he alluded to the principle again in his comments on the very next verse. In reflecting on God's creation of the expanse and the separation of the waters by that expanse, Calvin said he believed that it was "a certain principle" that the text was not treating anything other than the "visible form of the world." He intimated that Moses did not intend to teach a precise, technical account of the structure or the functioning of the heavens. The reader who might be looking to the biblical text to "learn astronomy, and other recondite arts" was strongly advised to "go elsewhere." As far as the text was concerned, the Spirit of God was interested in teaching "all men without exception." The waters about which Moses spoke, Calvin maintained, were but those which "the rude and unlearned may perceive" and that meant the ordinary clouds suspended in the air.[53] He did not suggest that Christian believers ought to be using the Bible as a sourcebook for the fundamentals of astronomy. In short, he thought that the text spoke the language of appearances with regard to the heavenly bodies.

The principle of accommodation came in for much more extensive treatment in the discussion of the work of the fourth day of creation on which God is said to have made the greater light, the lesser light, and the stars. We ascertain from Calvin's remarks that some of his contemporaries believed that there was a contrast between what the Bible said about the sizes of the heavenly bodies and what was known about their sizes from scientific investigation. He solved the problem by an appeal to accommodation. Even though Moses referred to the Sun as the "greater light" and the Moon as the "lesser light," Calvin argued that he was not philosophically discussing the sizes of the Sun or the Moon. Instead, he was addressing himself to our senses. Calvin chided those who rebuked Moses because he did not speak with greater exactness on the grounds that the great lawgiver of Israel was not speaking as an astronomer. Because he was speaking as a theologian, Moses was more concerned about us than he was about the stars. Although Moses was not ignorant of the fact that the Moon does not have sufficient brightness to light the Earth very much, he simply did not "descant subtilely like a philosopher about the secrets of nature." Moses' purpose was different from that of the philosophers or astronomers. He assigned a place in the heavens to the stars and planets, but the astronomers drew distinctions regarding the spheres. Moreover, Calvin noted, the astronomers had conclusively demonstrated that the planet Saturn is larger than the Moon. Being a theologian, he made no mention of which astronomers had conducted the demonstration, nor did he talk about what methods had been used for determining sizes of heavenly objects. At least he observed that the reason that Saturn does not appear to be larger than it does is because of its much greater distance from us compared with the Moon. He did not address the question as to whether Moses actually knew that Saturn is larger than the Moon. The point for him was that Moses, as the author of Genesis, was not interested in technical astronomy or in making a show of any advanced knowledge he might have possessed. Instead, he wrote in a popular style "things which, without instruction, all ordinary persons, endued with common sense, are able to understand." In contrast, the astronomers "investigate with great labor whatever the sagacity of the human mind can comprehend." It would be an unwarranted inference, Calvin insisted, to conclude that Moses wanted us to neglect astronomy, but as

> he was ordained a teacher as well of the unlearned and rude and of the learned, he could not otherwise fulfill his office than by descending to this grosser method of instruction. Had he spoken of things generally unknown, the uneducated might have pleaded in excuse that such subjects were beyond their capacity. Lastly, since the Spirit of God here opens a common school for all, it is not surprising that he should chiefly choose those subjects which would be intelligible to all. If the astronomer inquires respecting the actual dimensions of the stars, he will find the moon to be less than Saturn; but this is something abstruse, for to the sight it appears differently. Moses, rather adapts his discourse to common usage. For since the Lord stretches forth, as it were, his hand to us in causing us to enjoy the brightness of the sun and moon, how great would be our ingratitude were we to close our eyes against our own experience?

The astronomers are certainly entitled to "their more exalted knowledge," said Calvin, but for ordinary folk, "they who perceive by the moon the splendor of night, are convicted by its use of perverse ingratitude unless they acknowledge the beneficence of God."[54]

Calvin returned to this issue in his commentary on Genesis 6. As noted previously, Moses did not engage in fine reasoning about the geometry of Noah's ark, despite his advanced learning acquired in Egypt. In support of Moses' alleged application of accommodation in that passage, Calvin again referred his readers to Genesis 1 and reiterated the ideas that he had espoused in his commentary on that chapter. He reminded his readers that, in the first chapter, Moses did not treat the stars in a scientific manner, as a philosopher would do. On the contrary, he described the heavenly bodies, "in a popular manner, according to their appearance to the uneducated, rather than according to truth, two great lights."[55]

This last quotation may be jarring to contemporary Christians who place great emphasis on the idea of the inerrancy of Scripture. Many lay Christians who hold to inerrancy are prone to regard all assertions, statements, or affirmations of Scripture as truthful and literally accurate, even such affirmations as pertain to matters of history, geography, or science.[56] Calvin, however, maintained that Genesis 1 is not speaking "according to truth" when referring to the Sun and the Moon. In effect, he said that the Bible does not represent to us the actual reality about the heavenly bodies by providing an accurate picture of their true size. It certainly does not provide us with a scientific description. By no stretch of the imagination, however, did Calvin imply that Scripture had made a mistake or an error, either deliberately or unwittingly. After all, God, the ultimate author of Scripture is truth himself and can neither lie nor make mistakes. Implicit in Calvin's interpretation of the fourth day of creation, therefore, is that Scripture is not always interested in presenting an unerring picture of physical reality to its readers. As such, the Bible is not always concerned to affirm one kind of truth, namely, the truth of scientific exactitude or even of scientific reality.

Calvin also alluded to the heavenly bodies in his second sermon on Job 9, a chapter that forms a part of the discourse of Job in which he spoke of God as creator of the various constellations. In this sermon, Calvin preached that Christians should "mark well that Job's intent here is to teach us to be astronomers so far as our capacity will bear." The point of our being "astronomers" is that we "may refer all to the glorifying of God, so goodly order in the heaven as we see." In the sermon, Calvin again pointed out that the Moon is not larger than "the other stars or planets, for it is certain that there are stars in the sky which are bigger than the moon." The reason that the stars do not appear to be larger to us is "because of their far distance from us." As in his Genesis commentary, he neither mentioned the names of those astronomers who made measurements of size or distance of the heavenly bodies nor the methods used. It sufficed for him to observe that the stars "are exceeding high in respect of us, insomuch that they seem not so great as they be, by reason of the great distance that is between the skies and us. And God speaketh unto us of these things, according to our perceiving of them, and not according as they be." Calvin summed up the essential meaning of the text regarding the great lights by proclaiming that "all men attain not to so sharp understanding as to know how big the planets are, what is the proportion of the stars, and how they be divided. Every man knows not this; but open your eyes and look up, and you shall see the sun which is a lantern of light."[57]

In the Genesis commentary, Calvin observed that Scripture did not speak "according to truth," and in this sermon, he preached that God did not speak about the heavenly bodies "according as they be." His point again was that God does not always address us in Scripture by speaking in exact accordance with physical reality. The reality, the physical truth, the actual state of affairs may in some cases be overlooked or ignored by the biblical writer under the inspiration of the Holy Spirit to get across a more important spiritual point to the hearer or reader of Scripture.

Astronomy also came up for discussion in the commentary on Psalm 136. This Psalm speaks of God making the heavens by his understanding, spreading out the Earth upon the waters, and making the great lights, namely the Sun to rule over the day and the Moon and the stars to rule over the night. In reviewing this passage, Calvin asserted again that the Holy Spirit had no intention to teach astronomy. In proposing instruction meant to be common to the simplest, least educated people, the Holy Spirit made use of popular language by Moses and the other prophets so that no one "might shelter himself under the pretext of obscurity." Such a strategy by the Holy Spirit was necessitated by the fact that people sometimes "very readily pretend an incapacity to understand, when anything deep or recondite is submitted to their notice." That would certainly happen if the psalmist engaged in a technical discussion about astronomy.   In Scripture, therefore, the Holy Spirit speaks so plainly that this excuse for not understanding is removed. Accordingly, Calvin said that even though Saturn really is larger than the Moon, it does not appear to be so to the eye because of the greater distance of Saturn. But the Holy Spirit would rather speak "childishly than unintelligibly to the humble and unlearned."[58] He further believed that the same remarks were applicable to what the Psalmist added regarding God's having assigned the Sun and the Moon their roles of ruling the day and ruling the night respectively. By these terms, he observed, we are not to understand that the Sun and the Moon exercise any government in and of themselves. The point is that the administrative power of God is very manifest in this distribution of light to the heavenly bodies. The Sun in illuminating the Earth through the day and the Moon and stars by night may be said to yield a reverential homage to God. One may surmise that Calvin might have balked at the language employed by some contemporary scientists to the effect that the world is "governed" by the laws of nature or that chemical reactions are "governed" by the laws of chemical thermodynamics. The things or laws created by God do not act as governors, but God governs his creation and everything in it through the instrumentality of his creatures.

In summary, in dealing with astronomy Calvin used the idea of accommodation to make the point that the biblical text sometimes speaks in terms of the way things appear as opposed to the way that things really are. In some cases the truth stated in Scripture is the truth of appearance rather than the truth of reality.

Accommodation and Geography

Calvin also applied the principle of accommodation to discussions about geography. The principle of accommodation was clearly very much on his mind as he worked on the Genesis commentary. No sooner had he invoked the principle in his extensive remarks on the work of the fourth day of creation than he introduced it again in talking about the location of the Garden of Eden described in Genesis 2. Here he dealt with the problem of the four rivers. Then, as now, everyone agreed on the identity of the Tigris and Euphrates Rivers, but the identities of the Pison and Gihon Rivers posed difficulties. Some writers had identified them with rivers far from Mesopotamia such as the Nile, the Ganges, or the Danube, but he thought it more likely that the Pison and Gihon were obsolete names of two other rivers in the vicinity of the Tigris and Euphrates. The text also mentioned that one river divided into four heads, and the interpretation of that statement remained problematic. As we saw in chapter 4, Calvin rejected the solution of those who would free themselves from the difficulty by imagining that the deluge had so altered the surface of the globe that the courses of the rivers had been thoroughly disturbed and changed. Despite changes brought about by the curse and the possibility of the Earth being laid waste in places by the flood, Calvin asserted that "it was the same earth which had been created in the beginning." Then he wrote "that Moses (in my judgment) accommodated his topography to the capacity of his age." Unfortunately, he threw out the statement without specifying exactly how Moses accommodated his topography to the capacity of the age. Perhaps he meant that Moses wrote his description of the Garden of Eden in terms of geographical features that were known to his readers.

Calvin then attempted a solution to the problem of the four heads. The four heads, he said, included both the sources of the rivers and their mouths. The Euphrates had formerly been joined to the Tigris "that it might justly be said, one river was divided into four heads; especially, if what is manifest to all be conceded, that Moses does not speak acutely, nor in a philosophical manner, but popularly, so that every one least informed may understand him." As an example of such a popular manner of speaking, Calvin referred back to the first chapter of Genesis in which Moses "called the sun and moon two great luminaries; not because the moon exceeded other planets in magnitude, but because, to common observation, it seemed greater." In what way, however, did Moses speak popularly rather than philosophically regarding the rivers? Despite the fact that commentators have struggled with the meaning of the statement about the four heads for centuries, Calvin intimated that the meaning of the statement was clear to the "least informed." Moses seemed "to remove all doubt when he says that the river had four heads, because it was divided from that place. What does this mean, except that the channels were divided, out of one confluent stream, either above or below Paradise?"[59] A facsimile of an old map of Mesopotamia was included in some early French, English, and Latin editions of the commentary on Genesis to illustrate Calvin's contention. The map shows the Tigris and Euphrates joining below Babylon and flowing as one river for some distance but then dividing again into two separate streams prior to emptying into the Persian Gulf. The conjoined Tigris and Euphrates below Babylon represents the one river. The four heads are the separate Tigris and Euphrates Rivers upstream from the confluence and the separate Tigris and Euphrates Rivers downstream from a point where they diverge before flowing into the gulf. Four separate channels either flow into or emerge from the one stretch of united river. The implication for Calvin was that the Pison and Gihon were obsolete names for two of the channels of the Tigris and Euphrates Rivers.

Calvin applied the principle of accommodation in regard to the relative positions of land and sea. Psalm 24:2 is but one of a number of verses suggesting that a great body of water exists beneath the land. This verse states that God founded the earth upon the seas. Calvin maintained that David was not disputing philosophically concerning the situation of the Earth when he said that the Earth been founded upon the seas. As in so many other instances, he insisted that David was using popular language and adapting himself to the "capacity of the unlearned," an assertion that implies that the idea of a subterranean body of water amounted to the common belief of the people. Calvin acknowledged that there was some justification for speaking in the manner that David had spoken. Although the earth is beneath the waters because, as an element, it "occupies the lowest place in the order of the sphere," nevertheless, "the habitable part of the earth is above the water." How can we account for this separation of elemental water from elemental earth remaining stable, he asked, unless "God has put the waters underneath as it were for a foundation."[60] In the end, Calvin himself seemed to think that the habitable Earth actually is above some waters.

Zechariah 9:10 says that the coming Messianic king will "proclaim peace to the nations. His rule will extend from sea to sea and from the river to the ends of the earth." Although Calvin did not use his accustomed language of accommodation in commenting on this verse, the concept was in his mind, because he understood that Zechariah was speaking to the Jews in terms of their own comprehension of world geography. Calvin believed that the expression "from sea to sea" referred to the Red Sea on the one hand to "the Syrian sea, towards Cilicia" on the other, no doubt referring to the Mediterranean Sea. The river referred to the Euphrates. By the "ends of the earth" or the extreme borders of the Earth, Calvin insisted, the reader ought "not to understand the whole world, as some interpreters have unwisely said; for the Prophet no doubt mentioned those places already known to the Jews." In other words, the universalism of the prophet was expressed in terms of the farthest reaches of the world that were known to the Jews. In that sense, Zechariah accommodated himself to the contemporary, limited geographic knowledge of the Jews. It would have made no sense for the prophet to have spoken in terms of far distant geographic features completely unknown to his hearers to make a point about the global reach of the coming Messiah's kingdom.[61]

One final text pertaining to geography remains for our consideration. That is the Solomonic and Messianic Psalm 72. Verse eight makes the identical claim about the extent of the king's rule that Zechariah made. Calvin was much more verbose with respect to this verse than he was in regard to the Zechariah text, and he explicitly brought in his accommodation concept. He traced the geographic limits in Psalm 72:8 back to Genesis 15:18 where, he observed, the Lord had assigned these four boundaries when he promised the land of Canaan to his people for an inheritance. According to Calvin, the psalmist intimated that possession of the promised land would be entire so long as the kingdom continued to exist. The psalmist wished "to teach the faithful that the blessing of God cannot be fully realized, except whilst this kingdom shall flourish." Consequently, he declared that the king would "exercise dominion from the Red Sea, or from that arm of the Egyptian sea to the sea of Syria, which is called the Sea of the Philistines, and also from the river Euphrates to the great wilderness."

Calvin raised the objection of some that these narrow limits hardly corresponded "with the kingdom of Christ, which was to be extended from the rising of the sun to the going down thereof." In refuting the objection, he responded that "David obviously accommodates his language to his own time, the amplitude of the kingdom of Christ not having been, as yet, fully unfolded. He has therefore begun his description in phraseology well known, and in familiar use under the law and the prophets; and even Christ himself commenced his reign within the limits here marked out before he penetrated to the uttermost boundaries of the earth."[62] As with the Zechariah text, Calvin implied that it would have been poor pedagogy for David to have described Messiah's universal reign in terms of a geographical description that someone from the 16th century might have embraced, a description that would have included the global nature of the Earth and continents far removed from Israel's world on the other side of vast oceans. In effect, David chose to describe Messiah's universal reign not in terms of the way the globe really is but in terms of geographical locators with which the Jews were familiar and were a part of their world. These geographical texts accommodated or adapted themselves to the restricted knowledge of the readers. Unlike the astronomical texts, they do not adapt to the appearance of things.

To this point we have examined several instances in which Calvin stated explicitly or implicitly that the biblical author did not discuss some physical aspect of the created order as it really is or according to physical truth but only as it appeared to the sense of sight or else as common folk understood that aspect. Calvin was wary of treating biblical texts as scientifically accurate documents. Because he did not think that they provide precise technical information about the natural world, he encouraged those who would learn astronomy to go to another source. Given his comments about geography, he might just as well have said that he who would learn the details of geography and topography should also go elsewhere. Because the biblical authors were able to tolerate the common and less than accurate perceptions and beliefs that ordinary folk have about the world, they were thereby able to reach those people in spite of, or even through, those less than accurate perceptions in order to make valid theological

affirmations. The implication of many of Calvin's comments about accommodation is that the perceptions and conceptions about nature to which the biblical
authors accommodated themselves were incomplete, naïve, or conceivably, mistaken.

With respect to one text, Calvin explicitly brought up, and favored, the idea
that the conception of ordinary people to which the biblical writer accommodated himself was indeed in error. The passage in question is Psalm 58:4. In the
psalm David wrote about the wickedness and injustice perpetrated by rulers.
"Their venom," he wrote, "is like the venom of a snake, like that of a cobra that
has stopped its ears, that will not heed the tune of the charmer, however skillful
the enchanter may be." Calvin's extensive comments on this verse are sufficiently striking—and somewhat unnerving to the contemporary conservative
inerrantist ear—that a lengthy extract is quoted here:

> The more emphatically to express their consummate subtlety, he compares
> them to deaf serpents, which shut their ears against the voice of the charmer—
> not the common kind of serpents, but such as are famed for their cunning, and
> are upon their guard against every artifice of that description. But is there such
> a thing, it may be asked, as enchantment? If there were not, it might seem ab-
> surd and childish to draw a comparison from it, unless we suppose David to
> speak in mere accommodation to mistaken, though generally received opinion.
> He would certainly seem, however, to insinuate that serpents can be fascinated
> by enchantment; and I can see no harm in granting it. The Marsi in Italy were
> believed by the ancients to excel in the art. Had there been no enchantments
> practiced, where was the necessity of their being forbidden and condemned un-
> der the Law? I do not mean to say that there is an actual method or art by which
> fascination can be effected. It was doubtless done by a mere sleight of Satan,
> whom God has suffered to practice his delusions upon unbelieving and ignorant
> men, although he prevents him from deceiving those who have been enlight-
> ened by his word and Spirit. But we may avoid all occasion for such curious
> inquiry, by adopting the view already referred to, that David here borrows his
> comparison from a popular and prevailing error, and is to be merely supposed
> as saying, that no kind of serpent was imbued with greater craft than his ene-
> mies, not even the species (if such there were) which guards itself against en-
> chantment.[63]

In this passage, Calvin granted the possibility that snakes could actually be
enchanted by their charmers, perhaps through the working of Satan. But this
view he regarded as a "curious inquiry," and so he favored a view that denied
that snakes really can be enchanted by the charmers. In effect, the idea of enchantment of cobras or venomous serpents by snake charmers is merely "a
popular and prevailing error." The common lot may think that snakes can really
be charmed, but they are wrong in so thinking. But the psalmist, for the sake of
argument, assumes the truth of the popular, but mistaken, notion in order to
draw out his analogy between snakes and the wicked rulers. Here Calvin explicitly had the psalmist accommodating himself to an error in belief. The text
sounds like it accepts the reality of snake-charming, but it is doing so only to

call attention to the sinful behavior of certain people by way of an image or analogy.

To make matters even more interesting, the text involves a significant statement that Calvin failed to address, because he was not aware of the problem. The entire passage implies either that the enchantment of cobras is done through the sound of the music which the cobra hears with its ears, or it may be that the hearing with its ears is a part of the belief of common people about cobras. The fact of the matter is that cobras lack ears in the sense that mammals do. Cobras do not hear musical sounds although they may sense vibrations, and they do not respond to the music that is played by snake charmers. As a result, cobras cannot stop their ears, assuming they wanted to, from heeding the tune of the charmer because they do not hear the tune in the first place. Cobras used by snake charmers sway in response to the movement of the instrument played by the charmer, not to the tune. Among the snakes, cobras have remarkably strong eyesight, are extremely attuned to motion, and position themselves to strike a moving object when it gets too close.

Calvin seemed to go beyond assigning the accommodation to perception as he did with astronomical matters. He went beyond saying that snakes *appear* to be enchanted by music even though they really aren't. It is unsatisfactory to say that people in the Old Testament simply assumed that snakes *appeared* to be able to hear and to sway to music in the same sense that they assumed that the Moon appears to be larger than the stars. There is little reason to doubt that people of Old Testament times literally believed that snakes respond to music. Even today many people believe that such is the case. Nor do we have evidence that talking about snakes stopping their ears was simply a figure of speech. If it were, it would undoubtedly be based on the presumption that snakes can hear.

If we follow Calvin's line of thinking, this text takes advantage of and employs a popular misconception about snakes and snake charming. In effect, the Bible, on the face of it, seems to make an assertion about the natural world that is known to be incorrect. Calvin's doctrine of accommodation provides a solution to the problem. The assertion about snakes and ears and music is not the point the Bible is driving at. We should not come away from the text believing that cobras have musically attuned ears simply because the Bible seems to imply that it is so. Calvin's doctrine of accommodation is flexible enough to include even the possibility that the Bible employs a mistaken idea about the natural world in making theological or ethical points without making any attempt to correct the mistaken idea. In other words the text does not take the trouble to say that snakes cannot really be enchanted by "snake charmers" nor to say that snakes do not really possess the ability to hear music or sounds. This passage certainly raises the question as to whether Scripture incorporates other statements about the natural world without necessarily endorsing them.

We have seen that Calvin used the principle of accommodation in a wide variety of situations. As David Wright has pointed out, Calvin did not tolerate the possibility of ethical or religious accommodation in Scripture. For our purposes, however, we must note that Calvin did use the principle several times in the interpretation of texts that bear on phenomena or characteristics of the natural world. On more than one occasion, he stated or intimated that when Scripture accommodated itself to its readers, it did not necessarily speak in accord with the way things really are, and it sometimes employed the erroneous beliefs about the world entertained by common folk. In the final chapter we will explore how Calvin's principle of accommodation might be applied to contemporary discussions about science in the context of Christian faith.

NOTES

1.   D. Russell Humphreys, "Accelerated Nuclear Decay: a Viable Hypothesis?" in *Radioisotopes and the Age of the Earth*, ed. Larry Vardiman, Andrew A. Snelling, and Eugene F. Chaffin, (St. Joseph, Mo.: Creation Research Society, 2000), 333-79. See 351-56 for biblical references that allegedly allude to acceleration of rates of nuclear decay.

2.   Ford Lewis Battles, "God Was Accommodating Himself to Human Capacity," *Interpretation* 31, (1977): 19-38. This article is particularly valuable for an understanding of the broader application of Calvin's principle of accommodation.

3.   Battles, "God Was Accommodating Himself," 20.

4.   Ibid., 22.

5.   John Chrysostom, *Homilies on Genesis 1-17* (Washington: The Catholic University of America Press, 1986), Homily IV.11, and Thomas Aquinas, *Summa Theologiae* (London: Eyre and Spottiswoode, 1964), I.70.1. See also I.68.3 where Aquinas said that "Moses was speaking to ignorant people and out of condescension to their simpleness presented to them only those things that are immediately obvious to the senses."

6.   David F. Wright, "Calvin's "Accommodation" Revisited," in *Calvin as Exegete*, ed. Peter de Klerk (Grand Rapids, Mich.: Calvin Studies Society, 1995), 171-90.

7.   Battles, "God Was Accommodating Himself," 20.

8.   Clinton M. Ashley, "John Calvin's Utilization of the Principle of Accommodation and its Continuing Significance for an Understanding of Biblical Language" (Ph. D. Dissertation, Southwestern Baptist Theological Seminary, 1972), 64.

9.   Battles, "God Was Accommodating Himself," 21.

10.   Ibid., 20.

11.   Commentary on Romans 1:14.

12.   Commentary on John 3:12.

13.   Commentary on Psalm 78:60.

14.   Commentary on Ezekiel 9:3.

15.   Commentary on Romans 1:19.

16.   Institutes 1.13.1

17.   Commentary on Psalm 78:65.

18.   Commentary on Genesis 28:13.

19.   Commentary on Genesis 35:7.

20.   Commentary on Ezekiel 1:25-26.

21.   Commentary on Psalm 93:2.

22.   Institutes 1.17.13

23.   Commentary on Amos 7:3.

24.   Commentary on Jonah 3:10.

25.   Commentary on Amos 6:8.

26.   Commentary on Genesis 1:5.

27.   Commentary on Acts 12:10.

28.   Institutes 1.14.11.

29.   Institutes 2.11.13.

30.   Institutes 2.7.2.

31.   Institutes 2.16.2.

32.   Institutes 1.11.1. The mid-nineteenth century translation of Henry Beveridge uses the expression "in accommodation to the rude and gross intellect of man."

33.   Institutes 4.1.1.

34. John Calvin, *The Deity of Christ and Other Sermons*, trans. Leroy Nixon (Grand Rapids, Mich.: William B. Eerdmans, 1950). The quotation is from the sermon on "The Deity of Christ."

35. Commentary on I Peter 1:21.

36. Institutes 2.6.4.

37. Institutes 2.10.6.

38. Commentary on I Corinthians 2:7.

39. Institutes 1.14.3.

40. Commentary on Genesis 3:1.

41. Commentary on Hebrews 11:21.

42. Commentary on Jeremiah 10:2.

43. Commentary on Isaiah 40:12-13.

44. Commentary on Psalm 69:28.

45. Reijer Hooykaas, *Religion and the Rise of Modern Science* (Grand Rapids, Mich.: William B. Eerdmans, 1972), 117-30.

46. Commentary on Acts 7:22.

47. Commentary on Genesis 6:14.

48. Fifth Sermon on Job 36.

49. Commentary on Psalm 19:4.

50. Commentary on Psalm 148:3.

51. Commentary on Jeremiah 31:35-36.

52. Commentary on Acts 14:17.

53. Commentary on Genesis 1:6.

54. Commentary on Genesis 1:16.

55. Commentary on Genesis 6:14.

56. The classic article that spells out the concept of biblical inerrancy is Archibald A. Hodge and Benjamin B. Warfield, "Inspiration," *Presbyterian Review* 2, (1881): 225-60.

57. Second Sermon on Job 9.

58. Commentary on Psalm 136:7.

59. Commentary on Genesis 2:10.

60. Commentary on Psalm 24:2.

61. Commentary on Zechariah 9:10.

62. Commentary on Psalm 72:8.

63. Commentary on Psalm 58:4.

CHAPTER 8

CALVIN AND CONTEMPORARY SCIENCE

Let's conclude with a few observations and recommendations regarding the contemporary relevance of some of John Calvin's views about natural science, the natural world, and the interpretation of Scripture in relation to scientific matters. The spiritual descendants of the great theologian of the Protestant Reformation enthusiastically accept much if not most of what he had to say from a theological point of view. Calvinists still eagerly consult the *Institutes* and the commentaries as much as, if not more than, they consult recent commentaries and volumes on systematic theology to see what profound insights Calvin had to offer on a wide range of topics. The question before us now is whether we can learn anything of value from Calvin that is applicable to our modern situation in regard to natural science. Did he have anything worthwhile to say about how a Christian should relate to the natural world or must we simply view Calvin's thoughts on scientific study solely as a matter of historical curiosity? When I ask whether Calvin can teach us anything that is relevant to our modern situation I have in mind some of the following questions: was he hostile toward science, skeptical of science, accepting of science with qualifications, or uncritically accepting of science? Did he adopt positions regarding the structure of the cosmos on the basis of the biblical text that we ought to adopt today? Did he adopt views regarding the age of the universe and the Earth, the effects of the fall, and the nature and extent of the flood that ought to affect the way that we think about those issues? Lastly, exactly how did Calvin interpret those parts of Holy Scripture that appear to provide information about the physical character of the world?

Calvin's Attitude toward Scientific Activity

We begin with Calvin's general attitude toward the practice of the natural sciences. Although science was vastly different in the sixteenth century from what it is now, there were, nevertheless, many individuals who attempted to ascertain the character and behavior of physical and biological entities by careful observation, measurement, reasoned reflection, or whatever method seemed to yield fruitful results. Some of these individuals were not Christian believers. As we learned in Chapter 1, there is no question that Calvin very much approved of efforts to understand the structure and workings of the world, seeing in them a form of uncovering the glory of God that is revealed in his handiwork. Specifically, he repeatedly lauded the science of astronomy and regarded it as a very useful enterprise. He wished that we could all learn as much astronomy as matched our capabilities. He regarded astronomy as the handmaiden of theology. We see no hint of Calvin rejecting the entire scientific enterprise or of refusing to accept scientific conclusions because they had been drawn by persons who were not Christians. While ardently desiring that unbelieving philosophers who engaged in the study of the natural world would give glory to God and would recognize God's guiding providence in the functioning of the cosmos, Calvin never rejected their attempts to explain natural phenomena in terms of secondary causes.

Calvin projected a deep appreciation of the natural world as well as a very positive attitude toward scientific endeavor aimed at understanding that world. His positive attitude pervades the commentaries and his little book, *A Warning against Judiciary Astrology*. What struck me most forcefully, however, is the fact that Calvin not only expressed his positive feelings toward science in writing but that he also preached scientifically-oriented sermons that focused on natural phenomena! The sermons on Job are a case in point. He used several passages in Job to elaborate on the nature of animals or on the behavior and causes of various aspects of weather. He even encouraged his congregation in the pursuit and study of science! As a Christian professional geologist with an intense love of rocks and mountains, of birds, and of all God's creation, I deeply appreciate, heartily applaud, and enthusiastically endorse Calvin's positive attitude toward nature and science. I earnestly wish that both the contemporary church and individual Christians would emulate his attitude. What a wonderful development it would be if the church generally and theologians and preachers particularly would vigorously and passionately promote the pursuit of scientific investigation of God's creation! The church rightly encourages its young people to pursue the high calling of proclaiming the gospel as pastors, missionaries, or teachers in Christian schools. Without neglecting these utterly essential callings that lie at the core of its ministry, the church would also do well to encourage young people to use their God-given curiosity and talents to serve the Lord of creation by seeking careers in the various natural sciences, not to mention other worthwhile areas of endeavor. Moreover, the church would be acting more biblically if it were to promote among all of its members the development of a love and appreciation for God's creation. Would that the pastors would invite church members to escape on occasion from the computer, the television, the cell phone, and maybe even one more church meeting in order to spend time outdoors enjoying the sky, the trees, the birds, the rocks, and the butterflies! The church should encourage its members to learn about the natural world and to develop a hobby such as stargazing (Calvin would have approved!), butterfly chasing, mineral collecting, or bird watching. And the church ought to inculcate in its members a passion for preserving God's creation as well.

But why should the church encourage young people to pursue natural science as a career? The church should practice such encouragement precisely so that young Christians can bring glory to their Creator by disclosing some of the mysteries of his creation. Perhaps some of the scientific knowledge and discoveries made by Christians in the sciences will lead to applications that will alleviate human suffering or benefit people in other ways. Moreover, believing scientists can use their scientific work and their positions as means for spreading the good news of salvation through Christ. Perhaps the church needs to begin thinking about biologists, physicists, and astronomers, for example, as "people groups" to be evangelized in much the same way that it views Muslims, or Navajos, or Mormons, or Hispanics, or Vietnamese. How better to reach biologists with the gospel than through Christian biologists who understand how biologists think? Is not biology, then, a profoundly Christian calling and a legitimate way to proclaim the gospel?

And why should the church encourage lay believers to take an active interest in the natural world? Would it not be refreshing to hear a preacher encourage his congregation to learn as much about the natural world as they could in their spare time so that they could more fully appreciate the remarkable creative ingenuity of their Creator, the very God that they worship and serve? One would think that a church that truly believes in the doctrine of creation would do all in its power to encourage the exploration and enjoyment of the results of God's craftsmanship by believers. And surely a church that deeply believes that God reveals himself through the created order ought to do all in its power to encourage closer familiarity with that very important means by which God reveals himself. Would we not get to know God better if we knew his works better? To profess love for God and then to ignore, be bored by, or even misuse his magnificent creation is much like professing to be deeply in love with a great composer or painter while showing no interest in, or possibly even dislike for, their musical compositions or paintings.

If the church is going to engage in such encouragement, the onus of responsibility will fall on the shoulders of the people in the pulpit. I mentioned that Calvin preached nature- and science-oriented sermons. He even encouraged his congregation to learn as much about the stars as they were able. But when was the last time you heard a sermon in which the preacher promoted science as a career or nature study as a hobby? And when did you last hear a preacher expound a biblical text, move naturally to a simple explanation of the manner in

which some wonder of nature works, and then commend the abilities and dili-
gent hard work of the scientists who discovered the way that the natural wonder
works? It doesn't happen often, does it, if at all?

Not long ago a minister in the Christian Reformed Church, Scott Hoezee,
published a book entitled *Proclaim the Wonder* in which he strongly advocated
the idea that pastors ought to work toward becoming role models for their congregations in encouraging and developing positive appreciation for the work and
the results of the sciences.[1] After all, science is in the business of explaining
how God's creation works, whether or not particular individual scientists may
see it that way. Natural science gives us a window into God's ordinary providential action with regard to the world that he made. Hoezee strongly advocated that
pastors occasionally incorporate specific illustrations from the world of nature
and science into their sermons. He hardly meant that sermons should become
scientific lectures. Far from it. Scientifically-oriented sermons should not be
forced just for the sake of working science into the sermon but should flow naturally from the text under consideration. One of the attractive features of
Hoezee's book is the inclusion of five of his sermons that incorporated themes
from or references to nature and science. An obvious case in point would be a
sermon on creation. Another might be a sermon on Psalm 19, a text that speaks
of the heavens declaring the glory of God. Would this not be an appropriate time
for a pastor to summarize for the congregation some of the wonders of the sky
that astronomers have discovered over the years? I think it would.

I can well imagine that pastors who read either Hoezee's or this book are
rolling their eyes heavenward and saying, "Give me a break! I'm already so
busy that I can barely keep up with sermon preparation and all my other respon-
sibilities. I'm being pulled in a thousand directions at once by my congregation
and my family, and now you expect me to learn some science. Get real!" Fair
enough. The science of Calvin's day was vastly easier to grasp than contemporary science is. Most pastors are just as intimidated by the natural sciences as the
rest of the human race. They generally avoid science like the proverbial plague!
They wish to stick to something they know like Hebrew and Greek and even
those, as they will tell you, are difficult enough!

But what I am suggesting is not quite so terrifying as one might imagine.
Pastors don't have to become experts in solving differential equations or delve
into the arcane details of quantum mechanics. I suspect that pastors already
spend plenty of time consulting commentaries, Bible handbooks, theological
dictionaries, concordances, and the like. Well, why not try working through
some scientific popularizations or introductory textbooks in one or two of the
natural sciences from time to time?[2] Watch *Nova* and some of the other excellent
programs about science on public television. And by all means, pastors, take
advantage of the scientific expertise that might be available right in your own
congregation. Seek the advice of practicing scientists in your congregations before making pulpit pronouncements of a scientific nature. Take a scientist to
lunch and pick his or her brains! Consult a biologist within the congregation to
find out about biological evolution. Consult a geologist within the congregation

to learn about the age of the Earth or about the geological effects of the deluge. Consult an astronomer to learn about the expanding universe or the Big Bang. I confess to some frustration on this point because I do not recall being asked for advice by a preacher in regard to a scientific question in preparation for a sermon. My experience provides likely evidence that the pastors in my acquaintance studiously avoided dealing with any scientific matters. For those pastors who are courageous and daring enough to wade into scientific waters, be sure you know what you are talking about. Keep in mind that a Christian biologist or geologist, for example, will not appreciate hearing his or her profession or the findings of the discipline subtly or not so subtly denigrated. They will not appreciate scientific findings being misrepresented or misinterpreted or misused. Consult the *experts* that you know. If you don't have experts handy and are reluctant to preach a scientifically-related sermon, at the very least you can encourage your congregation to get involved in science. It is better if you can model that involvement and interest yourself. What Scott Hoezee urgently recommended for contemporary preachers is something that Calvin tried to do in his sermons. I would strongly encourage all pastors to read and re-read Hoezee's book and begin putting into practice many of his suggestions.[3]

Both the church and individual preachers also need to act as if they recognize that science is an extremely powerful and integral component of the modern world. Science has produced incalculable practical benefits to the human race, such as medicine, as well as opening up fascinating intellectual insights into our world. The scientific attitude of thought has helped to free us from superstition and has taught us to evaluate things carefully. Surely the church and the pulpit ought to express appreciation for natural science as one of God's great gifts to the human race. Surely preachers ought to express publicly the gratitude of the Christian church for the faithful and dedicated labors of Christians in science who have regarded their own work, not as an excuse for atheism, but as a vehicle for bringing honor and praise to the God who made this incredible world.

I have called upon the church to emulate Calvin's interest in nature and his positive, encouraging attitude toward natural science. Unfortunately, the reality is frequently very different. If and when church denominations or pastors deal with science, particularly those with a very conservative theological bent, they often do so in a way that casts science in either a negative or suspicious light. For example, how often has an ecclesiastical denomination issued a study report that affirms the practice of natural science as a natural outgrowth of the doctrine of creation? Instead, what frequently happens is that a denomination engages in a particular study because an office-bearer in the church has espoused views on the basis of scientific findings that are perceived as undermining biblical doctrine or distorting Scriptural texts. Or, there may be "unrest" within a denomination because people have been discussing biological evolution or the age of the Earth or the days of creation or some other science-related issue, and the church members become upset because they discover that there is a difference of opinion on these matters. And one of the reasons for the "unrest" is that people within the church are afraid that science is dictating how the Bible should be interpreted. Science is perceived as a dangerous threat to Christian faith.[4] The effect of these episodes in ecclesiastical life reinforces the sense that science bears careful watching.

Negative or suspicious attitudes toward science are also fostered when preachers make mildly disparaging comments about "science" or the "scientists" from the pulpit. In my experience, the great majority of references to science or scientists from the pulpit have carried at least a slightly negative tone. For example, it may be appropriate to critique the erroneous opinions of an "unbelieving," "godless," or "atheistic" scientist who thinks that science has disproved the existence of God or rendered Christianity obsolete. The problem, however, is generally not with the science of such a scientist. The problem is his or her religion or lack of it. And if it is necessary to refer to such individuals, perhaps it would be well to include some "godless" economists, historians, philosophers, sociologists, lawyers, politicians, doctors, and even theologians. "Godlessness" is not the unique preserve of natural scientists. Moreover, it would be wonderful if, for every mention of an agnostic or atheistic scientist like Cornell astronomer Carl Sagan (1934-1996) or co-discoverer of the double helix structure of DNA Francis Crick (1916-2004) there were two or three references to great Christian scientists of the past like chemist Robert Boyle (1627-1691), Scottish optics specialist David Brewster (1781-1868), experts in electromagnetism James Clerk Maxwell (1831-1873) and Joseph Henry (1792-1878), geologists James Dwight Dana (1813-1895), J. William Dawson (1820-1899), and Edward Hitchcock (1793-1864), or in our own day, Francis Collins of the human genome project, Princeton University geologist John Suppe, Harvard University astronomer Owen Gingerich, or the approximately 2500 members of the American Scientific Affiliation and its British counterpart, Christians in Science. If the only time that the words "scientist" or "science" are used in a sermon they are preceded by an adjective such as "godless," "atheistic," or "unbelieving," then the pulpit sends a message to the congregation, perhaps unintentional, that natural science is something that Christians need to keep at some distance.

It is wise for pastors to warn parishioners against believing that science can solve all the problems of the human race or that science is the only route to sure knowledge. Those beliefs, however, are not the fault of science itself but of faulty philosophies that are built around science. The church should warn against all theological error including any theological error that comes from individuals within the scientific community. My complaint is that if the church refers to science exclusively in a negative manner, it will gradually engender on the part of lay Christians and of young people in the pew a deep suspicion and mistrust of the scientific enterprise. In my judgment, large segments of the church and many pulpits have not modeled a balanced attitude toward science. Is it any wonder that the Christian in the pew does not have a very balanced attitude toward science?

Much of the general public is already poorly educated in regard to scientific matters. In the public schools, most students take some general science and a course in biology, but many students are not exposed to physics or chemistry unless they are college bound, and even then they may not have exposure to both sciences. Very few students learn anything about geology or astronomy apart from brief exposure in eighth or ninth grade. Rare is the high school in the United States that offers a full year course in geology. Rarer still is the school that requires college bound students to study geology. Sad to say, many Christian schools are afraid to provide in depth instruction about geology or biological evolution for fear of stirring up the ire of parents and having students pulled out of the school. In other cases, if students are taught geology, much of what they learn is young-Earth creationist flood geology, which, regrettably, is pseudo-scientific nonsense that is rejected by all but a handful out of tens of thousands of professional geologists including Christians. And for those students who attend college, it is rare that they are required to take more than two semester-long courses in the natural sciences, except, of course, for those choosing to major in a natural science. So, because the public generally does not have a strong background in the natural sciences by virtue of formal education, most people are not in a favorable position to see through the flaws in some of the widespread scientific nonsense that is espoused by well-meaning Christians, including pastors. Sadly, most of the science-oriented books available in the Christian bookstores must be regarded as science fiction. Moreover, many of the people in the pew with a weak scientific background may become quite vulnerable to the negative impressions that are unintentionally, and sometimes intentionally, conveyed to them from the pulpit.

But pastors are themselves products of the same educational systems that fail to provide a substantial education in the sciences. Because they are as ignorant of sound science as the rest of the general public, for the most part, many pastors lack the skills to detect the pseudo-science of young-Earth creationism and may think they are doing their congregations a service by passing on the faulty science of the "creationist" movement to them.

How can this situation be remedied? I believe that theological seminaries bear some of the blame for this unfortunate state of affairs. The majority of theological seminaries, thinking that science is not particularly germane to the work of the pastorate, do not require much, if any, college science for admittance into a seminary program, nor do they offer any course work in which a pastor is exposed to much science. The exception might be that an apologetics course could contain some science.[5] In my mind, this situation is a woeful one indeed, for we live in a culture that is powerfully shaped by scientific concepts. Our everyday lives are saturated with the fruits of scientific endeavor. And if we are to bring the gospel to bear on the scientifically oriented culture in which we live, pastors need to point out to congregations how the biblical message of creation, fall, and redemption bears on the entire scientific enterprise that so powerfully shapes their lives. Thus, seminaries should make sure that their graduates understand basic science and its functioning and that they have a good working grasp of the scientific issues that seem to plague the church perennially. And seminaries should make sure that pastors are able to distinguish legitimate science from the pseudo-science that abounds so prolifically in Christian circles. Seminaries need to require more science for admission, offer more science-related courses, and sponsor continuing education workshops on science in the pulpit for active pastors, perhaps in conjunction with one or more denominations. And, of course, if seminaries are going to be effective in equipping pastors to deal with scientific issues, then the professors of theology and apologetics must themselves become much more knowledgeable about scientific matters.

Denominations, seminaries, and pastors also need to face the issue of the evangelization of the scientist "people group." I have mentioned the crucial role that practicing scientists may play in evangelizing other scientists. But preachers play a role here, too. Scientists are sinners as much in need of the saving work of Jesus Christ as anyone else. But the gospel must be presented to scientists winsomely. Now suppose that a chemist or biologist, for example, is searching spiritually and finds himself or herself attending a Christian worship service. Or suppose that our scientist happens to overhear a Christian radio broadcast or to stumble onto the program of a television evangelist and decides to listen in or to watch just out of curiosity. Then suppose that the preacher begins to make a few remarks about science and scientists. Imagine the devastating impression that will be made on our scientist if the speaker insults, makes sarcastic remarks about, or denigrates the scientific profession or the personal intelligence and learning of scientists. Imagine the negative impression made if it is intimated that science or scientists are the enemy of the Christian faith. Imagine the negative impression made if it is suggested that geologists have it all wrong in their findings regarding the antiquity of the Earth. Imagine the negative impression made if it is suggested that there is no evidence for biological evolution. Imagine the negative impression made if it is intimated that the light reaching the Earth from the Andromeda galaxy, two million light years distant, was really created *en route* to the Earth only a few thousands of years ago rather than actually having traveled from there to here for the past 2,000,000 years. In no way will such suggestions or declarations help to win converts to Christ from among scientists. It will drive them away. Such pulpit pronouncements will only convince the scientists, who know their science, that Christianity must be wrong if one is forced to choose between Christianity, which they don't know yet, and science, which they do know. If the church wants to convert scientists along with everyone else, it should either say nothing at all about science or else get its science right and present it fairly and appreciatively. Above all, the saving work of Jesus Christ needs to be presented without the sarcasm, cynicism, and ridicule of scientists or their views that are sadly all too common. Scientists will also be far more inclined toward the message of the gospel if, instead of a diatribe against biological evolution or against an old Earth or in favor of flood geology or in favor of intelligent design, they hear that the biblical doctrine of creation lays the foundation for the pursuit of scientific investigation and knowledge and that the natural sciences are honorable professions that open up sweeping vistas of the glory of God.

I also suggest that denominational study committees that are erected to investigate issues that bear on scientific questions such as the proper interpretation of Genesis 1 ought to include not just theologians and ministers but also scientists from a variety of disciplines.[6] A committee with a broad-based contingent of scientists on it should normally be spared from egregious misrepresentations of the status of scientific knowledge. For example, I have seen a study committee report in which it was intimated that the issue of the antiquity of the Earth is still an open question. The report suggested that the church and individual Christians need to wait until the matter has finally been settled before committing themselves to a particular view. Whenever I see Christians make that statement I cringe.[7] Consultation with practicing geologists would help to avoid such unfortunate statements. During the past two centuries, thousands of geologists from around the globe have examined in astounding detail dozens of lines of evidence that bear on the question of the antiquity of the Earth. The issue is settled. It has been settled for a long time. The evidence overwhelmingly indicates that the Earth is vastly older than a few thousands of years. There is no longer any scientific justification whatsoever for maintaining that the Earth is only a few thousands of years old. That denomination, seminary, or individual Christian who is holding out just a little bit longer until "all the evidence is in," is in a state of denial. There may be room for further adjustment in our knowledge of the exact age of the Earth, but the fact that the Earth is extremely old with an age that is measurable in hundreds of millions to billions of years has been established to the point where no amount of evidence yet to be uncovered will ever convince a person of the great antiquity of the Earth who steadfastly refuses to accept that idea now.

Some measure of distrust toward science has been occasioned by the perception that its practitioners are generally hostile to the Christian faith. As a result, many believers feel warranted in rejecting scientific ideas that they find not to their liking. They suspect that a profound bias against Christianity on the part of scientists has unduly influenced what theories they espouse. But such beliefs and attitudes by Christians are inappropriate. After all, Matthew 16:2-3 indicates that even Jesus, God in the flesh, acknowledged that unbelievers are capable of properly interpreting the natural world. Moreover, scientific theory is adopted by a scientific *community*, not by isolated individuals.[8]

The fact that a given theory may be accepted by an individual non-Christian scientist in part because he or she perceives that theory to be incompatible with Christianity has little to do with the validity of the theory. A theory that should be taken seriously by the public generally and by Christians specifically is one that has generally been adopted by the scientific *community*. That community adopts a theory, not because either the theory or the community as a whole is hostile to Christianity, but because the community as a whole judges in light of its experience and expertise that the available evidence satisfactorily or generally supports the theory.[9] In developing a scientific theory, the community will weigh and sift evidence over time, offer arguments as to why the data are insufficient to support the theory, propose alternative hypotheses, offer additional supporting data, and so on. In short, a scientific theory gains support through a long, tedious process that entails research, publication, debate, and critique by colleagues that involves a large number of individuals of varying biases, temperaments, training, expertise, and religious, social, political, economic, and cultural backgrounds.

Scientists love to discuss and debate theories because that is precisely how the science is advanced. They do not hesitate to look for flaws in a proposed or existing theory in order to refute it or to improve on it. They sometimes enjoy searching for evidence that would undercut a proposed theory. This means that a scientific theory that is very widely held by the appropriate, knowledgeable community has already been examined and tested very critically and must have a great deal of evidential support. A generally held scientific theory, therefore, should not be dismissed and treated lightly by those who are ignorant of the supporting data and their significance. Sadly, that is how many Christians treat such theories as biological evolution or radiometric dating. They don't like the theories themselves or their implications because they think they are incompatible with their perception of what the Christian faith teaches. Therefore, they dismiss or actively combat those theories even though they may have little or no idea of the nature and amount of evidence that have been accumulated over the years by experts in support of those theories.

But another factor enters in. All too often, lay Christians assume that natural science is "under the control" of non-Christians. Science, or at least significant components of it, is virtually considered to be a non-Christian activity that has a built-in bias against Christian faith. The reality, however, is that there are hundreds of Christians in the natural sciences, and some of them are among the leaders in their fields.[10] That certainly was the case in the nineteenth century, and it is increasingly the case today. From time to time one hears comments to the effect that Christian practitioners of science are bullied or pressured into believing certain "unchristian" theories just to save face and to maintain standing in the scientific community. The Christians in science have almost been portrayed as cowards who accept theories on the authority of non-Christian leaders in the field without really having examined the evidence for themselves or even having the ability to examine and evaluate the evidence. Christians in science are sometimes viewed by other Christians as dupes or unwitting pawns of the non-Christian scientific hierarchy.

What an insult to the hundreds of competent, dedicated, thoroughly professional Christian astronomers, biologists, chemists, geologists, and physicists who view their work as a calling of God and, therefore, pursue that work with integrity, thoroughness, and caution. I am personally acquainted with dozens of practicing geologists who are Christians. They accept the idea that the Earth is extremely old, and they reject the idea that Noah's flood produced much of the world's geology. Now, the idea of an old Earth is anathema to a lot of well-meaning but ill-informed Christians. Moreover, the idea of a geologically significant global deluge is near and dear to the hearts of a lot of the same well-meaning, but ill-informed Christians. On the other hand, my Christian geologist friends have extensive academic training in geology and years of personal experience as geologists. They are actually thoroughly acquainted with the evidence for an old Earth. They are conversant with the wealth of geological evidence that undermines the idea that the Earth's stratified rocks were deposited in a global flood. They are quite capable of evaluating new evidence from field and laboratory. Some of them have discovered some of that evidence personally. Should lay Christians take the word of well-meaning believers who are not experts in geology that the Earth is a few thousand years old? Or should they take the word of competent Christian geologists that the Earth is probably billions of years old? Should sick persons seek medical treatment from friendly neighbors or from individuals with the appropriate medical training and experience?

In the late eighteenth and early nineteenth centuries when the idea of an old Earth was first accepted by geologists and the idea of a global deluge was rejected as an explanation for the world's strata, it was Christian geologists like Oxford professor William Buckland (1784-1856), Cambridge professor Adam Sedgwick (1785-1873), John Fleming (1785-1857), the Dean of Llandaff Cathedral in Wales, William Conybeare (1787-1857), and Hugh Miller (1802-1856), a leading figure in the establishment of the Free Church of Scotland, who were in the forefront of developing the evidence or explaining it to the public. Some of the very greatest geologists of the nineteenth century were Christians: James Dwight Dana of Yale, J. William Dawson of McGill, Arnold Guyot (1807-1884) of Princeton, Alexander Winchell (1833-1891) of Michigan, and Edward Hitchcock of Amherst, for example. Geology is not the infidel science that some believers have claimed for it.

Contemporary Christians would do well, then, to accept the scientific theories that have been widely adopted by the scientific community because any such theory has been painstakingly developed by that community, consisting of believers and unbelievers alike, from a wealth of evidence. I'm not talking about accepting the latest radical conjecture put forward by a publicity-seeking scientist that may happen to find its way into the newspaper or the nightly news broadcast on television. I'm not even talking about an important hypothesis that is presently being debated in the scientific community and that has many prominent supporters. Consider, for example, the idea that the dinosaurs went extinct at the end of the Cretaceous Period thanks to the impact on the Earth of a large meteorite or comet. Although that hypothesis has much to commend it and may well be correct, geologists are still sifting through the evidence for and against it. I'm suggesting that Christians accept theories that have generally been accepted by the community of appropriate scientific experts after years of testing and evaluation. Of course, there is always room for improvement, refinement, and adjustment of many widely accepted theories. The theory of plate tectonics, for example, is accepted by most geologists. There is a wealth of evidence to support it. Rival theories fail to account for that evidence as satisfactorily. And yet there is room for improvement in our understanding of the mechanism of plate tectonics. But that does not provide sufficient warrant for a non-geologist to reject plate tectonics without providing sufficient evidence to satisfy and convince the community of geologists. It is arrogant for Christians to reject what they don't like when it is accepted by those who have spent their lives gaining expertise in some field of science. And it is especially arrogant when the person who does the rejecting lacks sufficient knowledge and judgment to make any reasoned evaluation of the data.

So what can we learn from John Calvin along these lines? Much of the scientific knowledge of his day had been acquired by individuals who either did not belong to the Christian tradition at all (e.g., the Greek and Roman observers like Aristotle, Theophrastus, Pliny the Elder, Strabo, and Seneca) or by individuals who were not necessarily theologically orthodox in their thinking. Yet it didn't seem to matter to Calvin whether the scientific knowledge of the day had been gathered by an unbeliever or a Christian. Valid knowledge was valid knowledge, independently of its source and author because, in the end, God is the author of all truth. Calvin also warned against those who took pride in and were content with the little knowledge they possessed to the point that they refused to learn anything new. Many contemporary Christian critics of professional biology, cosmology, and geology seem to fall into that category. Their lack of knowledge and understanding of the fields that they criticize is matched only by the confidence with which they criticize them.

Why Was Calvin Sympathetic to Science?

What was the basis for Calvin's generally positive view of science? Clearly he appreciated the benefits to the human race that accrued from the practice of science. He appreciated the fact that science entails the study of God's creative handiwork, and he understood that the human mind is enlarged and enriched by an increased knowledge of the world around us. Beyond that, his overall theology was conducive to a scientific outlook on the world. Calvin never expounded a Christian philosophy of science or of nature in any of his writings. Nor did he ever talk systematically about his reasons for thinking as he did about science. He never tried to justify his acceptance of science. Nevertheless, we can glean rudiments of a Calvinist philosophy of science from comments scattered here and there in his writings.

No doubt Calvin felt as he did about science because of his commitment to the concept of a divinely created order of nature. According to Susan Schreiner, "the concept of order was central to Calvin's cosmology and, like Melanchthon, he frequently called attention to the order in creation as proof of God, creation, and providence."[11] The idea of an order of nature was not original with him. This commitment he shared with a host of other Christian predecessors and contemporaries. As far as he was concerned, not only did God create a functioning order of nature, but he also providentially sustains, governs, and upholds that order moment by moment. The order of nature, he thought, was such that each part of the world has its own properties and functions. The world did not, therefore, exist or operate autonomously and independently of God. Indeed, as Schreiner has said, "in Calvin's view, the order that God gradually brought into being out of chaos was not a stabilizing force which made nature more independent but, on the contrary, that order itself was dependent, requiring the direct, specific, and powerful providence of God."[12]

Calvin was no deist. He saw that the properties of the entities within the order of nature were not inherent to those parts. God continuously provides to the various entities the energy and ability to function in such a way that they behave and operate in a consistent, regular manner. Thus, although trees might have certain characteristics, yet, left to themselves, trees would do nothing unless supplied with the appropriate energy by divine will. But God does not energize his creation in a haphazard, whimsical manner such that a sheep behaves like a lion one day, like a fish the next, and like a sheep the third. Nor does a pebble lie passively on a stream bottom one day, roll upstream the next, and fly the third. Although God is free and able to do such things contrary to their created natures and might do so during a miracle such as the floating axe head (II Kings 6:1-7), he normally supplies that energy and effectiveness in a consistent manner to his creatures such that we can legitimately talk about the properties of trees or of any other creature. Creatures act in accord with their properties, but they do so because God enables them to do so.

But God's consistency with respect to nature does not exclude variety. Calvin was enormously impressed by the tremendous variety within the created order. The Sun does not track across the sky in exactly the same way every single day. The Sun rises and sets farther and farther to the north and tracks higher and higher in the sky as winter progresses toward summer. It reverses that trend as summer progresses toward winter. Moreover, the times when the Sun rises and sets progressively change throughout the year. As a result, the Earth experiences the various seasons with their various types of weather. The Moon, too, rises and sets at different times and locations each day. Throughout the course of a month, the appearance of the Moon changes from a full Moon to a gibbous Moon to a half Moon to a crescent Moon to a barely visible new Moon. The animal world and the plant world are characterized by unimaginable diversity. Human beings are wonderfully varied in terms of height, weight, hair color, eye color, complexion, bone structure, facial features, dispositions, and talents. This staggering variety captured Calvin's imagination. He regarded variety as a clear evidence of God's control of the universe, and he employed variety apologetically as an indication that nature is not a self-existent, self-running automaton. Extreme uniformity would characterize a hypothetical autonomous nature, and people might have warrant or excuse for thinking that nature is self-existent if it indeed acted in a monotonously uniform fashion. Calvin felt justified in appealing to diversity as evidence that nature is the product of God's creative imagination and sustaining grace.

Calvin still understood that there is an order to nature despite the diversity. Certainly it is a fundamental postulate of scientific activity that the world is in some way or other an orderly place. Underlying all the variation that we see in the world, there is still a fundamental order and regularity. There would be no science apart from that presupposition of order, for science is an effort to discover the fundamental patterns of the universe and to attempt to give an accounting of how those patterns function in such a regular fashion.

Without doubt Calvin's understanding of the natural order was not quite the same as that which characterizes the modern scientific outlook. He did not think about the order of nature in mathematical terms or in terms of laws of physics that underlie all the phenomena. When discussing order he would typically call to mind the biblical allusions to regularities in the world: the alternation of night and day (or the Moon and the Sun), the boundary between the land and the sea, the behavior of the animals. Still, the concept of order, even as espoused by Calvin, carries with it the idea that there are regularities and patterns in the natural world that, in principle, could be discovered. Thus, I think it is legitimate to claim that Calvin's conception of an order of nature provided him a justification for the practice of science. Had he entertained the thought that God upheld the world in a purely whimsical, unpredictable manner, he would likely never have paid much heed to nature, science, or even theology, for that matter!

Any discussion of Calvin's conception of the order of nature must also take into account the fact that he envisioned the original order of nature as somehow being disrupted by the entrance of sin into the world. The entire world, he thought, manifests signs of such disorder. Famine and drought, severe storms and other extremes of weather, and the hostile attitude of animals toward humans were all viewed as indications of disorder, according to him. Yet any disorder present in the world was not sufficient to eliminate the underlying order of nature. Despite famines and storms, the basic elements of weather still remain. The heavens continue on their daily journey around the Earth. The seasons still come and go in accordance with the influence of the constellations. Calvin talked about natural phenomena in terms of the action of secondary causes, and he did not see that secondary causes were eliminated from the world at the time of the fall. In fact, he believed that even some aspects of disorder in the world could be accounted for in terms of secondary causes. It is not as if the disorders were necessarily direct actions of God in the world, but rather actions of God whereby the Lord directed the elements of creation in such a way that they served as an irritant or punishment for humans on account of their folly and rebellion. Disorder was somehow providentially worked into the post-lapsarian upholding and governance of nature. Calvin interpreted extreme weather as a consequence of a fallen world, as a punishment for human sin. Yet he still could talk of natural, or secondary, causes for extreme weather. There is no sense that he envisioned the fall as destroying the original order of nature and replacing it with an entirely new one. God simply employed the created order to bring about these extremes.

Calvin also regarded humans as image-bearers of God who had been charged by the Creator with the task of exercising dominion over nature. Very likely he perceived that the possibility of discovery flowed from the exercise of that dominion. In short, his commitment to the notion of an order of nature and to human beings as image-bearers of God who exercise dominion very likely led him to appreciate the role of science in human life.

We do well to emulate Calvin here. Contemporary Christians should likewise find warrant for the idea that the world is amenable to scientific examination in the biblical doctrine of God's creation of an ordered universe and in his providential upholding of that ordered universe. And the creation of humanity as rational beings who have been entrusted with the task of subduing the Earth provides a basis for the actual doing of science inasmuch as the proper exercise of dominion necessarily entails the understanding of the world over which the dominion is to be established. And that understanding will involve scientific investigation. And we do well to remember that the blessing of subduing the Earth with its implied commission to find scientific truth extends to *all* of humanity including both believers and those who reject the gospel.

Should We Adopt Calvin's Science?

We should follow Calvin in taking delight in nature and science. We should follow him in finding reason for doing science in a providentially upheld, ordered creation. But if Calvin approved of scientific activity, should contemporary Christians also follow him in accepting the scientific views that he adopted? He believed that the Earth is only a few thousands of years old. Should we believe the same? He probably assumed that the great deluge was a global phenomenon that affected the entire human race. Should we also believe that? A great many contemporary Christians are in complete agreement with these conclusions and would be delighted to claim Calvin as a prime witness in support of a very young Earth and of a global flood. There is no doubt, either, that he was persuaded that these ideas were not just consistent with the biblical text but also derived from it. Ought contemporary Christians follow the reformer in adopting these views as part of their scientific outlook?

In response the following points need to be stressed. In the first place, Calvin was completely in line with his predecessors and contemporaries on these two issues. There were virtually no voices in his day making compelling arguments for acceptance of an old Earth or of a localized flood. As a result, it is dubious that he ever gave serious consideration to the possibility of an old Earth or of a localized flood.

In the second place, Calvin and his contemporaries lived two and a half centuries before students of the Earth began to uncover increasingly persuasive evidence for an extremely old Earth and three centuries before geologists began to be very suspicious about a global deluge of any kind. In short, Calvin was not confronted with any extra-biblical evidence that could have driven him to a textual re-evaluation of the creation and flood passages to see perhaps whether accommodation to the scientific beliefs of the original readers might be operative. It is one thing to make an assertion about the meaning of a biblical text in the complete absence of relevant extra-biblical information. Because it is something entirely different to make an assertion about the meaning of a text that flies in the face of persuasive and overwhelming extra-biblical data, it may fairly be asked whether Calvin would have maintained his positions on those two issues had he lived, say, in the nineteenth century. After all, a large number of Calvinistic theologians of the nineteenth century, such as Charles Hodge and W. G. T. Shedd, were convinced of the great antiquity of the globe.

As a third point, we may note from our vantage point that a staggering amount of geological, geophysical, and astronomical evidence has accumulated that virtually compels assent to the notion that the planet is billions of years old.[13] That being the case, why would anyone feel compelled to hang on to the "geological" beliefs of someone from the sixteenth century who lived long before the advent of the science of geology?

Lastly, I would ask those who feel compelled to accept Calvin's "geological" notions why they do not also feel compelled to accept his astronomy and physics. Calvin was very much an adherent of a generally Aristotelian-Ptolemaic view of the cosmos and the Earth. Like almost all of his contemporaries, he thought that the Earth is the center of the universe. He accepted the four fundamental elements of the sub-lunary world. He accepted Aristotle's theory of exhalations. His knowledge of plants and animals was adopted largely from that of classical Greek and Roman writers. He also was persuaded that these scientific views were mostly compatible with the biblical text. So should not Christians today accept science that is biblical? Well, every Christian and even every Calvinist knows full well that we have advanced scientifically far beyond Calvin's beliefs about the cosmos. Almost no Christian would dream of accepting geocentrism, the theory of four elements, the theory of exhalations, or the theory of natural places simply because Calvin adopted them or because he thought they were in accord with the Bible. Why then should we dream of accepting a 6000-year-old Earth and a global deluge simply because Calvin adopted them? If we are going to insist on a young Earth, let's be consistent and insist on a geocentric universe as well. If anywhere, we see how very much Calvin was a product of his times in the area of the content of his science. There is no need for contemporary Christians to adopt the science of another time. Calvinism hardly requires the adoption of outmoded and discredited scientific conceptions.

By its very nature as a process of continuing observation, testing, and reflection science is a self-correcting enterprise. As a consequence, contemporary understandings of the workings of the universe have superseded those of the ancient world and the Middle Ages because they are based upon a vastly superior (both qualitatively and quantitatively) set of observations and measurements often made possible by superior instruments, superior methods of data collection and analysis, and more productive theoretical concepts. Shall we return to a geocentric universe simply because Calvin was a geocentrist? After all, we are the beneficiaries of Galileo's instrument-aided observations of the phases of Venus and of the orbiting of the moons of Jupiter; of Kepler's mathematical analysis of orbital observations that enabled him to formulate the laws of planetary motion; and of Newton's theoretical formulation of the laws of motion and gravitation. The Foucault pendulum provided a remarkable confirmation of the rotation of the Earth. Modern astronomy has provided us with measurements of the velocity of light, the expansion of the universe, the amount of red shift, distances to galaxies, the chemical compositions of stars, and so on. Had Calvin lived to see all these developments, I suspect that he would have taken great delight in the results and enjoyed the progress of astronomical knowledge. Given his own attitude toward science generally and astronomy particularly, I also suspect that he would have become a heliocentrist after it became clear that the scientific community had adopted that view on compelling grounds. So, no modern Calvinist should even dream of adopting Calvin's scientific ideas. We should not follow Calvin in regard to the content of science, and that includes his belief in a young Earth and a global deluge.

God-of-the-Gaps

There were some instances in which Calvin was not fully satisfied with aspects of some of the scientific theories of his day. He was not comfortable with the Aristotelian explanation regarding the stability of the Earth at the center of the universe while the planetary and stellar spheres were thought to be whizzing around the Earth at enormous speeds. Nor was he convinced that the theory of natural places accounted in a fully satisfactory manner for the fact that the element, earth, is locally positioned above the water. According to that theory there should be a sphere of water above the element, earth. Calvin's solution in both cases was to introduce a providential miracle. It was God who, by an exercise of sheer divine power without necessarily using any second causes, kept the central Earth from spinning out of control because of the drag of the orbiting spheres. Likewise it was God who, by an exercise of raw omnipotence without necessarily employing natural causes, kept the threatening ocean at bay so that it did not overflow the continents in an effort to attain its natural place.

In the last chapter, I mentioned that Calvin more or less adopted the strategy known today as the God-of-the-gaps strategy. The idea behind the strategy is that if we cannot explain a certain phenomenon, cannot even think of a plausible explanation, and cannot even imagine that anyone else now or ever could come up with a plausible natural explanation of that phenomenon, then the phenomenon must be attributable to a miraculous, direct divine intervention. The direct, immediate action of God is invoked to fill in the gaps in our scientific knowledge. In centuries gone by, for example, disease was often regarded as a punishment directly from the hand of God until it was recognized that, in many cases, germs are the disease-producing agent. The God-of-the-gaps strategy has been adopted repeatedly and still finds its way into many current discussions about science and religion.

The God-of-the-gaps method is perhaps most commonly invoked today in regard to the issue of the origin of life on the Earth. Many Christians are predisposed, for whatever reason, to think that the origin of the first life must have required a sheer miracle. The scientific community has been exploring the problem for several decades now. Numerous hypotheses have been proposed to account for the beginning of life, but, thus far, all of them have encountered intractable difficulties. Likewise several laboratory experiments have been conducted that offer some hope for a scientific solution to the problem, but the experiments have been far from achieving a solution. One can almost detect an "I told you so" attitude on the part of some Christians in response to the presumed scientific "failures" at explaining the origin of life. Included among these are some Christians who might maintain that a natural mechanism for the formation of life would violate the known laws of thermodynamics. In the end, what these Christians suggest is that lack of convincing *scientific* evidence for the beginning of life pretty much compels us to conclude that God must have originated the first life miraculously. This line of argument illustrates pure God-of-the-gaps thinking. I sense that adherents of a divinely miraculous origin of life are eagerly looking for compelling evidence for the existence of God that they can use as an apologetic tool with which to convince unbelievers of the truth of the Christian faith.

Despite protests to the contrary, the intelligent design movement shows a similar tendency to fall back on the God-of-the-gaps approach in its dealings with biological phenomena.[14] Adherents of intelligent design point to what they consider as examples of irreducible, specified complexity at the cellular and molecular levels within organisms. The structures within cells or biological systems are said to be so unimaginably complex that they could not possibly have developed in terms of natural causes, especially the combined action of mutation and natural selection, no matter how much time we allow for that to happen. As a result, it is concluded that an intelligent agent must have designed these complex structures. Although many proponents of intelligent design are careful to point out that the identity of the designer is not specified by the scientific data, it comes as no surprise that Christians who are enamored of the idea of intelligent design assume that the designer must have been the God of the Bible.

The insistence of Romans 1:20 that the invisible things of God are clearly seen and understood by means of the things that have been made, however, strongly implies that the entire universe and all its component parts plainly show signs of having been created by an intelligent Creator *including everything that can be explained by natural causes.* Calvin certainly would have agreed. Christians tread on apologetically unstable ground in limiting the idea of intelligent design to irreducibly complex structures, because it gives non-Christians opportunity to claim with justification that other structures and phenomena such as rocks and rivers were not intelligently designed. I do not find warrant for restricting intelligent design to structures that cannot presently be explained in terms of natural causes. Moreover, it is premature to state that certain biological phenomena cannot (in the sense of "can never") be accounted for by natural causes generally or mutation and natural selection specifically. The appeal to the action of an intelligent agent to explain something that we cannot presently explain in terms of natural causes certainly smacks of the God-of-the-gaps strategy. Moreover, God is the creator of all, the explained and the unexplained alike.

Flood "geologists" have also used this strategy in a different kind of way. Adherents of flood geology have tried with might and main to explain *scientifically* the sedimentary rock strata, fossils, landforms, igneous intrusions, and many other geological phenomena in terms of an approximately year-long global deluge that allegedly took place a few thousand years ago. Their explanations are implausible, and professional geologists have satisfactorily accounted for these phenomena in terms of an old Earth.[15] Although flood geologists are convinced that they have provided valid and persuasive scientific arguments to sustain their conception of a global flood, sooner or later they encounter difficulties for which they cannot provide a scientific explanation that even remotely begins to convince and satisfy the very proponents of flood geology. And so they fall back on a God-of-the-gaps argument, namely, a miracle to explain the difficulties, in effect conceding that they have no scientific explanation. For example, how did pairs of all the existing land animals from every corner of the globe as well as pairs of all the extinct animals that are now preserved as fossils migrate from the places where they lived to the place where they could board Noah's ark? In such circumstances flood geologists have not hesitated to say of such difficulties that God must have performed a miracle. God-of-the-gaps has provided serviceable for adherents of all kinds of viewpoints.

The history of science, however, has demonstrated the danger of the God-of-the-gaps approach that was taken by Calvin and many other honorable Christians. The strategy has proved ineffectual over the years as, one after another, phenomena that seemed inexplicable on scientific grounds and that were at one time attributed to direct divine action, ultimately yielded to the insights of science. Christians today should abandon the strategy, even if Calvin may have adopted it. Christians need not deny for an instant that there are miracles in the sense of direct exercises of divine power as, for example, the virgin birth and the resurrection of Christ, but these miracles are clearly affirmed in the Bible. When it comes to scientific issues with no bearing on redemptive history such as the origin of life or the origin of species, Christians need to abandon their tendency to claim the necessity of a miracle. Instead they should get to work in the search for a divinely guided natural process, just as soil erosion, a volcanic eruption, or the growth of a child is a divinely guided natural process. With Calvin we should continue to insist that all secondary causes operate effectively under the establishment and supervision of God's providence. One may stubbornly hold out forever for the idea that the first life form must have been miraculously created, but sooner or later (it might take another millennium or two, but that's all right) the scientific community is likely to solve the puzzle of the origin of life and find a satisfactory mechanism to account for it. Rather than feeling disappointment that God has supposedly been shoved out of the picture when a scientific explanation for the origin of life is forthcoming, the reaction of Christians should instead be, "What an amazing God we have—a Creator who conceived and executed this incredible process that we have finally discovered, a process that ultimately led to the appearance of the first forms of life!" Perhaps the discovery of the process by which life originated will bring us to see that God performed a much greater wonder than if he had simply brought life into being by a direct, instantaneous act that entailed no natural process whatever. Perhaps we will find that the discovery of a natural process that God conceived and executed will result for us in an expanded conception of the glory of our God. Let's not follow Calvin in invoking miracles just because we can't explain some creaturely phenomenon.

The Principle of Accommodation

The final point of application of Calvin's thought to modern science concerns the manner in which Calvin handled biblical texts that bear on the natural world. We can learn a great deal from the way in which he handled Scripture that will help us in our current debates about the relation between Scripture and nature. His doctrine of Scripture is, of course, complex and multi-faceted. Theologians have made it abundantly clear that Calvin held a very high view of Scripture as the infallible Word of God.[16] In Calvin's view, Scripture makes no mistakes and possesses absolute divine authority in all of its parts. Within the confines of that basic belief, however, he freely made use of the principle of accommodation. Let's establish some context for the application of this principle.

The vast sums of knowledge that have been acquired about the natural world in the centuries since Calvin's day have put the Christian church in a somewhat awkward position. The awkwardness arises from the fact that, at many points, well established scientific knowledge is at odds with traditional interpretations of some biblical texts that refer to the natural world. Some of the traditional interpretations were very common in Calvin's era. By way of example, scientific evidence demonstrates that the Sun did not come into existence after the Earth. Geological evidence overwhelmingly indicates that the Earth is billions, not thousands of years old. Paleontological studies incontrovertibly show that a vast array of animals lived, died, and suffered disease and predation long before human beings appeared on the Earth. Geological evidence is totally inconsistent with the idea that a global deluge was responsible for the Earth's layered, fossil-bearing sedimentary rocks such as those that are exposed in the walls of the Grand Canyon, throughout the Colorado Plateau, throughout the Valley and Ridge province of the Appalachian Mountain chain, or in the Canadian Rockies. Finally, anthropological evidence indicates that human beings have been on the planet for at least tens of thousands of years.

Such disparities between the findings of the natural sciences during the past couple of centuries and the traditional views that many Christians have of the Bible have contributed to the widespread, although incorrect, impression that there is a "warfare" between science and the Christian religion.[17] Many well educated individuals who are not enamored of Christianity have seized on these disparities to argue that the Bible is full of errors and is so unreliable that its message of salvation can be dismissed. Christians must not respond to this situation by simply brushing the discrepancy problem under the rug. They must not shrug off the findings of science either by rejecting, ignoring, or distorting them.

One strategy that Christian apologists and scientists have adopted during the past couple of centuries to deal with this state of affairs is that of *concordism*. Concordism is a broad approach consisting of a variety of ways of showing how the scientific data allegedly really do mesh with the biblical text once the text is properly understood. For example, consider the fourth day of creation of Genesis 1. Numerous strategies have been employed to get around the problem of having the Sun, the Moon, and the stars created on the fourth day after the Earth was already in existence. Christian geologists and theologians have postulated that on the fourth day the Sun was not created *de novo*, but that the stuff of the Sun had already been created at the beginning. The Sun, then, was said to make its initial appearance as the cloudy atmosphere of the first three days of creation finally cleared sufficiently so that a hypothetical observer on the Earth could now distinctly see that big orange ball in the sky for the first time. Others have suggested that the Sun was first designated as a time measuring device on the fourth day. Still others have suggested that the present arrangement of the solar system came into being on the fourth day, even though the Sun and the Moon may have previously existed. The problem for all of these strategies of interpreting the events of day four is that they distort the text by evading the statement that God *made* these objects. The text does not say that the objects *appeared* or had previously existed somewhere else. The problem with such concordist efforts is that very often they have resulted in distortion of the biblical text. Moreover, concordism faces the problem of attempting to tie down the Bible to the science of the present day. A growing number of Christian scholars have concluded that concordism is a failed enterprise.[18]

Because the biblical text must be allowed to speak for itself, it should not be forced to speak to *contemporary* scientific issues that were not a concern of the author and that were not pertinent to the ancient culture in which the text was originally composed. The text must not be altered to solve a modern scientific problem but must be interpreted in light of its own context. Proper interpretation must take into account the imagery, figures of speech, idioms, literary conventions and genres, and thought worlds of the Old and New Testament times. If after we have determined what the text says, we discover a discrepancy with contemporary knowledge, then it is quite appropriate to ask why the discrepancy exists. Quite possibly some of these discrepancies might be explained if we accepted the text for what it really says and then applied Calvin's principle of accommodation. Specifically, I am suggesting that, in some of the texts in which we perceive a conflict with science, the Bible is addressing itself to the ancient Hebrews in terms of the very conceptions they held about the structure and behavior of the natural world so that they would not be distracted from hearing the thrust of the message, namely, "what man is to believe concerning God and what duty God requires of man." In other words, in bringing his message of redemption to fallen human beings, God adapted his message to the original recipients by couching it in terms with which his readers and hearers were familiar. We will explore examples of what I have in mind a bit later.

Accommodation in the Conservative Calvinist World

Before we look at these examples, however, I am compelled to urge reconsideration of the use of the principle of accommodation by followers of Calvin because I have the impression that Calvin's concept has not always fared well in the theological writings of his admirers. Yes, one does encounter discussions of accommodation from time to time. The Dutch Calvinist theologian Herman Bavinck (1854-1921), for example, discussed the use of anthropomorphisms in the Bible in reference to God in his *magnum opus, Reformed Dogmatics.* "If God nevertheless wants us to know him," Bavinck wrote,

> he has to come down to our level and accommodate himself to our limited, finite, human consciousness and speak to us in human language. Thus those who would deny the propriety of using anthropomorphisms in effect denied the possibility that God revealed himself to his creatures. Anthropomorphisms were considered an example of God's accommodation.[19]

What I am getting at is the relative lack of attention given to accommodation in connection with discussions of the proper interpretation of biblical texts. Also missing are extended discussions of the application of accommodation to texts with relevance to the interpretation of nature. Invocations of accommodation and appeals to Calvin in such invocations are scarce in biblical commentaries. I do not recall ever hearing a preacher mention divine accommodation to human conceptions in preaching on a particular text. In contrast, one repeatedly runs into the appeal to accommodation in Calvin's writings. David Wright confessed that he did not think that "attempts to spell out how Calvin viewed Scripture have taken the full measure of some aspects of the accommodation motif."[20]

One is also hard pressed to discover much discussion of the idea of accommodation by those who have written on the inspiration of Scripture. In particular, mention of Calvin's principle of accommodation is glaringly absent from the work of many of the most able advocates of biblical inerrancy. Clinton Ashley, who wrote a doctoral dissertation on Calvin's doctrine of accommodation, observed that there has been "a reaction against the usage of the principle of accommodation for interpreting the language of the Bible" on the part of evangelical Christian scholars. He charged that "the negative, illegitimate use of the principle of accommodation by liberal theologians has influenced some evangelical biblical interpreters either to ignore or to reject altogether this method of interpreting Scripture." Regarding this rejection of the accommodation method as detrimental, Ashley claimed that such rejection had "robbed evangelicals of one of the most balanced and most effective principles for interpreting biblical language."[21] I find this lack of attention striking because Calvin's principle of accommodation bears in important ways on how one might properly understand

and interpret texts for which infallibility and inerrancy are claimed. Certainly accommodation provides a viable method for getting a handle on apparent textual errors. Whether inerrantists have felt threatened by the misuse of the idea of accommodation as Ashley maintained, or are simply unfamiliar with the concept, I leave to others to determine.

Without claiming exhaustive familiarity with all writings in support of biblical inerrancy, I offer the following exhibits in support of my contention that advocacy of accommodation is largely absent from the writing of inerrantists. Most of my examples come from the writings of theologians in the Old Princeton-Westminster tradition of Calvinism. I am aware of only one instance in the writings of theologians from this tradition in which an appeal to accommodation was raised in connection with a scientific matter and was linked to the idea of biblical inspiration. I will introduce that instance toward the end of the chapter.

For now let's look at some examples that ignore or downplay accommodation. The volume entitled *The Inspiration and Authority of the Bible* is an anthology that consists of nine articles by B. B. Warfield in defense of the Bible's teaching about its own inspiration and of the traditional church doctrine on inspiration.[22] In his article on "The Real Problem of Inspiration," Warfield rejected the idea that Jesus and the apostles did not personally accept the traditional doctrine of inspiration but simply accommodated themselves to the widely held belief of their Jewish contemporaries that the Old Testament is a divinely inspired, fully trustworthy text of indefectible authority. Calvin's principle of accommodation, however, is never once mentioned in any of his articles on inspiration. Nor is it mentioned in the classic paper by Archibald Alexander Hodge (1823-1886), a professor of didactic and polemic theology at Princeton Theological Seminary, written in conjunction with Warfield that spelled out in detail the notion of inerrancy that is so close to the heart of modern evangelicals.[23]

In 1946, the faculty of Westminster Theological Seminary published *The Infallible Word*, a symposium on the inspiration of Scripture. The article by Paul Woolley (1902-1984), a professor of church history at the seminary, on the relevancy of Scripture dealt with questions of application of inerrancy to textual interpretation. The essay touched on questions pertaining to natural science and the Bible. It also recognized the importance of taking the cultural context of the biblical authors into account. Nevertheless, no explicit acknowledgment of the principle of accommodation is anywhere in sight. None of the other articles contain a single reference to the principle of accommodation.[24]

One of the more influential expositions of biblical infallibility and inerrancy was *Thy Word is Truth* by Edward J. Young (1907-1968), a professor of Old Testament at Westminster Theological Seminary.[25] This popular treatise offered a wealth of possible solutions to apparent discrepancies and supposed errors in the biblical text, and various harmonizing strategies were proposed, but not once was Calvin's principle of accommodation introduced as a viable interpretive strategy.

John Murray, a systematic theologian and a contemporary with Young at Westminster, was a student of Calvin's thought. In an article on "Calvin's Doctrine of Scripture," Murray defended the position that Calvin held a high view of errorless Scripture.[26] He addressed passages in Calvin's writings that seemed to talk about textual mistakes including Hebrews 11:21, the verse that refers Jacob's leaning on his staff. Hebrews 11:21 is one of the verses for which Calvin invoked accommodation, but in his argument as to why Calvin's discussion of the verse espoused nothing contrary to inerrancy, Murray essentially by-passed the reference to accommodation and did not take advantage of the occasion to examine Calvin's use of accommodation.

Inerrancy and Hermeneutic, a more recent product of the Westminster faculty included a paper by professor of missions Harvie Conn (1933-1999). Conn did acknowledge that the principle of accommodation might play a role in the proper interpretation of texts. He addressed the cultural setting of texts pertaining to the status and role of women in church and society.[27] He provided, however, no examination of the application of accommodation to texts bearing on science or to texts that might contain time-bound conceptions.

British evangelical scholar James I. Packer, then of Trinity College, Bristol, acknowledged that there is a doctrine of accommodation in Calvin's writings.[28] He suggested that one of the four key notions that pervade Calvin's treatment of the Bible is "condescension." In summarizing Calvin's concept of "condescension," Packer noted that God, as an expression of his love, talked to us in our language in an earthy and homespun manner so that we might understand him.[29] Packer reviewed instances where Calvin was alleged to have found errors in Scripture. In one instance, Packer suggested that God may have accommodated to "rough-and-ready" forms of speech where he was not concerned to speak with the high degree of accuracy. As an example, he mentioned Calvin's assertion that Moses spoke in phenomenal language so that we cannot expect to learn astronomy from Scripture. As a second instance, Packer referred to points of formal inaccuracy where no assertion was intended by the text so that no error had really been made." As an example, he referred to Calvin's denial that the gospel writers intended to write strictly chronological narratives.[30] Although Packer recognized that accommodation was very important in Calvin's handling of Scripture, he denied that one should make Calvin out as someone who did not espouse biblical inerrancy. He did not examine Calvin's use of accommodation in relation to questions pertaining to nature or science.

Baptist theologian Bernard Ramm (1916-1992) showed some awareness of the relationship of accommodation to inspiration. On the one hand he was critical of theories that postulate accommodation by Jesus, Paul, or other New Testament writers to the religious or ethical views of their contemporaries, thus rendering such doctrines as that of the atonement as not binding on us. Clearly such liberal views of accommodation eviscerate Christian doctrine. In contrast, Ramm recognized that Scripture does accommodate to the culture of the ancient readers in such a way that inspiration is unaffected. As an example, he mentioned the mustard seed, described by Jesus as the smallest of all seeds. "The mustard seed is not the smallest seed known to botanists," Ramm stated, "but among the Semites it passed as the smallest of seeds." It would have been grotesque and unintelligible, said Ramm, for Jesus to have given the Latin terms of the smallest seed. Ramm did not find the Lord's use of the maxim about the mustard seed either contrary to or an argument against the inspiration of Scripture. Perhaps more than any of the writers in the Reformed-Presbyterian tradition Ramm grasped something of the significance of the Bible's accommodation to the "science" of biblical times.[31]

Arguably the most thorough treatments of Calvin's principle of accommodation are those of Ford Lewis Battles, Clinton Ashley, and David Wright.[32] Yet none of these three explored to any degree exactly how Calvin used the principle in relation to natural science. Nor did they develop the application of accommodation to texts that contain possibly erroneous human conceptions. Nor did they suggest biblical examples other than Calvin's own examples where the principle might be applied today.

From time to time church denominations have produced lengthy study reports on biblical inspiration. For example, the 1961 Synod of the Christian Reformed Church reviewed a very long report on "Inspiration and Infallibility in Light of Scripture and the Creeds" and recommended the report for study by individual congregations with the denomination.[33] The report strongly supported the notions of infallibility and inerrancy but took pains to point out that inerrancy is not to be equated with pedantic precision or scientific accuracy of statement. The report noted that readers of the Bible needed to take into account the influence of the ancient Near Eastern context of the Old Testament. Although Calvin was discussed to some degree, there was no reference to his frequent employment of the idea of accommodation. A few years later, another report was produced on "The Nature and Extent of Biblical Authority."[34] Building on and presupposing the findings of the earlier report, the study committee examined the nature and extent of biblical authority in relation to the Bible's content and purpose. The report acknowledged that Scripture was originally addressed to particular situations and circumstances, thus affecting what was said and how it was said. Insights into the history, religion, and culture of the nations surrounding Israel provided by archeology were recognized and accepted, as were insights from the natural sciences. It was noted that scientific discovery compels biblical interpreters to re-examine the text to see if a traditional interpretation really reflects Scripture's intent or if that reading is out-of-date. The report has many valuable and helpful observations in interpreting Scripture, particularly the early chapters of Genesis. Yet, despite the fact that the report cited Calvin's treatment of the fourth day of creation, a passage in which the idea of accommodation comes to the fore, there is no mention, let alone development, of the principle of accommodation in relation to textual interpretation or infallibility.

I suspect that evangelical scholarship has neglected to avail itself of a helpful interpretive tool by paying scant heed to Calvin's principle of accommodation. In what follows, I make a preliminary attempt at some applications.[35] In the last chapter we examined a host of instances in which Calvin applied this principle to the interpretation of texts. On numerous occasions, he evaded the literal, face-value understanding of the words of a text by asserting that God or the human author of the Bible, e.g., Moses or David, was accommodating himself to the capacity of his hearers or readers so that they could understand the point of the message. We saw that there are several types of application of accommodation. God is portrayed anthropomorphically so that readers can form some concept of what he is like. In some instances, accommodation or adaptation meant nothing more than the author's making the message very simple by presenting it in layman's terms rather than in technical terms. In other instances, accommodation meant the omission of a host of details but supplying only a few examples to represent the point being made. In still other cases, however, Calvin applied the principle of accommodation to cases in which the hearers held a particular, arguably erroneous, idea about nature. God or Moses or whichever human author wrote, applied the principle by assuming the validity of the reader's opinion in order to reach the reader rather than attempt to correct the mistaken or less than accurate opinion. To do the latter would have distracted the writer from the main point he was making. The reader would have been baffled by being given a new interpretation of nature that did not make sense either to him or to anyone else around him. This last use of the principle of accommodation occurs most strikingly in the passages dealing with the sizes of the heavenly bodies and with the cobra having ears.

Accommodation and Pedagogy

The beauty of the principle of accommodation is that it keeps in mind the central pedagogical concern of the Bible. The Bible has a message of eternal consequences to convey: the message of salvation through Jesus Christ. Over a period of 1500 years the Scriptures tell the story of how God formed a people for himself out of the whole human race that had fallen into sin and rebellion against the Creator, gave them his laws and covenants, brought them into the promised land, gave them priests and sent them prophets, and promised them a Messiah, an anointed one who would be the great king of righteousness. God designed that great blessing would be brought to the entire world through the people of Israel and the Messiah. In time, Jesus was born as the Savior who would save his people from their sins. He kept God's law perfectly and gave up his life on the cross as a sacrifice to satisfy divine justice. The New Testament tells us that Jesus is the promised Messiah and that salvation is available to all who put their faith in him. The message is a matter of eternal life and death, of eternal joy in the presence of God or eternal separation from God. It is, therefore, imperative that human beings understand the message of the Bible in order to act appropriately on it. God wants us to "get it." He stops at nothing to make sure that we grasp the message. In a sense, then, God acts as a teacher who reaches down to the level of his pupils, a point that Calvin made more than once.

Because the Lord did not address the Bible just to the highly educated, philosophically minded people, he did not normally employ elaborate technical arguments nor arguments that require a mass of arcane knowledge. He typically employed the language and the concepts of ordinary people so that they could understand the message of salvation.

This condescension, adaptation, or accommodation is something that good teachers engage in all the time. They meet their students at the level of their understanding. We do not speak to third-graders as if they had the level of knowledge and experience of college sophomores. The typical third-grader is not intellectually ready to be taught the details of calculus or absorb the fine points of crystallography. Teachers work with students where they are. As a result, there are times in the educational process when aspects of truth may be overlooked so that the teacher can get across the point of immediate importance. For example, when college students take an introductory geology course, one of the first things that they learn is that there are three categories of rocks: igneous, sedimentary, and metamorphic. Not until a student becomes a major in geology does he or she learn that some rocks don't fit neatly into any of these three categories, and they discover that there are such things as vein rocks and tectonic breccias. In the interests of simplicity, time, and the fact that most rocks *do* belong to one of the three major categories, however, instructors of introductory geology courses normally don't mention that there really are more than three rock categories. The instructor does not tell the whole truth, and may even distort the truth somewhat, in the interest of helping the student learn the categories of the most abundant rocks.

Introductory geology students also learn the differences among the igneous, sedimentary, and metamorphic rocks. In becoming familiar with common rocks, they often discover that some igneous rocks, such as granite, look very similar to some metamorphic rocks, such as gneiss, in terms of the general size of the mineral grains and of the mineral content. To help students learn to distinguish the rock types, geology professors generally make the point that many metamorphic rocks, including gneiss, display a property known as foliation. That is, gneisses and many other metamorphic rocks possess banding, preferred alignment of most of the mineral grains within the rock, or some other oriented structure. In contrast, the igneous rock samples that the students will see, including granite, are characterized by randomly oriented mineral grains. The idea is to get students to recognize a very important distinction between the great majority of granites and the great majority of gneisses. If the student goes on to major in geology and ends up taking a course in petrology, he or she will probably learn that in some localities a body of igneous rock, such as a granite, is characterized by very pronounced layering or preferred orientation of mineral grains. The petrology professor will explain how the layering in the granite might form and how it differs from the banding of a gneiss despite the superficial similarity. At the introductory level, however, the students lack sufficient background in geology to appreciate this nuance. They would only become confused and frustrated by telling them that some granites have the banding of gneisses. Nor do instructors have the time to go into the exceptions to the rule that we establish regarding preferred orientation of mineral grains in rocks. Teachers don't always tell the whole truth about a particular topic, and sometimes, in the interest of making a larger, more basic point, the actual state of affairs may be distorted in instruction.

The same thing happens when geologists talk about the internal structure of the Earth or about bond types in crystals in an introductory course. For example, students learn that in the common mineral halite, which is sodium chloride, the sodium and chlorine atoms are held together by ionic bonds in which the atoms are attracted to one another by virtue of their opposite electrical charges. In contrast, in a diamond, composed of pure carbon, the carbon atoms are held together by covalent bonding, an arrangement that entails sharing of electrons between adjacent atoms. Instructors may mention these two minerals as examples of minerals that have two very different kinds of chemical bonding. At the elementary level, most students are not yet ready to be "confused" by the fact that ionic-bonded crystals like sodium chloride also possess a small percentage of covalent character. The important point for introductory geology students is that there are several distinct bond types in minerals and that these two minerals serve as examples of two of those types of bonds. Not until a student takes a course in mineralogy will he or she face some of the subtleties of chemical bonding in minerals.

When a small child explains a concept to his or her parent and clearly has grasped the main thrust of the concept, but perhaps has some of the facts supporting the concept mixed up, the parent may often express pleasure that the child has grasped the concept without necessarily attempting to correct any and every factual error that may have been made. That can come with time. Most of us know that a lot of small children assume that the baby inside Mommy's tummy is in the stomach, because they don't know about the uterus just yet. And many mothers don't feel the need to give a two-year-old a lesson in the female internal anatomy and to correct the error until the child is much older. Good pedagogy sometimes allows mistakes to stand in the interests of driving home the point at issue.

If we keep the pedagogical thrust of Scripture in mind, it makes sense to assume that God is so desirous that we understand the message of the Bible that he tolerates the imperfections of our state of knowledge in peripheral matters. What we believe or what the ancient Hebrews believed about the structure of the cosmos is relatively unimportant compared to the knowledge that God is our maker and redeemer. The apostle John does not say in his gospel that he wrote it so that we would have an improved or corrected knowledge of the way the world is put together. He says he that wrote his gospel so that we might believe that Jesus is the Christ, the Son of God, and that believing we might have life through his name. And Paul in writing to Timothy did not say that the God-breathed Scriptures were given to teach us the fine points of cosmic structure or the mechanics of rock deformation but rather that they are profitable for doctrine, reproof, correction, and instruction in righteousness so that we might be made perfect and thoroughly equipped for every good work.

Scientific Knowledge of Bible Times

If we postulate that God addressed the ancient Hebrews *through* their ideas about the nature of the cosmos without attempting to alter those ideas, then the question arises as to what state of knowledge of the world the ancient Israelites had. Given that the overwhelming majority of significant scientific discoveries have been made within the past few centuries, we obviously cannot expect that the Old Testament Hebrews thought about the world in the same way that we do. We now routinely talk about the Earth going around the Sun, spinning on its axis, and being a globe. We talk about earthquakes and mountain belts forming in response to the movement of tectonic plates. We understand that many diseases are caused by germs such as viruses and bacteria. We know that living organisms and tissues are composed of cells. We know that genetic information is passed from parent to offspring by means of genes and DNA. We know that the heavens include a host of mind-boggling objects such as galaxies, black holes, quasars, and nebular clouds. We talk about supernovae, the red shift, the expanding universe, and the stretching of space. We think of the Earth as being 4.5 billion years old. We talk about the development of life through time. These entities and concepts were completely unknown to Calvin in the sixteenth century. How much more obvious that these concepts and entities were unknown to the Israelites of the Old Testament era. Aristotle's conception of the cosmos had not even been formulated when the Old Testament canon was completed.

We learn about ancient Near Eastern conceptions of the world from some of the archeological discoveries that have been made throughout the Middle East. There was widespread acceptance of the idea that the Earth is a flat disk rather than a sphere. For most ancient cultures the heavens were thought of as a hemispherical dome covering the Earth-disk. That dome was regarded as a solid with a crystalline nature.[36] Some cultures envisioned the existence of primeval waters located above that dome or firmament.[37] Many cultures, likewise, believed that there are substantial bodies of subterranean waters. If these beliefs were widespread among the neighbors of ancient Israel, it should not surprise us that the ancient Israelites themselves entertained these notions. After all, the Israelites trace their ancestry to Abraham, a citizen of Ur in Mesopotamia. They undoubtedly inherited Mesopotamian beliefs about the structure of the world. They sojourned in Egypt for several hundred years before the Exodus. They also undoubtedly acquired some of their ideas from the Egyptians, particularly because their leader Moses had been educated in the royal courts of Egypt as the adopted son of Pharaoh's daughter. The children of Israel at last made their way into the promised land where they struggled for years to evict the resident Canaanites. Failing to extirpate the inhabitants of the promised land completely, they undoubtedly also picked up ideas about nature from the Canaanites and the

Philistines. There is no question that conceptions about the structure of the world were tinged with polytheistic religious overtones in these heathen cultures. No doubt some individuals among the Israelites had a difficult time shaking off those overtones. Israel constantly battled the polytheism and idol worship in its midst. Rachel brought the household gods out of Mesopotamia. Joshua urged the Israelites to abandon the gods of their forefathers and to follow Yahweh. The entire history of Israel throughout the Old Testament is permeated with Israel's repeated lapse into idolatry that variously involved the worship of Baal, Ashtoreth, Moloch, and other gods. So there is no question that many Israelites mixed up their conception of the physical world with pagan cosmogony, mythology, and practice.

Nevertheless, stripped of its pagan, polytheistic elements, there is nothing inherently wrong, nothing inherently anti-monotheistic, nothing inherently anti-Judaic in the physical world pictures in and of themselves or of then current ideas about the behavior of animals and plants. Given a world in which the scientific enterprise had barely begun, a world in which scientific methods of observation, testing, experimentation, measurement, and use of instruments were not commonplace, people developed conceptions of the way the world is put together and functions in the best way that they could. Generally those ways were based on superficial or common sense observation. To any one simply observing the sky it is obvious that the Sun and the Moon go around the Earth. There is no compelling observational reason in the immediate environment of an ordinary observer to think that the world is a globe. To think of a globe requires a much more sophisticated analysis of the situation such as the recognition that stars occupy different positions in the sky when observed at exactly the same moment from locations that are very widely separated from one another. But to discover that situation would have required an amount of travel that would have been beyond the opportunities of most individuals, or it would have required careful observation, record keeping, and ongoing communication between distant observers, a rare circumstance. The sky does resemble a dome, and the stars do look like little points of light attached to the dome. Perhaps it is a little less obvious why one would assume that there are primeval waters above that dome, although those living in areas with lots of blue, cloudless skies day after day might be persuaded that the blue sky resembles a vast upside-down ocean. Likewise, it makes some sense to think that there are substantial bodies of water underground. After all, people frequently encounter springs or see water flowing out of fractures in rock outcrops.

In addition to a physical world picture that makes perfect sense in a prescientific age, there would undoubtedly be other beliefs about the world that might be based on superficial observation. We might expect that beliefs about the behavior of animals and plants or about the medicinal values of plants would arise. Think of Jacob and the mandrakes as an example. Some of these beliefs strike us as superstitions now, but some of them may simply have been based on hasty observation and then passed down to succeeding generations. The idea of spontaneous generation is also a common sense observation. Throughout history people have seen tiny organisms appear in mud or maggots on spoiled meat. Lacking the tools to see the eggs of flies, the ancients may be excused for thinking that these organisms grew directly out of the mud or meat.

Applying Accommodation to Scientific Issues

Let's turn now to the Bible and particularly the Old Testament, and let's think about God addressing the people of Old Testament times. Would not God address them in terms of the world that they knew? Would he not have addressed the ancient Israelites in terms of the language that they knew, the idioms with which they were familiar, the symbols and figures of speech with which they were acquainted, and the literary conventions that they used? By the same token would he not have addressed them in terms of the physical world picture with which they were acquainted, and in terms of their beliefs about animals, places, history, and the structure of the world? Why would he do otherwise? The Bible is a book about God and about his relationship with human beings. It is a radical book that makes a drastic break with the religious, moral, and ethical beliefs of all the cultures around Israel. The Bible is unequivocally monotheistic. It tells us that humans are neither an annoyance to the gods, nor gods themselves. Rather we learn that humanity bears the image of God and that humanity is in a state of sin and rebellion against God and is under his curse. Scripture tells us that no amount of human effort can bring about deliverance from our bondage to sin. It tells us that God's action alone can do so, and it tells us how God has done so through sending his Son to take on human flesh, live a perfect life in obedience to the one who sent him, suffer the punishment of our sin in his own death, and rise victoriously from the dead. Moreover, the Bible tells us what God's will is for our lives.

The clear thrust of the Scriptures is religious and ethical in nature. Given that the message of the Bible is so radically different from everything else in the world religiously speaking, would not God couch his message in a way that would not completely put off his hearers? In other words, would he not couch his message in terms that were already familiar to the readers? Suppose that God had addressed the Israelites by way of Scriptures that also corrected all their notions about the structure and behavior of the cosmos, that corrected all their notions about pre-history, or that addressed them in language forms that were totally different from what they were used to. Would not the effect have been to put off the readers? Who would pay any attention to someone who told you that the Earth really goes around the Sun when everyone knows full well that the Sun goes around the Earth? The message of the Bible could then legitimately be dismissed as a message from a rather unreliable source.

Suppose that God is addressing the human race for the first time during *our* lifetimes. Imagine that he is describing the work of creation for us. Given that most of the world now is aware that the Earth spins on its axis and goes around the Sun, would not the Creator be more likely to cast the descriptions of creation in heliocentric terms? Might we not find an occasional reference to a galaxy? Or maybe a black hole? Wouldn't Scripture be addressed to us in terms that are familiar to us? But now if we step back for a second, we realize that our current talk about an expanding universe, a Big Bang, electrons, and quantum mechanics is only the current scientific understanding of the world. In another 2000 years, we will have learned vastly more about the universe. Our current world picture will undoubtedly be modified in significant ways that we can't imagine right now. Remember that God is writing the Scriptures for *our time* in this hypothetical scenario. Would he do so in terms of a world picture that would be valid 2000 years from now, or in terms of some ultimately true picture of the world? I think it is unlikely that God would do that. If the object of God's revelation is to reach his hearers, would he throw unnecessary roadblocks in the way by talking about matters that are way beyond the knowledge and comprehension of the original hearers or readers, in this case by introducing a scientific world picture that lies thousands of years in the future? We talk in terms of what we know now, or think we know. Had God given us a Scripture cast in terms of a scientifically valid world picture for 2000 years in the future, we would very likely become suspicious of the author and begin to wonder if we were dealing with a reliable book. We would more likely suspect that we were reading science *fiction.*

It makes perfect sense that God addressed the ancient Hebrews in terms of the "scientific" world picture with which they were familiar and comfortable. It would have made little sense for God to have talked about billions of years of Earth history, about biological evolution, about the Big Bang, or about early hominids in Genesis. The ancient Hebrews knew nothing about all that. What they did know was that the world is full of mystery, that there is a deep dome-like sky out there chock full of stars that orbit the Earth along with a Sun and Moon that do the same.

Biblical prophecy is handled in a manner along the lines that I am suggesting. The Old Testament prophetic books are filled with passages that look ahead to events in a distant future which, even for us, thousands of years from the time of the prophets, still seem yet to be fulfilled. The careful student of the Bible will take note that many of the glorious prophecies are cast in terms that were familiar to the Old Testament Israelites, terms that would convey a sense of the pinnacle of pure religion: the rebuilt temple, the restoration of sacrifices and pure worship in the temple, the nations coming to Jerusalem to worship, David as king over restored Israel, and the like. The Old Testament Israelites were not quite ready to hear about the abolishment of animal sacrifices, the indwelling of the Holy Spirit, the worship of the resurrected Messiah in churches throughout all the nations of the world, the observance of the Lord's Supper, missionary activity, or the proclamation of the gospel by people who were not descendants of Levi. Thus the restoration of God's people and the establishment of the coming kingdom were prophesied in terms that the Israelites knew. As a result, literal interpretation of many of these prophetic utterances misses the point that the prophecies were cast in terms that the original hearers would relate to. Not even the prophets themselves fully grasped the import of their own prophecies. Although they understood that God was going to do something wonderful, even they could not see clearly beyond the Jewishness of their utterances.

Possible Examples of Accommodation

Let's now look at a few examples in which we might apply the principle of accommodation. Genesis 1:6-8 records the events of the second day of creation. The text mentions that God made an expanse or a firmament. He then separated the waters that are below the firmament from the waters that are above the firmament. But what exactly is that firmament or expanse? Many contemporary scholars, particularly in the evangelical community, have said that the sky or atmosphere is in view here. Calvin himself was one of the earliest commentators to suggest a similar position. In his commentary on Genesis, he referred open air and everything open above us to the firmament. Interestingly, however, in his commentary on Psalm 19:2, published a few years later than the Genesis commentary, he spoke about a revolution of the firmament that drew the fixed stars with it, suggesting a conception of a somewhat more solid firmament. Today, a growing number of scholars insist that the text is not talking about empty space or the atmosphere.[38] The Hebrew term that the various English versions have translated as firmament or expanse is *raqia'*. According to the standard Hebrew lexicons, *raqia'* conveys the idea of something that has been hammered or beaten out into a thin sheet and refers to a *solid* dome that covers the sky and serves as a dam to prevent the ocean of waters above from collapsing onto the Earth. According to the Hebrew text, the stars are in this dome, possibly embedded in it, and the birds fly *across the face* or surface of the dome, not in it (Genesis 1:20). In effect, the text says that God made a solid dome or vault to separate the waters.

What is the biblical evidence that *raqia'* is a solid vault? The vision of Ezekiel in which the prophet saw the wheeled cherubim refers to the *raqia'* (Ezekiel 1:22-26; 10:1-2). The appearance of a throne is said to occur above the *raqia'*, and the appearance of a man is seated on the appearance of the throne. The impression is given in the vision that the likeness of the throne is resting on the solid floor provided by the *raqia'*. The consensus of commentaries on Ezekiel is that this *raqia'* is solid.[39] In Job 37:18, Job's friend Elihu refers to the sky as being beaten or spread out (verb form of *raqia'*) as hard as a mirror of cast bronze (NIV) or strong as a molten, i.e., cast, looking glass (KJV). Other passages in the Old Testament in which the verb form is employed include Jeremiah 10:9 (hammered silver, beaten silver), Isaiah 40:19 (a goldsmith overlaying, spreading over, or plating with gold), Exodus 39:3 (hammer out, beat thin sheets of gold). Texts like Psalm 136:6, Isaiah 42:5, and Isaiah 44:24 refer to spreading out of the Earth. In all these cases that which is beaten, hammered, or spread out is a solid substance. So the various biblical references to *raqia'* are consistent with its being a solid object. Paul Seely has demonstrated that the ancient Near Eastern cultures had a strong belief that the sky is solid, that is, that there is a solid domed vault above the clouds in which the heavenly bodies are located.[40] The Babylonians believed that the dome or vault served as a barrier or dam to keep a heavenly ocean at bay so that it would not fall on the Earth. Given their origins in Mesopotamia, there is no reason to believe that the early Israelites would have thought any differently about the structure of what is above. An Israelite reading Genesis 1:6 around the time of King David would understand the text quite naturally as saying that God made the solid vault of the sky. There is no reason to think that a hypothetical exegete living in 200 B. C. would read the text as saying that God made *the appearance* of a solid dome. Verses such as Isaiah 40:22 speak of God's spreading out the heavens like a tent or a canopy. Here poetic language is used. But with *raqia'*, God doesn't make the sky like a *raqia'*--it is a *raqia'*.

For the ancient Hebrew, the sky didn't simply *look like* a solid dome, there *was* a solid dome or at least a resistant dome up there. Virtually everyone believed that it was so. Several of the early church fathers believed it was so. Origen referred to the firmament as "the corporeal heaven." He went on to say that "every corporeal object is, without doubt, firm and solid."[41] In his third homily on the hexameron, Basil questioned whether the firmament was composed of solidified or hardened water, but he did maintain "concerning the firmament that it is something firm." Moreover, Basil's response to certain critics indicates his belief that there is a dome up there. The critics of Scripture had questioned just how the fluid waters above the firmament with their slippery nature would keep from sliding off the top of the dome. Basil's solution was not to deny that there is a firm dome-like barrier above. Instead he said that when viewed from the inside the firmament does appear to be shaped like a vault, dome, or orb. But it's not that way on the outside. The top of the firmament doesn't have the shape of a sphere because "there is a level place constructed above it." In essence, there is a flat roof above the dome.[42] Ambrose asked in his comments on Genesis 11:6, "if the nature of the elements is taken into consideration, how is it possible for the firmament to be stable between the sky?" The reason that the stability of the firmament posed a potential problem was that "the one is liquid; the other solid." Later he asserted that "the specific solidity of this exterior firmament is meant." Moreover, he noted that the "firmament cannot be broken, you see, without a noise. It is also called a firmament because it is not weak nor without resistance."[43] In discussing writers who addressed the question whether the firmament was stationary or moving, Augustine said that they "must certainly bear in mind that the term 'firmament' does not compel us to imagine a stationary heaven: we may understand this name as given to indicate not that it is motionless but that it is solid and that it constitutes an impassable boundary between the waters above and the waters below."[44] Chrysostom was non-committal about the substance of the firmament. Asking what "firmament" meant he concluded that "no sensible person would be rash enough to make a decision" on whether it consisted of congealed water, compressed air, or some other substance. He thought it best just to accept what we were told and not reach "beyond the limits of our own nature."[45] His agnostic position regarding the substance of the firmament, of course, does not rule out the possibility that he conceived of it as a solid dome.

In fact, most people continued to believe in a solid covering to the sky well into the Middle Ages. The Bishop of Lincoln, Robert Grosseteste (c. 1175-1253), for example, recognized that many had accepted the solidity of the firmament, and he seemed to concur on the grounds that inasmuch as rock crystal was believed to be formed from water by freezing it should be no surprise that the upper waters should be solidified into one great crystal. The temptation to interpret the text as referring to what *appears* like a vault is *our* problem, brought about by the fact that, in the modern scientific age, we know that there is no *solid* vault up there. So what should we make of this? If the text of Genesis 1:6 is saying that God made a solid vault of heaven to separate an ocean of waters above from the waters below, then are we not bound by the Word of God to believe that there is indeed a solid vault in the sky no matter what the astronomers may tell us? With this kind of syllogistic logic many Christians have attempted to sweep away the dilemma by arguing that *raqia'* does not mean a solid dome.

But there is another way around the difficulty if we keep in mind the purpose or the point of the biblical statement. And here is where accommodation comes in. Application of the principle of accommodation would tell us that God accommodated himself to the scientific belief of the original recipients of the biblical message in order to make a point that he didn't want them to forget. And what was that point? The teaching of Genesis 1:6 is that *God, later to be identified with Yahweh, is the creator of the raqia'*. Yes, the original readers would naturally take it in the following sense: "You know that sky up there which you believe to be a solid dome that holds back the primeval ocean? Well, God made it. It isn't there all by itself. It isn't a divine entity in and of itself. It wasn't made by the pagan gods. It didn't come into being in the course of squabbles among the heathen gods. It is a creature, brought effortlessly into existence by the word of the one and only living God who made all of heaven and earth." The point of the text is not that God made *a solid sky*. The point is that *God made* the "solid sky," the *raqia'*. The text is not *teaching* either the original hearers or contemporary readers about the physical structure of the cosmos. *Scripture is teaching us about the relation between the author of the cosmos and of the cosmos and its physical structures* (however we may conceive of them). The text is not making a binding scientific claim. It is making an inerrant theological claim.

But what of us who live today? If we keep in mind the idea that God was speaking through the science of the ancient culture, we should come away with much the same conclusion. Perhaps we could capture the idea in the following sense: "You know that sky up there with all those stars that shine down on us from outer space far above the Earth, that region of the world that the ancients believed was a solid sky dome over the Earth, a *raqia'*? Well, God is the maker of all that. The sky and the heavenly bodies are not there all by themselves. The sky and the universe did not just spontaneously appear on their own out of the void. The sky and the universe are not eternally self-existent entities. They are the products of divine creation (no matter how you may conceive of them scientifically), brought into being effortlessly by the word of the living God who made heaven and earth." Again, the point is not that God made the physical structure of the sky or the stellar bodies or galaxies exactly *as we currently understand them with our contemporary scientific knowledge*. The point is that God made what we take as the sky with all the objects that appear in it or above it. *Whatever is actually out there is a creation of God. What we should take away from Genesis 1:6 is the infallible theological claim that the one God is the Creator of what we see (and what we do not see), not inerrant instruction about the physical constitution of the sky or the stellar regions beyond.*

The Genesis text is indeed inerrant in the sense that it teaches us that *God created* the *raqia'*. That is the purpose of the text. To extend the concept of inerrancy to the existence of a solid vault or to our current scientific conception of the structure of the sky or universe goes beyond what the text is attempting to teach.

Some readers may complain that I have fallen prey to adopting an interpretation of *raqia'* that not only violates the notion of biblical inerrancy but is also suspect because it is widely accepted among theologically liberal writers who don't mind partitioning Genesis into several primitive documents that were compiled by an editor some time after the exile and who also look with great favor on finding Mesopotamian influences on the biblical text. In reply I would remind the reader that when I first suggested that the Reformed tradition had generally ignored Calvin's idea of accommodation and then gave several examples, I mentioned that there was an important exception in the linkage of accommodation and biblical inspiration. The exception was Charles Hodge (1797-1878), a revered professor of exegetical, didactic, and polemic theology at Princeton Theological Seminary throughout much of the nineteenth century. In his 1857 article on "Inspiration," Hodge wrote that the inspired biblical writers were not elevated in secular knowledge above the age in which they lived. Even though inspiration did preserve those writers from teaching error in regard to secular and scientific truths, nevertheless, to the sacred writers "the heavens were solid, and the earth a plane; the sun moved from east to west over their heads." But such matters were "no part of the faith of the sacred writers."[46]

Then years later in his *Systematic Theology*, Hodge, in writing about objections to the Mosaic account of creation, noted that one of the objections is that Scripture represents the visible heavens as a "solid expanse." Rather than denying that Scripture represents the heavens as a solid expanse, Hodge conceded that interpretation, noting that the Bible when dealing with such matters "is framed in accordance with the common usage of men." He asked that "if we speak of the concave heavens, why might not the Hebrew speak of the solid heavens?" Remarkably, at that point, Hodge quoted (in Latin) Calvin's statement from the *Institutes* that "although Moses, in accommodation to the ignorance of the generality of men, does not in the history of the creation make mention of any other works of God than those which meet our eye." Charles Hodge accepted the idea that the firmament in biblical times was regarded as a solid and then invoked the principle of accommodation to account for the reference. In effect, he regarded the statement that the firmament is solid as not part of the inerrant *teaching* of Moses.[47]

But now let's look at another example. In Matthew 5:45 Jesus taught his disciples that God causes his Sun to rise on the evil and the good. Psalm 19:5-6 very poetically speaks about the Sun rejoicing to run his race across the sky. Ecclesiastes 1:5 tells us that "the sun rises and the sun sets, and hurries back to where it rises." The English translations of several other Old Testament texts make reference to the going down of the Sun, to the place where the Sun sets, or to the west (Deuteronomy 11:30, Joshua 1:4, 23:4; Psalm 50:1, 104:19; Malachi 1:11). The Hebrew term employed by these texts refers to an entrance. Joshua called upon the Sun to stand still. In response to Joshua's prayer, the Sun stood still while the Israelites vanquished their Gibeonite enemies.

Contemporary evangelicals typically claim that these texts are employing phenomenal language. After all, today *we* speak of sunrise and sunset, do we not? But that's *our* problem. Jesus did not say that God caused the appearance of the Sun rising on the evil and the good. Psalm 19 does not say that the Sun looks like it is running a race across the sky. Ecclesiastes does not say that the Sun looks as if it were hurrying. The cluster of texts that use the word for "entrance" do not say that there appears to be an entrance for the Sun. Joshua did not ask the Sun to look like it was standing still. Readers of the Old Testament texts that mentioned the "entrance" of the Sun would have interpreted the verse literally given that many ancients believed that the Sun passed through a tunnel or slot in the dome or firmament at its setting. Every last one of Jesus' listeners would probably have interpreted his words in Matthew 5 literally for the simple reason that every one of his contemporaries assumed that the Earth is stationary and that the Sun daily moves across the sky and around the Earth. The Sun and the Moon obviously will look like they are moving around the Earth because they are moving around the Earth. Everyone thought that. Common sense observation compelled acceptance of that belief. The Greek astronomers all believed as much, with the exception of Aristarchos of Samos. Virtually nobody accepted his claim that the Earth moves. Geocentric belief persisted universally until the sixteenth century when Copernicus proposed his heliocentric ideas. So there is no reason to think that either Joshua or Jesus, in his human nature, were thinking in terms of the language of appearance when they called on the Sun to stand still or mentioned that the Sun rose. Nor would the early interpreters of these texts. Not until the time of Galileo when it was realized that the Sun only appears to rise and move across the sky because of the rotation of the Earth on its axis did exegetes begin to make the claim that the text is merely employing phenomenal language.

I suggest that we have here another instance of the principle of accommodation in which the divine author was accommodating himself by speaking in terms of the world picture of that day. God made no effort in authoring his written Word to correct the early scientific notion that the Sun moved around the

Earth. The divine author took the belief as it was and used it to make far more important points. On the one hand Matthew 5:45 teaches the power that God exercises over nature. On the other hand, God also teaches in this text that his compassion and kindness as displayed in the ordinances of nature are daily and lavishly made available alike to those who put their faith in him and to those who do not.

Again, suppose that God wanted to teach "correct" science and that in the Sermon on the Mount, Jesus had launched into a discussion about the Earth's daily rotation on its axis with the result that the Sun simply looked like it is moving whereas, in fact, it is we who are moving. Would it have served any purpose? Would it not have served as an enormous distraction to have brought in more advanced science? Jesus had enough detractors as it was. Why start making claims about the Sun and the Earth that everyone could see were plainly false? Would not Jesus then have undermined his credibility?

I suggest that God accommodated himself to the scientific beliefs of his hearers and readers so that his main point would be clear to them and so that they would not be distracted from it. In the case of the Sermon on the Mount, the text is inerrant, but it is inerrant with regard to the point being made, not with regard to statements made in abstraction from the point being made. The text inerrantly teaches that God graciously provides sunshine for all people no matter what their scientific understanding of the physical, geometrical, or mechanical relationship of the Sun and the Earth to each other may be. The text may say, *but it does not intend to compel assent to the idea*, that the Sun moves around the Earth.

There may be other instances in Scripture in which the Lord of creation has accommodated himself to less than accurate conceptions about the natural world entertained by the early recipients of the biblical message. Among some of the possibilities might be the references to the chewing of the cud by the hare (Leviticus 11:6), the foolish or cruel egg-laying behavior of the ostrich (Job 39:13-18), and the existence of satyrs or goat-demons in the desert (Isaiah 13:21; 34:14). I will leave it to readers to explore these issues further. Suffice it to say that rabbits do not chew cud, ostriches turn out to be pretty conscientious parents, and satyrs don't exist.

It might be objected that I have pushed the principle of accommodation beyond what Calvin did. After all, in the classic example of accommodation in his exposition of Genesis 1, he specifically interpreted the text about the creation of the Moon and stars as using phenomenal language, the language of appearances, as opposed to speaking "according to truth." I make no judgment here as to whether he should have done this or not. I simply note that he did. But I have suggested that there are passages in the Bible that should be taken at face value and that are not merely speaking the language of appearances. When taken at face value the texts seem to make assertions that we know are incorrect. Such a strategy can be acceptable and compatible with an infallible Bible.

Consider, for example, Calvin's application of accommodation to geography. The description of world geography in terms of the river to the ends of the

Earth (i.e., the Arabian peninsula) is deficient compared to our present knowledge. The geography is the geographic knowledge of that day, not the geography of the world as we know it today. God condescended to speak to the hearer in terms of the geographic knowledge of that day. But, one might argue, the geographic knowledge of the ancient world was not incorrect, it was merely limited. That may be so, in a sense, but when Messiah's universal reign is portrayed, it is portrayed in the very narrow terms of the knowledge of the time and is less than fully accurate. But how else could Messiah's future reign be portrayed to Old Testament readers?

More telling, however, is Calvin's discussion of Psalm 58:4 where he specifically applied accommodation to an erroneous but commonly held opinion that snakes can be charmed by music. The text taken at face value seems to imply that snakes can be charmed, enchanted, or hypnotized. Calvin said that maybe that can happen by virtue of diabolical action, but he was inclined to think instead that the Bible accommodated itself to the erroneous opinion of the common folk of the day that snakes can be enchanted. A belief that snakes can be entranced by the playing of music is scientific in nature, for whether snakes respond to music is a matter of observation in the realm of nature. The false belief about snakes being enchanted by music was assumed by the psalmist, in Calvin's judgment, for the sake of making a point about the wicked behavior of those who, likened to venomous snakes, rebelled against the Lord. In the process, it sounds like the Bible is supportive of a false belief.

I do not think that I have pushed the principle of accommodation beyond what Calvin himself did in these two cases. I have, however, applied the principle to verses that he did not. Many readers might wonder, however, about the wisdom of applying this principle. Are we not in walking to the top of the slippery slope? What is to prevent us from applying accommodation to any verse in the Bible, to any text that we don't understand, to any text we disagree with or don't like, for example? The big question is, then, in what situations should we apply the principle of accommodation?

For starters, let's reiterate that the stated purpose of Scripture is to tell us what to believe about God and Christ and to tell us how to live. This stated purpose would seem to rule out theological, religious, or ethical accommodation. The clear testimony of Scripture is that, apart from the revelation of Scripture, the human race, by virtue of its rebellion against God, is not at all a reliable guide to religious or ethical truth. The Bible condemns the vain speculations of people. Thus, when the Bible is making religious assertions (especially when they are strikingly different from what the mass of people typically believe), it is to be doubted that the author accommodated himself to the religious views of his contemporaries simply to gain their attention.

Nor should we invoke accommodation to explain away miracles. In no way should the virgin birth or the resurrection of Jesus be dismissed as accommodations to the naïve superstitious beliefs of his disciples about their remarkable leader. Nor should we invoke the idea to discredit other miracles. Nor does a philosophical speculation that disagrees with a biblical teaching provide adequate grounds for undercutting the force of the biblical teaching by means of the principle of accommodation.

On the other hand, it seems to me that the appropriate time to consider invoking the principle is where Scripture includes a statement about the natural world that is clearly contrary to firmly established and empirically verified knowledge. This is particularly the case where we can see that Scripture might be referring to beliefs that could easily be drawn from superficial observation of nature. As we have seen, superficial observation of a snake charmer playing a pipe in front of a swaying cobra could very easily be interpreted as musical enchantment of the snake. The interpretation of the observation, although sensible, would be incorrect. It has been established empirically that snakes do not hear music in the sense that we do and that snakes sway to the movement of the pipe which is perceived by the snake as a possible threat. Many Christians have inferred from the biblical text that the Earth is only a few thousand years old. However, it has been firmly established by numerous lines of empirical evidence that the Earth is vastly older than a few thousands of years. If the Bible really seems to suggest that the Earth is young, then it may be that Scripture has merely accommodated itself to that belief. In my judgment, judicious application of Calvin's principle of accommodation would go a long way toward solving some of the problems concerning the relation of science to the Bible. Accommodation of the type suggested should in no way undermine the doctrine of creation or any other basic Christian doctrine, nor should it be seen as incompatible with a divinely inspired, infallible Bible. The idea of accommodation should, in fact, help us to see more clearly how the Bible actually functions, and it should help to make us better interpreters of Scripture. The principle of accommodation helps us to see the extent to which God descends to our level to make sure that we grasp the good news of salvation. As Paul Seely put it, accommodation is a "manifestation of amazing grace."[48]

If we learn nothing else from the way in which John Calvin approached nature itself and the scientific study of nature, we need to recognize that his careful, reasoned, and judicious application of the notion of divine accommodation to human concepts about the natural world provides us with another valuable tool that enables us to unlock the meaning of the biblical text. His application of the principle of accommodation serves as a potent reminder that Scripture was written, not to teach us inerrant scientific data, but to lead us to believe that Jesus is the Christ, the Son of God, and that believing we might have life through his name.

NOTES

1.   Scott E. Hoezee, *Proclaim the Wonder: Engaging Science on Sunday* (Grand Rapids, Mich.: Baker Books, 2003).

2.   Those who are interested in learning about scientific findings should consult the very readable popularizations of geology by John McPhee and of physics and astronomy by Paul Davies and Timothy Ferris. Kenneth Miller, a Roman Catholic cell biologist who rejects the blatantly materialistic philosophy of anti-religious popularizers such as Richard Dawkins and Daniel Dennett, has written *Finding Darwin's God*, a very clear exposition of the scientific basis for biological evolution. Readers can also benefit from articles in *Scientific American* and the excellent programs of *Nova* broadcast on public television. The   Affiliation   of   Christian   Geologists   (ACG)   maintains   a   website (www.wheaton.edu/ACG/) with a feature entitled "Ask a Geologist."

3.   Hoezee briefly flirted with John Polkinghorne's suggestion that God established the overall plan and goal of the cosmos but did not predetermine all its minute details and events, a clear departure from Calvin's view that even the smallest details of nature are under the guidance and control of God as well as the larger picture. The reader who forgives this transgression will receive great benefit in the book.

4.   In recent years, several denominations within the Reformed tradition have issued reports on creation in relation to science. These include the Report of the Committee on Creation and Science, Synod of the Christian Reformed Church (1991); Report of the Special Committee to Articulate the Doctrine of Creation, 253rd Synod of the Reformed Church in the United States (1999); Report of the Creation Study Committee, 28th General Assembly of the Presbyterian Church in America (2000); and Report of the Committee to Study the Views of Creation, 71st General Assembly of the Orthodox Presbyterian Church (2004).

5.   C. John Collins, a professor of Old Testament at Covenant Theological Seminary, teaches a course entitled "Christian Faith in an Age of Science." Collins received his bachelor's and master's degrees from Massachusetts Institute of Technology in electrical engineering, a course of study that would entail a solid grounding in physics. As a theologian with formal training in a natural science, Collins is an exception. Other exceptions include Robert C. Newman of Biblical School of Theology and Christopher Kaiser of Western Theological Seminary, both of whom have Ph.D. degrees in astrophysics.

6.   The members of the ecclesiastical committees mentioned in note 4 were predominantly pastors and theologians. The OPC committee consisted of seven members, none of whom are scientists. The PCA committee consisted of twelve members including a chemist, physicist, and biologist. The CRC committee of eight included three scientists (a chemist, physicist, and biologist) and one philosopher of science. In my judgment, the CRC committee produced the most balanced report of the four and fairly represented scientific data and theory.

7.   The report of the Presbyterian Church in America (PCA) concluded with the recognition that there is a difference of opinion about the age of the Earth among Reformed scientists. Observing that the heliocentric view won out over the geocentric view "because of a vast preponderance of facts favoring it," the report said that "likewise, in the present controversy, a large number of observations over a long period of time will likely be the telling factor." The committee that authored the report believed that the issue of the age of the Earth is "a continuing effort, not a completed one." They wisely noted that "the church is not the authoritative source for determining what is or is not scientific truth. Traditionally, this has been left to the scientific community to decide." But then the

committee, indulging in wishful thinking, indicated unwillingness to accept the fact that the scientific community long ago decided the question in favor of an extremely old Earth, not because of perceived hostility to the truths of special revelation, but because of an overwhelming preponderance of data from a wide range of sources and collected over a long period of time by thousands of geologists.

8.   There is a wide range of definition of the terms theory, hypothesis, and fact among scientists and philosophers of science. In most cases, theory is employed in preference to hypothesis when the degree of acceptance is much greater. As scientists use the term, a theory is not simply an educated guess. It is rather an explanation that successfully accounts for a wide range of data, has repeatedly and successfully been tested in a variety of ways, and is consistent with other bodies of accepted knowledge. A really good theory will continually be tested, challenged, and refined. Theories may be considered as valid for long periods of time and eventually be discarded when new information becomes available and better theories supersede them. The theory of phlogiston and the geocentric theory were considered as valid, the latter for hundreds, if not thousands, of years, before being discarded. An established theory, however, will not be rejected by the community of scientific experts until it can be shown to the satisfaction of the community that the theory no longer accounts for many new facts and that a different theory accounts for those facts more successfully.

9.   On theory acceptance in science see Ernan McMullin, "Values in Science," *PSA 1982: Proceedings of the 1982 Biennial Meeting of the Philosophy of Science Association* (East Lansing, Mich.: Philosophy of Science Association, 1983), 1-25 and Del Ratzsch, *Science and its Limits* (Downers Grove, Ill.: InterVarsity, 2000).

10.   Many prominent scientists are orthodox Christians. The membership of the American Scientific Affiliation (ASA), an organization consisting primarily of evangelical Christians, includes Nobel Prize winners, members of the National Academy of Sciences, and professors at major universities, for example.

11.   Susan Schreiner, *The Theater of His Glory: Nature and the Natural Order in the Thought of John Calvin* (Grand Rapids, Mich.: Baker Books, 1995), 22.

12.   Ibid.

13.   See Dalrymple, *The Age of the Earth* and Young, *Christianity and the Age of the Earth.*

14.   There is a vast and growing literature on intelligent design. Among many others, see Phillip E. Johnson, *Darwin on Trial* (Downers Grove, Ill.: InterVarsity, 1991); Michael J. Behe, *Darwin's Black Box: The Biochemical Challenge to Evolution* (New York: Simon and Schustser, 1996); William A. Dembski, *Intelligent Design: The Bridge Between Science and Theology* (Downers Grove, Ill.: InterVarsity, 1999); and Del Ratzsch, *Nature, Design and Science: The Status of Design in Natural Science* (Albany, N.Y.: State University of New York Press, 2001).

15.   For critiques of flood geology see Davis A. Young, *Creation and the Flood: An Alternative to Flood Geology and Theistic Evolution* (Grand Rapids, Mich.: Baker Book House, 1977), Young, *Christianity and the Age of the Earth*, and Young, *The Biblical Flood.*

16.   See John Murray, *Calvin on Scripture and Divine Sovereignty* (Grand Rapids, Mich.: Baker Book House, 1960) and James I. Packer, "Calvin's View of Scripture," in *God's Inerrant Word: an International Symposium on the Trustworthiness of Scripture*, ed. John Warwick Montgomery, (Minneapolis: Bethany Fellowship, Inc., 1973), 95-114.

17.   The warfare metaphor has been critiqued by James R. Moore, *The Post-Darwinian Controversies: A Study of the Protestant Struggle to Come to Terms with Darwin in Great Britain and America 1870-1900* (Cambridge: Cambridge University Press, 1979)

and David C. Lindberg and Ronald L. Numbers, eds., *God and Nature: Historical Essays on the Encounter Between Christianity and Science* (Berkeley, Calif.: University of California Press, 1986).

18. On the failure of concordism, see Paul Seely, "The First Four Days of Genesis in Concordist Theory and in Biblical Context," *Perspectives on Science and Christian Faith* 49, (1997): 85-95 and Davis A. Young, "Scripture in the Hands of Geologists (Part Two)," *Westminster Theological Journal* 49, (1987): 257-304.

19. Herman Bavinck *Reformed Dogmatics*, vol. 2. *God and Creation* (Grand Rapids, Mich.: Baker Books, 2004), 104.

20. Wright, "Calvin's 'Accommodation' Revisited," 179.

21. Ashley, "John Calvin's Utilization," 30, 34.

22. Benjamin Breckinridge Warfield, *The Inspiration and Authority of the Bible* (Philadelphia: Presbyterian and Reformed Publishing Co., 1948).

23. Hodge and Warfield, "Inspiration."

24. Paul Woolley, "The Relevancy of Scripture," in *The Infallible Word: A Symposium by Members of the Faculty of Westminster Theological Seminary* (Philadelphia: Presbyterian and Reformed Publishing Co., 1946), 196-215.

25. Edward J. Young, *Thy Word is Truth* (Grand Rapids, Mich.: William B. Eerdmans, 1957).

26. Murray, *Calvin on Scripture and Divine Sovereignty*.

27. Harvie M. Conn, "Normativity, Relevance, and Relativism," in *Inerrancy and Hermeneutic: A Tradition, A Challenge, A Debate*, ed. Harvie M. Conn, (Grand Rapids, Mich.: Baker Book House, 1988), 185-209.

28. Packer, "Calvin's View of Scripture."

29. Ibid., 104.

30. Ibid., 106.

31. Bernard Ramm, *Protestant Biblical Hermeneutics* (Boston: W. A. Wilde, 1950).

32. Battles, "God Was Accommodating Himself"; Ashley, "John Calvin's Utilization"; Wright, "Calvin's 'Accommodation' Revisited."

33. Infallibility and Inspiration in the Light of Scripture and the Creeds, Supplement No. 24, Acts of Synod 1961, Christian Reformed Church, 253-328.

34. The Nature and Extent of Biblical Authority, Supplement—Report 44, Acts of Synod 1972, Christian Reformed Church, 493-546.

35. I am indebted to Paul Seely for showing how Calvin's principle of accommodation can be applied to biblical texts bearing on contemporary scientific issues.

36. Paul Seely, "The Firmament and the Water Above, Part I: The Meaning of *raqia'* in Gen. 1:6-8," *Westminster Theological Journal* 53, (1991): 227-40.

37. Paul Seely, "The Firmament and the Water Above, Part 2: The Meaning of 'The Water Above the Firmament' in Gen. 1:6-8," *Westminster Theological Journal* 54, (1992), 31-46.

38. Among recent biblical scholars and theologians who have interpreted *raqia'* as a solid dome are John Currid, Paul K. Jewett, John Walton, and Claus Westermann.

39. Commentators on Ezekiel typically refer to the *raqia'* in Ezekiel 1 with such expressions as a platform, a crystalline platform, a crystalline firmament, or a crystal dome. Among these commentators are scholars across the theological spectrum including Leslie Allen, Charles R. Biggs, Daniel Block, Ronald E. Clements, Patrick Fairbairn, E. Henderson, E. W. Hengstenberg, J. A. Motyer, Bruce Vawter, and J. W. Wevers.

40. Seely, "The Firmament and the Water Above," 227-36.

41. Origen, *Homilies on Genesis and Exodus*, trans. Ronald E. Heine (Washington: The Catholic University Press of America, 1982), Hom. I.2.

42. Basil, *The Syrian Version of the Hexaemeron* (Lovanii: In Aedibus Peeters, 1995), Hom. III.4.

43. Ambrose, *Hexameron, Paradise, and Cain and Abel,* trans. John J. Savage, The Fathers of the Church, vol. 42 (New York: Fathers of the Church, Inc., 1961), 48, 60, 62.

44. Augustine, The Literal Meaning of Genesis, John Hammond Taylor, trans., *Ancient Christian Writers*, vol. 41 (New York: Newman Press, 1982), Book I.61.

45. John Chrysostom, *Homilies on Genesis 1-17*, trans. Robert C. Hill (Washington: The Catholic University of America Press, 1986), Hom. IV.7.

46. Charles Hodge, "Inspiration," *Biblical Repertory and Princeton Review* 29, (1857): 660-98.

47. Charles Hodge, *Systematic Theology*, vol. 1 (Grand Rapids, Mich.: William B. Eerdmans, n.d.), 569-70.

48. Paul Seely, "The Date of the Tower of Babel and Some Theological Implications," *Westminster Theological Journal* 63, (2001): 15-38.

INDEX OF NAMES AND SUBJECTS

INDEX OF SCRIPTURE TEXTS
COMMENTED ON BY CALVIN